ABRAHAM GEIGER'S
LIBERAL JUDAISM

Jewish Literature and Culture
Alvin Rosenfeld, editor

ABRAHAM GEIGER'S LIBERAL JUDAISM

Personal Meaning and Religious Authority

Ken Koltun-Fromm

INDIANA UNIVERSITY PRESS
BLOOMINGTON AND INDIANAPOLIS

The author and the publisher wish to acknowledge the generous support of The Lucius N. Littauer Foundation.

This book is a publication of

Indiana University Press
601 North Morton Street
Bloomington, IN 47404-3797 USA

http://iupress.indiana.edu

Telephone orders 800-842-6796
Fax orders 812-855-7931
Orders by e-mail iuporder@indiana.edu

The paper used in this publication meets the minimum requirements of American National Standard for Information Sciences—Permanence of Paper for Printed Library Materials, ANSI Z39.48-1984.

Manufactured in the United States of America

Library of Congress Cataloging-in-Publication Data

Koltun-Fromm, Ken.
Abraham Geiger's liberal Judaism : personal meaning and religious authority / Ken Koltun-Fromm.
p. cm. — (Jewish literature and culture)
Includes bibliographical references and index.
ISBN 0-253-34744-0 (cloth : alk. paper)
1. Geiger, Abraham, 1810–1874—Teachings. 2. Reform Judaism. 3. Authority—Religious aspects—Judaism. 4. Meaning (Philosophy)—Religious aspects—Judaism. I. Title. II. Series.
BM755.G4K65 2006
296.8′341092—dc22

2005037578

1 2 3 4 5 11 10 09 08 07 06

For David and Barbara Fromm

CONTENTS

Acknowledgments

A book like this attempts to acknowledge authority both more and less than it should: more, because my debts to others are innumerable, yet less, for I could never repay them. But I accept that burden of authority as my blessing. Indeed, that blessing exceeds my own grasp to fully account for the authority of personal meaning that informs my own life. Still, I am grateful for all the encouragement, support, and advice I have received in years past that helped to advance this project forward. Members of the religion department at Haverford College—David Dawson, Tracey Hucks, Naomi Koltun-Fromm, John Lardas, Anne McGuire, and Michael Sells—have all (in ways they may not even recognize) made this book possible. I am so very much at home in this department, and my respect for its faculty is sincere and binding. Haverford College too has been overly generous, supporting leave requests and funding through faculty grants. For a liberal arts college dedicated to teaching young students, Haverford cares mightily about academic excellence and the intellectual life. My colleagues in other departments here—too many to mention—further and sustain that excellence, and I have become the better scholar and teacher for it.

I have not been isolated within a small circle of friends and supporters, and have sought guidance from beyond my more immediate surroundings. My colleagues in religious studies—Susannah Heschel and David Ellenson, chief among them—have always extended their precious time to review and critique my work. Members of the Works in Progress Group that meets yearly at the Association for Jewish Studies Conference in December have read versions of chapters in this book, and their counsel has been judicious and well received. My semester at the Oxford Centre for Hebrew and Jewish Studies during my year leave in 2000–2001 proved both rewarding and necessary for embarking on this book project. The serene Oxford landscapes, bountiful libraries, and the elusive but real sense of sabbatical time all encouraged a good life of friendship, research, and leisure. My family enjoyed the international community at Yarnton Manor and Wolfson College, together with punting on the river and, at least for me, local escapes to nearby pubs. My friends at Indiana University Press, especially Janet Rabinowitch and Joyce Rappaport, have guided this manuscript through some rather tortuous paths. I am forever in their debt. The generous support from the Lucius N. Littauer Foundation brought this book to completion, and their dedication to academic scholarship is a model for us all.

My wife Naomi, with our three children Ariel, Talia, and Isaiah, find me at the computer more often than they should, and I regret that. Yet their authority over me is unequivocal: Naomi leads, Talia runs, Ariel transforms, and Isaiah blesses my life.

That life, I have come to understand, has roots that extend far deeper than I am usually willing to admit. Abraham Geiger has taught me that authority has many sources, and not least among them are my parents. I dedicate this book to them for their unflinching love, warmth, and grace. But even more, I recognize that authority, in at least one of its visages, is a form of ancestor worship. I am fortunate, and certainly blessed, to have ancestors worthy of veneration. I am honored by them, and hope this dedication, however small and inadequate, still persuades my parents that my life is good because theirs is too.

ABRAHAM GEIGER'S LIBERAL JUDAISM

Introduction: Abraham Geiger, Religious Authority, and Personal Meaning

As the leading theorist and intellectual founder of the Jewish Reform movement, Abraham Geiger (1810–1874) appealed to the authority of personal meaning to both ground and challenge modern Jewish practice. His prodigious works offer a local and dynamic account of religious authority rooted in personal meanings that inspire and command. Neither objective in appeals to foundations "out there," nor purely subjective in focusing on the self, religious authority for Geiger mediates between social life and individual commitments, historical memory and liturgical worship, texts and their interpretation. Situated at modernity's door, Geiger's religious works uncover the roots of contemporary Jewish experience, even as his appeal to personal meaning bridges modern and post-modern Judaism. His world, to be sure, is not ours, but the complex issues he faced—the value of historical memory, textual authority, the politics of gender and religious practice, rabbinic authority, and the challenge of Jewish education—all remain with us nonetheless. A sympathetic but critical reading of Geiger on these issues, as this book offers, can help shape and inform present-day reflection on these very subjects. Indeed, contemporary Jews will come to recognize the sources of their commitments and conflicts in Geiger's own.

Yet even with Geiger's importance for modern Jewry, we still lack an extended critical study of his religious works and their significance for modern Jewish practice. To be sure, Michael Meyer has published a number of important essays on Geiger, and other leading historians of modern Judaism—Jay Harris, Jakob Petuchowski, Ismar Schorsch, Andreas Gotzmann, to name but a few—have discovered in Geiger's works significant contributions to the study of Jewish midrash, prayer book reform, and Jewish history.[1] Geiger's son Ludwig (himself a distinguished scholar of German Jewry) published the most comprehensive biography and collection of critical essays—and to this day, despite its rather hagiographic tone and Max Wiener's more recent collection, it still remains the best account of Geiger's life and works.[2] Yet a critical, focused, and book-length study of Geiger's Jewish thought has so far eluded scholarly attention. Even Susannah Heschel, who has written the only extended study in English, focuses her work on Geiger's obsession with early Christianity. Geiger proposed a "counterhistory," argues Heschel, in order "to demolish the standard portrayal of Western history by looking at the Christian West from the perspective of Jewish experience." He attempted, in Heschel's phrase, to "Judaize Christianity."[3] Although Heschel recognizes that Geiger "raised the problem of how religious authority in the modern world might be established,"[4] she focuses on Christian authority through Geiger's portrayal of the Jewish Jesus. Geiger reverses the gaze, such that his critique "should be understood not as an effort at assimilation, but, in light of postcolonial theory, as an attempt to subvert Christian hegemony and establish a new position for Judaism within European history and thought."[5] If so, then we need to understand as well how Geiger positions *Jewish* religious authority within the modern world.

Geiger's religious thought offered a cogent and provocative defense of liberal Judaism and, as this book argues, is pivotal for understanding the sources of authority in contemporary Judaism. Meyer notes, for example, how Geiger's "intellectual and scholarly eminence [was] recognized even by those who differed with his religious views," and "his dilemmas were shared by others in his generation and thereafter; his resolutions set a permanent seal on the [Reform] movement."[6] Even Heinrich Graetz, the great German-Jewish historian of the nineteenth century, fashioned his scholarly works to directly assault Geiger and his movement.[7] Geiger penetrated to the heart of nineteenth-century debates on history, memory, texts, education, and religious practice, and suffered the inevitable stings of criticism, some motivated by jealousy, that come with intellectual prominence. Yet through his contested analysis, contemporary Jewry is better equipped to face the challenges of authority in modern and post-modern life.

This book analyzes how the authority of personal meaning energizes and informs Geiger's account of modern Jewry. If Heschel directs Geiger outward to confront Christian identity, I turn him inward to challenge Jewish identity and the dynamics of religious authority that inform it. Through focused chapters on history and memory, sacred texts, gender practices, rabbinic office, and Jewish education, I argue that Geiger consistently appeals to personal meanings and their authority to command Jewish religious practice. In rewriting Jewish history to reflect the passions and concerns of modern Jewry, Geiger turns to memories that inspire, and rewrites Jewish prayer books to better access and ground these memories. He also situates the authority of personal meaning within sacred texts, showing how Jewish readers appropriate those texts as their own through translation and, at times, through altering the written words on the page. This aggressive control of meaning carries over to ritual practices, where Geiger recoils from feminine influence in traditionally male domains. This anxiety was provoked by an idealist rhetoric that promoted feminine interiority and spirituality but restricted female religiosity from becoming materially present in public spaces. Yet even with males at the center of Geiger's imaginative public realm, rabbinic authority had noticeably weakened there as well. Liberal rabbis such as Geiger recognized this, and convened a series of conferences in the mid-1840s to reassert it. Geiger defends the local autonomy of rabbis who, armed with scholarship that broadens and informs contemporary experience, respond to the lived practices of individual Jewish communities. But, as Geiger well knew, these communities were ever open to secular pursuits and studies, and parents often channeled their children away from Jewish education to seek broader knowledge in the liberal arts. When Geiger opened his Jewish school in Breslau in 1843, he did so within the marketplace of competing educational choices. He therefore transformed Jewish pedagogy to invoke the personal meanings that could still command Jewish allegiance. In doing so, Geiger underscored his central hermeneutical and theoretical focus: to ground liberal Judaism in the authority of personal meaning that underwrites Jewish history, text, gender constructions, rabbinic practice, and education.

But that grounding proved less than secure for Jewish liberal practice. To moor it tighter, Geiger justified his reform by appealing to religious idealism. His liberal Judaism discovers in the Jewish "spirit" an original moral source that undergirds and empowers material history. These eternal moral ideas are realized in ever-changing religious practices. Rituals undergo change in new religious contexts, but the pure moral ideas in Judaism remain ever-present and commanding. That idealism underlies the three basic principles of Geiger's liberal Jewish religion: 1) Judaism is an original expression of the pure religious and moral consciousness; 2) that consciousness remains unchanged despite new historical circumstances, such that the same Jewish "spirit" informs but remains distinct from its material expressions; and 3) those material products identify a specific people who embrace Judaism as a world religion.[8] Geiger formulated this neo-Kantian religious idealism very early in his rabbinic career, and remained committed to it for much of his life. In his defense of that ideal Judaism, Geiger relocates the weight of authority from personal meaning to the captivating power of secure moral foundations. Jewish moral sources move through, even if unmoved by, history, and they command by the pure force of their divine origins.

The contingency of Geiger's reading practices, together with his account of Jewish memory, stand in tension with the safe borders of Jewish moral authority. We recognize this conflict in Geiger's most popular work, *Judaism and Its History* (1864/65). There, in the first chapter, religion echoes the "jubilation of the soul" and the "flight of the spirit after the ideal." Rather than a set of moral truths,[9] religion exposes a deep personal yearning for meaning. The religious search itself elicits authority, and provokes ever-renewed commitment.[10] This sense of personal journey or quest, as I argue in the conclusion to this book, is now a central feature of post-modern American Jewish experience. But in the very next chapter of *Judaism and Its History,* Geiger stifles this personal rhetoric of "inborn longing," and appeals instead to eternal moral truths. Judaism carries these truths throughout its history, and yet it stands above contingency and change. Even as Judaism represents true, progressive religion, it still remains universal in its moral scope. Jewish history, as it turns out in this text, witnesses neither to the struggle for textual meaning nor to the power of memory to command religious practice. It is not a yearning or spiritual flight toward an ideal that commands through personal resonance and meaning. Instead, Judaism embodies eternal moral laws that forever and everywhere remain in force. Appeals to personal meaning reflect local, particular, and personal attachments that generate religious authority. Yet talk of universal moral ideals jettisons such contingency for the safe harbors of religious foundations. Geiger's religious idealism stands in sharp contrast to, and at times even suppresses the power and authority of personal meaning.

These tensions surface throughout Geiger's analysis of liberal Jewish practice.

When he confronts the power of Jewish historical memories, Geiger triggers moral reflection even as he appeals to personal commitment. This dual strategy underlies his reform of Jewish prayer books as well. When reading sacred texts, Geiger often recovers moral sources, although his great critical study of the Bible, the *Urschrift* (1857), stands alone in debunking religious idealism. But when Geiger and later critics reflect back upon his tour de force, they discover an idealism originally missing from that 1857 text. Geiger and his followers must recover moral ideals even if, or especially when, none can be found. In gender practices, Geiger reasserts male moral authority in public ritual acts, even as he supports (and even encourages) inner spiritual movements of female piety. But Geiger also defends the new modern rabbi who unites Jewish moral ideals with the ever-changing, and often frightening practices of modern culture. The rabbi bridges personal attachments with the moral standards of ideal Judaism. Finally, in Jewish education, Geiger redirects Jewish pedagogy to stimulate personal meanings that inspire, although he too, as was the case with many of his colleagues, turned to religious catechisms to ground Jewish ideals when inspiration proved too thin. But these conflicting movements in Geiger's thought should not surprise us. The tension between the authority of personal meaning and grounding moral authority runs throughout Geiger's works—as it does, I believe, in the lives of many modern and post-modern Jews.

Geiger's conflicted allegiance to a grounding authority, on the one hand, and one more open to personal reflection, on the other, arises out of his own personal narrative. Like many of his contemporary German-Jewish reformers, Geiger was nurtured in a traditional religious home and schooled in the classic rabbinic texts as a young child.[11] His parents wished him to become a learned Talmudist, an ambition Geiger shared as well. So three years after his birth on May 24, 1810 in Frankfurt am Main, he began studies in Bible—though not to learn Hebrew, Geiger tells us in his journal, but to instill "piety" (*Frömmigkeit*).[12] His father was himself a teacher and rabbi, and his mother the daughter of the Rosh Yeshivah of Frankfurt.[13] No wonder, then, that Geiger recalls little time for child's play (*Kinderspielen*) as he continued studying Mishnah and Talmud to please his parents. By eleven years of age, however, Geiger harbored doubts about his traditional education, and revealed some embarrassment in his youthful comparisons of Moses' teaching to Greek and Roman writings.[14] But the floodgates had opened, and after learning Greek and Latin, Geiger yearned for knowledge beyond his insular Jewish education—and he regarded this period of schooling as a time of "innocence," and, not without sorrow, as a time wasted upon him.[15] When he finally entered the University of Bonn in 1829 after less than a year's study in Heidelberg, he had chosen to focus on oriental languages and so to "begin a new life." There he met his young friend and later rival, Samson Raphael Hirsch, with whom he met every Sunday so both could study and deliver sermons.[16]

At the end of his university studies, Geiger wrote an essay on Jewish sources of the Qur'an (in Latin, no less), which later received a prize in 1832 and was published in German as *Was hat Mohammed aus dem Judenthume aufgenommen?*

(What has Mohammad taken from Judaism?—but published in English as *Judaism and Islam*). Heschel claims that this text produced the groundwork for much that would come in Geiger's later writings, for Geiger there established a "counter-historical argument" that placed rabbinic Judaism at the center of religious history.[17] Soon after completing his doctorate, Geiger accepted a rabbinical post in Wiesbaden, a small Jewish community that Geiger found rather dull and ignorant of the massive reform changes in Europe. There he became engaged in 1833 to Emilie Oppenheim (1809–1860), whom he had met a year earlier in Bonn. They did not marry until July 1, 1840 in Frankfurt, and only visited each other occasionally while in Wiesbaden.[18] But even with personal happiness, Geiger found little professional success despite all his work,[19] and after five years he left for Breslau where he would spend the great part of his rabbinic career (1840–1863) and write the bulk of his scholarly texts. In Breslau, Geiger established new educational programs for young boys and girls, published the first of his two reform prayer books, wrote his most significant piece of scholarship (the *Urschrift*), edited the second of his journals on Jewish scholarship (he published his first in Wiesbaden), and raised four children with his wife. But Emilie's health slowly deteriorated in 1850 after she gave birth to her fourth child, and when she died in 1860, Geiger sought the comforts and support of home in Frankfurt.

Yet his move there in 1863 proved disappointing. Frankfurt appeared less "the light of the world," as Geiger had once called it as a young man of fourteen, and seemed more like a sleepy little Orthodox town.[20] That three of his children no longer lived at home (with only his youngest daughter remaining) only increased Geiger's sense of loneliness. As his son Ludwig tells it, the house seemed practically empty. Even more, most of Geiger's relatives were religiously Orthodox and disapproved of his more liberal views.[21] Indeed, home proved far less comforting than Geiger had previously imagined, and so he spent much of his free time visiting his numerous old friends, even as he tirelessly worked on his studies. It was during this time that he published what would become his most popular text, his public lectures on Jewish history, *Judaism and Its History*.[22] When the Berlin Jewish community sought a liberal rabbi to replace Michael Sachs after his death in 1864, Geiger jumped at the opportunity to live in the center of German cultural life and Jewish learning. As a faculty member at the new *Hochschule* in Berlin, Geiger delivered lectures on Jewish thought and history, and served as rabbi from 1870 until his death in 1874. Though both he and his wife were buried in Berlin at Schönhauser Tor, Geiger's life is one of wanderings and searches. With little to ground his own life, he devoted much of his writings to discover what grounded other modern Jews like himself.

Religious *authority,* as I will employ the term in this book, refers to the sources of obligation to the history, culture, and ideals of a religious tradition as embodied in sacred texts and ritual practices. It is, to be sure, a vast and well-traversed field of research. Though numerous works discuss features of authority in detail,[23] still others explore the dynamics of authority without naming it as such.[24] Indeed, religious texts are vitally concerned with authority, whether revealed at specific locations or within historical persons and sacred writings. Religions often provide that "sacred canopy"[25] within which persons discover meaning and authenticity. But with the onslaught of modernity, together with the movements that scholars understand as comprising it—the Enlightenment, industrialization, urban and economic expansion, social emancipation, and secularization, to name only the most pronounced changes—that protective canopy quickly collapsed. With such radical dislocation in their social, cultural, and religious lives, modern religious thinkers had to do more than appeal to revelation in order to reconstitute religious authority. Jewish thinkers like Geiger lost their belief in Torah from Sinai, and they badly needed new authoritative sources to maintain Jewish continuity and practice in a modern world of religious and secular culture. Jews now faced choices they did not have to confront only a generation earlier, and they were attracted to new sources of authority—progress, nationalism, science—that often uprooted their Jewish commitments. Many of Geiger's contemporaries turned to history or reason to shore up Jewish obligations, and still others revisited sacred texts to discover innovative meanings for a changing world.

Geiger turned to the self, and discovered therein the authority of personal meaning that could recapture modern Jewish allegiance. Each of the five central chapters in this book engages features of personal authority—historical memory and the observance of religious Judaism, the reading of sacred texts, gender performances, rabbinic leadership and communal lived religion, and educational training. Geiger sought to engage modernity rather than deny it, and he recognized that Jews would look inward for authentic meaning as more religious and cultural options became available to them. Those who turned to the self—informed by Enlightenment conceptions of reason and autonomy, and the cultivated personal ideal of *Bildung*[26]—would discover sources within that would motivate and confirm their allegiances outside the self.

The authority of personal meaning refers to those sources that command because they are felt as inner, more authentic commitments. These personal sources help to explain and confirm the choices we make regarding our social, religious, and cultural lives. Geiger will explore religious memory, for example, together with a more balanced narrative of Jewish history, because personal memories infuse that history. The resonance of personal reflections makes Jewish history speak in tones that inspire, and perhaps even command. Religious authority begins with the self, so Geiger argues, but it ends with new and stronger attachments to historical, communal, and religious goods. If the sacred canopy can no longer be discovered, at least now it can be fashioned to respond to personal meaning, and be that much more commanding in the very making of it.

To recover the authority of personal meaning in Geiger's thought, I draw upon a legacy of scholarly research. But none are more important to this study than the work of Moses Mendelssohn and Max Weber. Their reflections on religious authority undergird this critical project. Mendelssohn himself was a formative influence on Geiger's religious thinking (as he was for the entire generation), even if, in the end, Geiger rejected much of his work. And Weber helps us understand why Geiger could not follow Mendelssohn and instead discovered other sources to regain Jewish commitment in the modern world.

The problem of religious authority underlies Mendelssohn's famous distinction between "divine legislation" for Jews alone, and "revealed religion" for all rational persons.[27] In *Jerusalem, or On Religious Power and Judaism* (1783), Mendelssohn recognized that Jewish observance would surely become voluntary in the modern period. He encouraged European Jews to adopt personal meanings to empower their still-commanded practices. Absent a common belief but still united in ritual, Jews could discover new sources of meaning and authority in continued practice of *mitzvot.*[28] But for all the "play" in religious meaning, the commandments were always and everywhere in force:

> He [God] gave his laws the most solemn sanction, publicly and in a never heard-of, miraculous manner, by which they were imposed upon the nation and all their descendants as an unalterable duty and obligation.
>
> In fact, I cannot see how those born into the House of Jacob can in any conscientious manner disencumber themselves of the law. . . . No sophistry of ours can free us from the strict obedience we owe to the law; and reverence for God draws a line between speculation and practice which no conscientious man may cross.[29]

The commandments obligate regardless of the meanings ascribed to them. Jewish observance will surely decline without personal attachments, but Jewish practice proves no less commanded without them. For Mendelssohn, personal meaning is necessary but nonetheless optional for continued Jewish observance. One discovers authority in practices that obligate independently of the meanings attached to these rituals. Jews may indeed fail to heed those commitments, but the commanded practices stand nonetheless. The commandments retain their authority apart from our need to discover meaning in them.

This is not so for Abraham Geiger, for whom authority and personal meaning remain closely intertwined. Observing commandments that no longer compel through personal significance betrays not Mendelssohnian loyalty but the lack of personal integrity. The personal meanings evoked by religious practice mark all the authority such practice can hold. Geiger justifies liturgical reforms, educational policies, historical analysis, textual readings, and gendered politics by appealing to personal meaning and significance. Without personal resonance and inner power, the commandments lose their force and authority.

But for Geiger, personal meaning does not devolve into personal preference. By locating authority within the power of the self, Geiger in no way removes that self from its social location and cultural influences. Indeed, he interweaves personal identity with historical narratives and texts that remain social and political in character. But without the inner relevance and the personal convictions that obligate modern selves, Jewish observance becomes a dead letter in Geiger's liberal Judaism. For Mendelssohn, *mitzvot* obligate regardless of their personal value and significance. But his *mitzvot* have become *ceremonies* in Geiger's rereading, such that Jewish practice commemorates a significant claim or moral truth in religious Judaism, and does so in a way that moves and inspires. Without motivating practices, Jews search for alternatives that better fit contemporary needs and emotions. The meaning things have for us, Geiger argues throughout his scholarly work, resides in historical, communal, and political acts that resonate with personal attachments. Authority is made, not discovered or inherited, by meaningful acts that cultivate social, political, and religious obligations.

Weber's distinction between charismatic authority and democratic legitimacy helps to explain why Geiger moved away from Mendelssohn's more traditional understanding of commanded practices. In Weber's account, the recognition of charismatic authority is a duty (*Pflicht*) in the sense that one ought to acknowledge it. The German word *Herrschaft* (translated in English as *authority*) connotes a strong sense of mastery and control upon persons subject to a commanding authority. Although the validity of charismatic authority "rests entirely upon the recognition of the ruled [*die Beherrschten*]," this acknowledgment is nonetheless felt as a duty (I feel an obligation to grant you authority even if I concede that your mastery relies upon my recognition). Weber calls this kind of commanding respect a "consequence of legitimacy" because it submits to what appears as genuine authority. But when my recognition becomes the *ground* of authority, such that a duty to submit no longer applies, charismatic authority turns into democratic legitimacy. Authority as *Herrschaft* deforms into pure *Legitimität* (legitimacy) and the ruled (*Beherrschten*) become "the community" (*die Gemeinde*) that "can enact, recognize, or abolish laws as it pleases."[30] In the democratic community, duties and obligations are imposed from within, as it were, rather than commanded from external (charismatic) sources.

Weber describes charismatic authority as a chosen master, but the democratic leader as a servant of the community.[31] In so doing, he draws out the distinctive features of authority for both Mendelssohn and Geiger. If Mendelssohn defends a notion of charismatic authority, then Geiger weakens it through appeals to democratic legitimacy. The *mitzvot* are not chosen but imposed in Mendelssohn's *Jerusalem,* but they obligate and command in much the same way as Weber's *Herrschaft.* Jews recognize a felt duty to submit to *mitzvot,* even if that commitment relies upon personal acceptance. Authority comes from outside the self, but is recognized from within. In Geiger's democratic turn, commandments serve communal ends and needs, and the Jewish community too "can enact, recognize, or abolish laws as it pleases." But even if created, those laws command nonetheless. Personal meaning stands as the source of their legitimacy, for they inspire commitment through evocative expression. Authority comes from within for Geiger because personal meaning does too. But those personal attachments reach out as well to communal sources, and inform (and are informed by) social and political ends. Geiger stretches the site of authority to encompass both social and personal goals, to frame both historical narratives and personal memories, and to mediate between communal practices and rabbinic leadership. Mendelssohn finds comfort and security in an authority beyond the self; but Geiger discovers it within a social self that creates, rewrites, and rereads the sources of religious authority.

This book contains five chapters, each devoted to Geiger's democratic turn in rethinking the authority of personal meaning. They do not cover all of Geiger's many works, nor do they pretend to offer a general account of his corpus. Instead, these chapters focus on Geiger's penetrating analysis of religious authority that still resonates today for contemporary Jewry. I indicate at the end of each chapter how Geiger's thought bridges the divide between his world and the contemporary scene, and I focus exclusively on this issue in the conclusion to this book. But the power of my claim resides in Geiger's own analysis of authority and in his ability to challenge readers to reinvigorate their religious commitments. Even as I situate Geiger firmly within nineteenth-century religious debates, especially among his Jewish intellectual peers, this book is less concerned with rooting Geiger in a particular intellectual tradition—whether that be Romanticism, Idealism, or some other. It is more engaged in a project of recovery to better understand the sources of modern religious authority. Reading Geiger can help us read ourselves, and enable us to uncover, and thus recognize, those personal sources that motivate and inspire.

The first chapter discusses Geiger's appeal to religious idealism as a moral authority for liberal Judaism. Geiger published historical studies and important articles on memory that explored how narratives fashion modern Jewish identity. His was not a positivist history of any sort, but a creative reworking of historical memory to produce a religious Judaism grounded in moral truths. Geiger discovered in Jewish history the foundation for Jewish ethics, and he justified the reform of Jewish liturgy upon this moral bedrock. He challenged, reworked, and at times completely erased historical memories in order to recover a recognizable and meaningful past. Personal memories, rooted in Jewish moral ideals, would inspire commitment to Jewish practice. The past proved to be "usable" in imaginative retrievals of forgotten moral sources. To be sure, Geiger devoted his work to *Jüdische Wissenschaft* as a scientific and enlightened study of Jewish history. Yet he focused on the *ways in which* historians tell the past, and the various strategies employed to protect an ideal Jewish ethic from enlightened critics. Religious authority would be grounded upon religious ideas and the ways in which Jews embody those moral ideas in liturgical worship.

In the second chapter, I explore Geiger's hermeneutical approach to classical Jewish texts, and the personal meanings discovered therein. Here I focus on what Geiger himself called his most important and significant contribution to Jewish scholarship, his *Urschrift und Übersetzungen der Bibel* (1857). The biblical editors, so Geiger claims, reworked the original text in order to read in all that they hoped to discover within it. Such consistent reworking produced new meanings, and in some cases, new texts as well. Indeed, Geiger subverted the sense of an "original text" by exposing the textual discrepancies in the Bible's many translations and revisions. Translations mediate and therefore establish biblical authority, and force the "original" text to speak in a different language, in a new voice, and through new meanings that reflect contemporary political, religious, and social debates. For Geiger, textual interpretation mirrored the movements of religious history and polemics. That history reflects the contours, dynamics, and historical dimensions of religious traditions that impose authority on a text through transformative readings. In Geiger's *Urschrift,* the search for biblical origins reveals a social and political history of religious authority.

But if political history lies at the center of Jewish religious authority, then so do the males who practice it. The third chapter examines the gendered politics of religious authority in Geiger's reading of biblical and rabbinic texts. In configuring public male and private female characters to reflect bourgeois standards of taste and morality, Geiger also helps to produce that very ideology. He defends this bourgeois position through appeals to religious idealism. Geiger believed that ideas and religious convictions transform material practices. Ideas empower when they infuse public political life. But Geiger also engendered this religious idealism so that domestic females would discover within the public sphere those ritual performances that fittingly embody private virtue. The public, male space becomes the expressive arena for rituals that correspond to the interiority of faith. Yet a critical reading of Geiger's religious politics unravels this idealist project to show how public male bodies determine and appropriate private female power. Male political acts inform spiritual female content—the precise inverse of Geiger's religious idealism. Geiger's liberal Judaism is, in this deconstructive reading, a gendered politics that protects male authority within the public realm of ritual performance. But Geiger's work also points to a more robust account of religious ritual, one in which physical, expressive performances themselves produce meaning and commitment.

The fourth chapter turns to the problem of rabbinic authority in liberal Judaism, especially as lay challenges to that authority surfaced in the mid-1840s. Geiger and his liberal colleagues were acutely aware of the burdening crisis in rabbinic leadership in nineteenth-century Germany. In fact, Geiger and others helped to create this predicament, for they contested the learning, status, and religious sensibilities of their rabbinic teachers. Geiger and his peers entered the very establishment they had earlier mocked with scorn, and found that much of their rabbinic authority over communal matters had rapidly deteriorated. The rabbinical conferences of the mid-1840s witnessed to this impoverished command among liberal rabbis. At the first of the three conferences, they confronted the problem of rabbinic authority and their weakening influence to control Jewish practice. Scholars such as Zacharias Frankel openly questioned rabbinic power and influence, and publicly endorsed learned scholars rather than official rabbis. Lay leaders had brashly criticized the elitism and legal judgments pronounced by rabbis too far removed from communal life. They challenged the rabbinic leadership to better support communal authority and Jewish lived religion. Geiger shared much with these critics, for he located religious authority within particular communities and their local customs. But he also sought to reinvigorate the rabbinic office, and so portrayed the rabbi as the grounded, local writer who unites passionate scholarship with committed community engagement. Yet in reaffirming rabbinic authority through the new "Jewish-theological writer," Geiger also exposed the tensions and anxiety of rabbinic leadership. If rabbinic authority lies ultimately within the lived practice of Jewish communities, then it must be made there—in and through communal practice—rather than blandly asserted by rabbinic assemblies too far removed from local communities.

Nowhere is rabbinic influence more keenly felt than in the new educational programs then blossoming in Germany. The fifth chapter explores Geiger's theory of Jewish education and the dynamics of religious authority in Jewish learning. The authority of Jewish education, Geiger admits, rests in how well it prepares Jewish boys and girls for a future in Europe. It is an education *in* and *by means of* the Jewish community, but it is still an education *for* a broader cultural audience. Parents wanted their children schooled in the arts, dance, and European languages that opened social and political goods. Geiger recognized that Jewish education must speak to a range of religious and secular concerns beyond Judaism. But to move beyond Judaism also meant to instill it within, and so Geiger sought to access, through his educational program, the inner life that motivates and sustains Jewish history and religion. He dismissed pedagogical approaches that schooled in doctrine, memorization, and other heuristic techniques. Instead, Geiger accessed personal sources that provoked religious practice and commitment. Jewish education, properly conceived, unlocks sources of authority that command through personal significance.

Religious authority for Abraham Geiger expresses the sources of obligation to a history, practice, text, and culture. Through a close reading of selected texts in Geiger's massive writings, I argue that even as that authority comes in many forms, all of them relate to the authority of personal meaning. To be sure, Geiger appeals to "highest-order meanings"[32] such as "ethical monotheism," the "mission of Israel," and the Jewish "spirit." These religious ideas occupy a good deal of Geiger's intellectual energy, and he defends them with rigor and wit. But Geiger also engages personal sources that inspire commitment to liberal Jewish practice. For his liberal home truths to command, they must activate strong personal attachments and resonate with meaningful ritual acts. Religious authority does not come to us clean, as it were, ready-made and revealed in sacred space. It must stir a sense of obligation by appealing to personal meaning. I conclude that Geiger sheds important light on how modern liberal Jews practice religious authority. For in the end, religious authority cannot be blandly asserted but must be passionately lived in local communities, and expressed in cultural, political acts. In this communal setting, religious authority becomes so through the practices of everyday life.

Historical Memory and the Authority of Religious Judaism

1

Many of Geiger's closest friends were his fellow students of oriental studies in Bonn during the early 1830s. With them he maintained close personal ties and literary correspondence, especially with Joseph Derenbourg—like Geiger a leader in the critical historical study of Jewish texts and thought (*Wissenschaft des Judentums*). After leaving Bonn and accepting his first rabbinical post in Wiesbaden, where he remained until 1838, Geiger wrote often to Derenbourg of his struggles there, and even more of his own doubts and concerns about liberal Judaism's future.[1] Discouraged by the Wiesbaden Jewish community, Geiger was fortunate to have Derenbourg close by as a preacher in Mainz. But when Derenbourg left for Amsterdam in 1835, Geiger maintained his friendship less through joint vacation visits and more through personal letters.[2] Here Geiger confesses to his many battles, including this pressing question about Jewish history, written to Derenbourg late at night in 1836:

> For the love of Heaven, how much longer can we continue this deceit, to expound the stories of the Bible from the pulpits over and over again as actual historical happenings, to accept as supernatural events of world import stories which we ourselves have relegated to the realm of legend, and to derive teachings from them or, at least, to use them as the basis for sermons and texts?[3]

As was the case with many of his colleagues who promoted a more scientific and critical approach to Jewish texts, Geiger expresses both frustration at the innocent adoption of legends as historical facts, and uncertainty about how to reimagine those legends as religiously meaningful. When biblical historical texts lose their authority "to derive teachings from them," how can preachers like Geiger employ that history "as the basis for sermons and texts"? If "actual historical happenings" no longer command modern Jewish practice, then what kind of usable past[4] can Geiger draw from to enliven contemporary Judaism?

This notion of a usable past is at the heart of Jan Assmann's perceptive study of the biblical Moses in European memory, in which Assmann distinguishes between "history in its radical form of positivism" and "mnemohistory" as the study of a remembered past.[5] Though memory is certainly related to history, Assmann opens new questions about how one imagines the past and its heroes, while he sets aside factual issues concerning what "really" happened. Assmann stands in good company in this turn to memory in historical studies. With Yerushalmi's influential *Zakhor*, together with his *Freud's Moses*, new works have canvassed the various terrain of historical memory, and have resurrected forgotten texts that deserve the historian's attention.[6] For many historians of memory, discovering what "really" happened in the past is either unfathomable or simply unnecessary for understanding how persons narrate and imagine that past. Assmann, for example, evinces little concern about whether Moses ever existed, or even if he had been an Egyptian. Those remain historical questions. Moses as a figure of memory "is modeled, invented, reinvented, and reconstructed by the present."[7] Even if Assmann's notion of history appears overblown, he still argues persuasively that a remembered past is a usable one, revealing not an innocent memory but a motivated projecting of contemporary debates about identity onto a past. In this way, the past becomes meaningful, and its heroes become authoritative sources for modern identity and authenticity.

Assmann's mnemohistory as a modeling and reinventing of the past undermines the very possibility of immediate access to past events. Though Assmann himself may still harbor a precarious belief in objective, positivist history, practitioners of his brand of remembering could very well forgo such attachments, and instead appeal to the ways in which we access and account for our past. History turns from a one-sided, professional activity to an imaginative retelling that invents authority through constructed memories. Historical accounts create authority, but make it appear as if those authoritative sources had already been there to discover. Indeed, to speak of memorializing, modeling, or reinventing the past actively subverts history as a fact-gathering, objective reading. Yet this represents less a post-modern turn than it does one of the many ways in which historians reconstitute the past.

Abraham Geiger responded to this historical challenge, and to his own questions posed to Derenbourg in that 1836 letter, by arguing that effective history memorializes a past in order to ground new religious possibilities. This seems odd, because as a leading practitioner of *Wissenschaft des Judentums,* Geiger would presumably defend the very kind of "positivist" history that Assmann associated with historical fact and objective study. Geiger, to be sure, believed in the power of *wissenschaftliche* studies to enlighten and strengthen modern Jewish identity, and his understanding of Judaism had always been, as he himself claimed, a historical one.[8] Yet Geiger did appeal to memory and inventions of the past, and in so doing reconfigured the "objective" standards of a movement that he belonged to and supported. He focused on the *ways in which* historians tell their past. And it is *their* past, for historical narratives reveal authorial intentions and desires, and these and other passions illuminate the motivated retrieval of a past. Geiger's writings on and about history, in other words, are really meditations on historical narratives as modern authority for Jewish identity.

Geiger published both seminal historical studies of Judaism and important articles on memory and the process by which it fashions identity in public worship. In both his historical pieces and essays on Jewish liturgy, Geiger stressed the centrality of a remembered past to historical and liturgical studies. He reimagined historical memories in order to ground his reform in a recognizable and meaningful past. But Geiger remodeled that past in the image of contemporary concerns. His *Wissenschaft des Judentums* confronted modern Judaism by appealing to a different, once forgotten but now remembered past. Geiger set aside and replaced "history in its radical form of positivism" with the power of memory to forge new futures through reconstructed history. These new historical memories would create the authority of personal meaning for contemporary Jewish practice.

The synergy between the personal meaning of historical memories and the moral centrality of religious Judaism highlights a typical feature of Geiger's historical approach. Geiger truly believed that moral ideals create and ground personal meaning. Historical memory retrieves those moral sources, and in doing so creatively situates religious authority in Jewish moral history. From the very beginning of his publishing career, Geiger understood that historical narratives embody claims to religious authority. We can see this in his reply to Bruno Bauer's controversial essay in 1842, in which Bauer denied a role for Jews and Judaism in world history. Some twenty years later, in his *Judaism and Its History* (1864/65), Geiger emphasized again the historical and religious character of Judaism, and the role it serves to ground liberal Jewish identity. His groundbreaking theoretical pieces on liturgical reform, and his two edited prayer books of 1854 and 1870 (both would have wide-ranging impact in Europe and America)[9] revealed how Geiger reconfigured historical memory to mirror his idealized religious Judaism. For Geiger the prayer-book reformer, the most complex dilemmas surfaced when powerful historical memories distorted his vision of modern Jewish identity. The various techniques and strategies Geiger employed to deal with such inflexible problems were also his most insightful explorations into the dynamics of historical memory and religious authority.

Geiger's focus on an ideal moral Judaism as meaningful religious authority becomes ever more significant when compared to the historical writing of Heinrich Graetz, the foremost and most popular historian of Jewish religion in nineteenth-century Germany, and Geiger's most outspoken critic. Where Geiger turned to *Judaism* and its material expressions in persons and events, Graetz focused instead on *Jews* and how great men creatively reinvented and fashioned Jewish practice. Indeed, this difference comes to the fore in the very titles of their magisterial historical works: Geiger's *Judaism and Its History,* and Graetz's *The History of the Jews.* Yet in both histories, the telling of the past returns Jews to the authoritative sources for modern Judaism. In that telling, Geiger argues, historical memories of an idealized and moral Judaism generate and ground religious commitment and identity. Modern Jews discover the authority of personal meaning in Jewish moral history.

Writing History and Historical Memory: Geiger and Religious Judaism

Geiger called his first edited journal "A Scientific Journal for Jewish Theology" (*Wissenschaft Zeitschrift für Jüdische Theologie*). From 1835 until 1847, he published six volumes that covered Jewish history, religion, liturgy, and theology. Like other Jewish editors of the time, Geiger wrote many of the articles himself. The breadth of his knowledge is extraordinary, with important essays published on Jewish liturgy, women and Judaism, contemporary theology, Karaite literature, biblical and Talmudic studies, and, to be sure, passionate defenses of *Wissenschaft* and its role in fashioning modern Jewish practice.

But the leading article in the journal's first volume did much to undermine *Wissenschaft* as an objective ground for modern Jewish identity. This article established the tone for the new journal, and its title, "The Judaism of our Time and Its Endeavors," witnessed to the romantic and global vision that advanced the journal's goals and faith. Geiger expressed such hope in the article's concluding page: "A new dawn has broken, the heart of the synagogue is strong and healthy, the spirit of God hovers over the water, and so very soon he will utter: let there be light!"[10] As God creates a new day in Genesis with ever-hopeful possibilities, so too Geiger's journal marks a new stage, a new dawn in Jewish scholarship that creates a vibrant future of Jewish life. Such strength and health, Geiger argues, can be found in "a *historical critique* of the highest level," one that reveals the organic relations between the past and present so that we become, this very day, "an organ of history."[11] But Geiger also cautions his readers about organic wholeness: "Not everything that we see before us in a self-contained arrangement has been a pure development of the religious idea that governs a community of faith. Not everything has followed *consciously* its sense and spirit. . . ."[12] Scholars must weed out the "pure development" from its deformations, and discover those spiritual movements that consciously follow the religious idea. Organic history, then, remains partial, and modern Jews reconnect only to the most conscious, and thus most free and spiritual features of their Jewish heritage.

In his appeal to the spiritual features of historical progress, Geiger echoes the Hegelian philosophy of history so prevalent in the nineteenth-century German academy. As Michael Meyer and others have noted, Hegel's hold on Jewish historians was powerful, and Jewish thinkers as diverse as Samuel Hirsch, Solomon Formstecher, Nachman Krochmal, and Solomon Steinheim all reacted to Hegel's dramatic account of spirit's progressive movement to ever-greater consciousness of itself as world spirit.[13] Ismar Schorsch has rightly observed that "equipped with the idealistic conceptual apparatus of Hegel, they [*Wissenschaft* scholars] tended to reduce the tortuous history of the Jews to the progressive unfolding of the idea of Judaism."[14] Geiger, too, was moved by Hegel's sweeping vision and method. Like Hegel, he tracked progressive spirit as it advanced to greater awareness, and left behind those moments of lesser spiritual import. In this organic, evolving model of historical progress, Geiger evinces that early exuberance for a dominant model of history that captivated the European mind. But where Hegel's philosophical Christianity superseded an outmoded Judaism, Geiger's Judaism revealed the steady but ever-increasing spiritual movements of Jewish history.

Geiger searched for the most essential (*wesentlich*) in Jewish history, for only this limited purity evoked an organic relationship with the past. Yet he offered no other criterion for distinguishing purity than "a *historical critique* of the highest level." Only this kind of critique could decipher the "pure development of the religious idea" from other, impure movements. In another article published in the same journal, Geiger described how the researcher considers the "inner, religious, ethical and intellectual development" of the times.[15] For Geiger, the guiding light of a new dawn relied upon the academic study of history (*Wissenschaft*) to highlight and strengthen the organic relations of Jewish life.

But then "historical critique" becomes the central problem for a progressive Judaism. If it fails, and if it is not "of the highest level," then pure moments mix with impure developments, and conscious, free decisions become enslaved obedience. The *study of history,* the *way in which* scholars decipher organic relations from inorganic ones, carries the weight of Jewish progress. Geiger emphasizes how we discern pure from impure (unconscious) history, and thereby evoke, like God before us, a new dawn. History becomes organic history only through a historical critique of the highest order.

Geiger's focus on method in historical studies marked his journal as part of a new Jewish movement in rethinking the past. Scholars as diverse as Graetz, Samuel Holdheim, Zacharias Frankel, Samson Raphael Hirsch, and Geiger himself all sought to loosen the traditional moorings of accepted history and offer a more reflective, academic approach less moved by religious ideology and more concerned with accepted scholarly practice.[16] Ismar Schorsch has catalogued what he views as the five central pillars of *Wissenschaft* scholarship: 1) the turn from the category of being to one of becoming; 2) the claim to absolute free inquiry; 3) the expansion of Jewish sources; 4) the focus on "problem-orientated, systematic, and ultimately synthetic" exegesis of the sources; and 5) the political struggle for emancipation.[17] When Geiger highlighted method in the telling of history, he signaled both his commitment to *Wissenschaft* scholarship and his critique of received Jewish history that could no longer serve as an authoritative source for contemporary Judaism. There was indeed a historical narrative to tell, as Geiger's appeal to an "organ of history" attests. But the content and meaning of that history would now rely upon the adequacy and rigor of historical critique. Historical appeals would have to convince through methodological rigor. So Geiger naturally turned to the Hegelian mode of reading history and its command of historical scholarship.

Geiger's appropriation of the Hegelian method also explains why he belittled Heinrich Graetz's work in Jewish history. For even as he knew the sources well and discovered important new ones, Graetz simply had no idea what to do with them, and lacked a sophisticated understanding of historical background.[18] Graetz offered a history without the higher criticism necessary for understanding the "pure development of the religious idea." Geiger challenged *the way in which* Graetz studied history, and in so doing focused on method to undermine Graetz's narrative. For Geiger, Graetz was incorrect because, though he knew his sources (and, Geiger admits, even the right ones!), he failed to read them critically. This emphasis on reading, on the approach to the sources rather than the sources themselves, located Geiger's history within Schorsch's fourth pillar of *Wissenschaft* scholarship (methodological critique). Geiger displaced a positive history of fact-gathering with an active historical reading that distinguished pure from impure moments, and affirmed a "higher criticism" that recovered organic relations between past and present Judaism. The story of Jewish tradition could no longer stand alone and simply stake a claim to modern commitments and practice. The focus now lay squarely on how one tells that story.

The new emphasis on historical critique also clarifies the explosive impact of Bruno Bauer's essay, "The Jewish Question,"[19] on historians like Geiger. Bauer's essay appeared in a series of installments in *Deutsche Jahrbücher für Wissenschaft und Kunst* in 1842,[20] a liberal journal that Geiger, for one, held in high regard. As the heated responses by Geiger and other Jewish thinkers attest, Bauer's essay incited a shock wave through the community of German-Jewish intellectuals and rabbis, echoes of which can be gleaned from Geiger's other essays of the period as well.[21] It also came at a time of increased tensions among Jews in Prussia as they awaited the outcome of government deliberations on a new Jewish law.[22] The force of Bauer's article, in this anxious climate, remains twofold. Bauer was a respected and noted liberal scholar who, as Hegel's student, pioneered a more radical (left) Hegelian approach to religious studies. His essay could not easily be dismissed as the wild ravings of a conservative lunatic against Jewish emancipation and its place within a Christian state. So Bauer's status and reputation moved many Jewish thinkers to take his claims seriously and respond to them in kind.

But more to the point here, Bauer's essay focused on historical method and narrative, and to these issues Jewish historians were no strangers. They had secured modern Jewish life on the shoulders of critical historical studies, and now faced a sophisticated Hegelian thinker who challenged their liberal views, and one who knew a thing or two about historical critique. Bauer's would not be a simplistic Christian supersessionist argument, although he did believe Christianity had overcome the "inconsequence" of Judaism. Instead, Bauer claimed that the Jew "does not recognize a purely human development of history, a development of human consciousness and even a development of his own historical consciousness."[23] Only a historical critique would justify Bauer's argument against Jewish emancipation. History would be the arbiter of modern politics, and the arbiter of history would be historical critique.

Bauer wanted to study "the being of the Jew as a Jew." To do so, he had to begin with "the right kind of question [*die richtige Stellung der Frage*]."[24] Methodological considerations took first priority, for only the right "position" would yield a true understanding of the Jew's essential being. The key methodological question turned on whether the Jew lived within or outside the progressive dynamics of history. Bauer repeatedly told his readers that history marks the patterns of development, freedom, and spiritual creation. But Jews react "against the movements and changes of history": "History wants development, new formations, progress and alterations; the Jews wanted always to remain the same, they strove against the first law of history."[25] The change in tense—from history "wants" to Jews "wanted"—clearly indicated Bauer's method and agenda. History continually develops toward ever-new progressive developments. But Jews remain in the past, actively working against such historical progress. Removed from progressive history, Jews have no true history of their own.

Bauer went even further and suggested that such a motionless existence is only an "illusion." Jews are a "chimerical" people who retain a ghostly presence outside the very movements of history:

> Who worked for eighteen hundred years for the education [*Bildung*] of Europe? . . . Who had created the Christian and modern art and filled the cities of Europe with eternal monuments? Who had developed the scientific studies [*die Wissenschaften*]? Who had worked on the theory of state constitutions? One cannot name a single Jew. Spinoza was no longer a Jew when he created his system, and Moses Mendelssohn died in grief when he heard that Lessing, his late friend, had been a Spinozist.[26]

Living in "the gaps and crevices of civic community," Jews actively oppose "the general interests of art and science." They maintain an "unhistorical character" grounded in an "oriental being" that denies "the possibility of development."[27] So how can one emancipate the Jews within European society if the Jew fights against its very possibility? The Orient is not Europe, just as the Jew is not a human being. To be truly human means to be a historical agent, but this the Jew cannot be:

> There is no more consequential spirit of a people as the Jewish one, which in the course of progress really does not progress, which in the course of development does not develop, and despite the highest ideas which have been imposed upon it, this Jewish spirit remains what it is. This consequence is nothing but egotistical stubbornness.[28]

The anti-Judaism here is palpable, and even more so in Bauer's claim that Christianity has overcome "this false appearance of the existence of a people."[29] But Bauer's position lies firmly rooted in historical critique, and in the grounding claim that Jews live outside history and actively work against historical progress. It would be wrong, and perhaps even unjust, to liberate a people that consciously struggles against the very notion of liberation. The Jews cannot be emancipated until they recognize the value of history. But then the Jew must become a human being, and so finally overcome Judaism and Jewish existence.

Despite the Christian rhetoric and supersessionist ideology, Bauer's essay on the Jewish question adopted the Hegelian position that historical critique arbitrates political and religious debates. Appeals must be made within the historical arena, and not within theological or even political circles. Geiger understood that, and so his response to Bauer did not evade the historical issues but tackled them head-on. He battled Bauer on his own turf, and adopted the explicit Hegelian terminology that Bauer himself had utilized with such power.

This is all the more striking when one notes the response by Gotthold Salomon, Geiger's liberal colleague. Salomon's response was, like Geiger's, an apologetic attempt to shore up Jewish history before the onslaught of Bauer's Christian bias. He defended Mendelssohn and Spinoza, as Geiger would, as prominent *Jewish* thinkers who actively participated in and furthered European *Bildung* and culture.[30] But Salomon's defense of Judaism relied upon the Kantian appeal to ethics, and not Hegelian historical dialectic. Indeed, Salomon accepts Bauer's claim that

Judaism remains outside history and progress. But this timeless purity reveals instead Judaism's eternal truth and beauty. The Talmud, Salomon explains, "modifies everything according to time and place that does not belong to the fundamental teachings." These teachings, as stable as mountains, cannot be altered nor improved, and "we cling to them with all our power and soul."[31] Only within this moral purity can one attain true freedom and ethical life (*Sittlichkeit*). Salomon is even willing to reject everything else in Jewish tradition—the ritual sacrifices, priestly constitution, purity and dietary laws—and yet "there remains left over in Mosaism the most exalted teaching out of which the founder of your religion . . . wanted to form his Christianity."[32] To Salomon, Judaism signifies a purified Christianity that contains the fundamental ethical teachings "for all humanity."[33] The historical critique, then, only helps to weed out all the unessential contingent forms, and to free ethical teachings from their historical baggage. Judaism's value and authority reside in its eternal ethical truths that remain stubbornly universal in scope and dimension.

Though Salomon rejects many of Bauer's claims about Jewish history and religion, he nonetheless accepts the historical critique only to dismiss it as irrelevant. Ultimately, Salomon cares less about contingent claims and more about grounding ethical truths. But Geiger could not so easily abandon history, even if he, like Salomon, would appeal to a similar set of moral universal truths. For to Geiger as for Bauer, the authority and authenticity of Judaism stands or falls with a "historical critique of the highest level."

Still, Geiger was not keen to attack Bauer or the journal that had published his articles. He respected both the man and the journal, and he hesitated before responding to "the professor of anti-theology." Geiger knew that Bauer had, in other works, challenged the religious Christian orthodoxy of his day, and had lost his chair at the University of Bonn because of it.[34] But such a historical assassination of modern Judaism could not go unanswered, and Geiger responded kind for kind. Like Salomon, Geiger structured his essay around Bauer's, quoting at length and refuting each point in turn.

Geiger responded by offering a counterhistory of his own,[35] one that would exonerate Judaism from the libel of Bauer's critique. Where Bauer anchored his critique in the notion of historical progress, Geiger turned to the central tension in that progress. Beginning with the Roman Empire, and even in Bauer's own "confessional state," two elements—the church and feudal (or civic) society—struggle to exert a one-sided supremacy over the other. The church has always demanded a Christian state, Geiger argues, while feudal society has concentrated power for the wealthy few. Only Judaism overcomes these two disintegrating forces, where the prophet conquers priest, and Judaism's spiritual life supplants worldly church ambitions.[36] To be sure, the new state should be "an organic member of a greater whole that is humanity." But the present German state remains far from that lofty goal, for Jews suffer the kind of vitriolic exclusion represented in Bauer's essay.[37] The state proclaims freedom and equality, yet it cannot deliver. But Judaism does, for it can show Bauer and others how to overcome the dialectical tension of priestly and feudal power, and so move all Germans to become members of a greater organic unity. Judaism, but not Christianity, represents "the historical religion" (emphasis on *the*). To drive the point home, Geiger titles this section of the essay "The historical Religion: Judaism and its Development."[38] Geiger had argued this point with force in an earlier article on Jewish equality in 1835: "For the principle of tradition, to which the whole Talmudic and rabbinic literature owes its emergence, is nothing other than the principle of constant progress and timely development."[39] Judaism, as the most historical of religions, is on Bauer's own terms the most universal and human.

Geiger accepts the preeminence of historical critique, but he tells a very different story than Bauer's. Both are rooted in Hegelian premises, and Geiger draws heavily from the Hegelian rhetoric, speaking of "reality" and "negation," as well as three levels of development and the process of overcoming.[40] Geiger's narrative reads like a counterhistory, for he inverts Bauer's narrative even as he appeals to the same sources. Put simply, he provides a counterimage of Judaism by reading Bauer's sources differently. Geiger interprets the same texts in a new way. He chides Bauer for missing just how integrated Jews have become in the civic, political, and scholarly affairs of modern Europe; emancipated, certainly not, but worldly and here to stay, to be sure. Geiger could not dismiss, as Salomon had done, the historical dimensions of Bauer's essay. His defense of modern Judaism would be historical too. In doing so, Geiger has focused attention on the ways in which scholars like Bauer tell the story of Jewish history.

Even more, Geiger recognizes the importance of authorial voice in that telling. Geiger focuses his essay both on Bauer's historical narrative and on Bauer himself as the preeminent master theologian of Christian liberalism. Even the title of Geiger's essay marks it as profoundly personal: "Bruno Bauer and the Jews." It is significant that Bauer, and not some less worthy opponent, wrote *Die Judenfrage.* Geiger's response turns Bauer's article about Jews into a personal statement *against* Jews. It truly shocks Geiger, as it surely did his peers, that such an esteemed German liberal could argue so forcefully against Jewish emancipation. But with Bauer's prestige, his article "has become a true litmus test for German liberalism."[41] Bauer's reputation precedes his article, and his public standing would encourage readers to accept the competence and "level" of his historical inquiry. Geiger worries that less sophisticated readers might well judge the historical narrative not according to its critical method, but on the reputation and standing of the author.

Although history remains the battleground for emancipation politics, Geiger alerts his readers to how one tells that story, and to the politics and convictions of authors who weave only a partial narrative thread. Geiger substitutes history as a simple unfolding of events, or what Assmann might call a "positivist" history, with a far more complex, polemical, and motivated telling of a past. With all his focus on intentions, meanings, and method, Geiger backdrops historical narrative and foregrounds hermeneutical concerns about reading texts. Only after such preliminary considerations can the "level" and meaning of a historical narrative unfold. In this, Bauer and Geiger agree. One should consider the meaning of historical narratives and the purposes they serve. But historical scholarship, as Bauer's essay makes explicit, serves contemporary political ends. History is neither innocent nor obscure, but materially embedded in the communities it serves and seeks to persuade. Telling a good story challenges the present as much as it recovers a past. Historians like Bauer and Geiger provoke only by recovering a meaningful past for the present. For *Wissenschaft* scholars like Geiger, history writing is a form of identity politics.

History informs identity only when it meets Geiger's test of "historical criticism of the highest level." Geiger adopts this view in his *Judaism and Its History* (1864/65)—his popular series of public lectures offered in Frankfurt and Berlin.[42] In the opening lecture, Geiger distinguishes between two views of Jewish tradition. The first understands Jewish history as a "great world-historical phenomenon," the second as "merely a historical consideration."[43] Only Judaism as a grand phenomenon can yield contemporary significance and, most on Geiger's mind, win the sympathy of his audience. Geiger's lectures are not detached historical studies, but motivated retrievals of the Jewish past that still offer meaning to the present; not a factual history of Judaism, but a Judaism meaningfully recalled and remembered. Yet it is a history of *Judaism:* Geiger recovers the most essential and spiritually "organic" phenomena, and then searches for historical materials that express the spiritual core.

Geiger's history is a retrospective one governed by his liberal and cultural environment. The opening lecture, titled *The Essence of Religion,* readily appeals to the contemporary idiom of religion so popularized by Schleiermacher's influential work.[44] For Judaism to be meaningful, Geiger must prove that, despite Kant's assertion, the essence of religion can be found in Judaism too. Geiger will offer a new reading of the past that highlights those Jewish principles that still resonate with a contemporary audience of "religious" believers. He weaves a drama that consciously subverts traditional Judaism in order to replace it with a more spiritual, organic, and liberal one.[45]

Yet as Schleiermacher had noted earlier, the very term *religion* was in Geiger's time under siege, held in contempt by many who recoiled from religious hypocrisy, and ridiculed by those who attacked religious superstition, heterodoxy, and claims to supernatural revelation. A new religious Judaism would have little appeal for these skeptics. Geiger recognized, like Schleiermacher before him, that religion did indeed have its "cultured despisers." Geiger mockingly called them "the knowing ones" (*die Wissenden*), for they rejected all religious observance in pursuit of rational enlightenment, and challenged religious authority and the received wisdom from the past. He designed his first lecture to undermine their misperceptions about the nature of religion, and to replace them with a conception of religious identity that could be universally shared and vindicated. For "the knowing ones," religion witnessed only to an antiquated and mere historical consideration better left in the past. Moderns should abandon religions without any contemporary significance or authority for a more enlightened, cultured approach that valued the "autonomy of the spirit [*Geist*]."[46] "The knowing ones" redeployed Geiger's distinction between a historical consideration and a world-historical phenomenon, but with more destructive ends in mind. All religions were merely historical curiosities that once commanded great respect and honor, but were now reactionary before an age of reason, enlightenment, and science. The first lecture on religion represented Geiger's response to this charge of irrelevance, and he defended the authority of Jewish history to command modern Jewish commitment. But that history would now come in the form of Judaism as universal religion.

To defend a Judaism still meaningful and significant for the present, Geiger attacked the conception of autonomy that grounded the misguided critique of religion. He did this by examining the nature of human identity, and conceded that natural science had opened areas of research and knowledge unimaginable by previous generations. There would be definite limits to how far science could proceed, but Geiger expressed genuine enthusiasm for scientific discoveries. Indeed, he believed science had discovered in nature a controlling will and rational purpose that could only be divine in character. To be sure, humans were embodied, limited, and natural beings who obeyed laws of nature. In this regard, they were fitting subjects for scientific research. But Geiger turned to another human feature—spirit (*Geist*)—to mark the distinction between human beings and all other natural phenomena. This would not have surprised his audience, for Jewish thinkers often adopted the term *spirit* as an act of accommodation and shoring up of a weakened Jewish tradition.[47] Geiger appealed to spirit in both senses by appropriating a culturally dominant account of religion that could highlight Judaism's distinctive and still meaningful features.

But the rhetorical function of spirit revealed more than the mere appeal to the term itself. The human power of recollection defined the peculiar nature of human spirit:

> Man, who is bound to time and space like all other corporeal and earthly creatures, individual man who is tied to a particular place, who lives and moves within a small period of time, nevertheless overcomes time and space in his innermost being. He is able to transplant himself to the most distant regions, can conjure up the past before him, presuppose the future, and have a conception of what is beyond the present. This capacity cannot be a function of the body. The body is circumscribed by space and time. Man has the power of recollection [*Erinnerung*], he bears within him that which is past, can recall it, and bring back the most various things from his memory [*Gedächtnis*]. Knowledge has become his property . . . Yet, where, in what part of his body is it? Let us pronounce the word which would not exist at all if the thing did not exist: Spirit [*Geist*].[48]

Note, to begin, how Geiger challenges "the knowing ones" and their conception of spirit as "autonomy." For Geiger's religious despisers, knowledge displaces the authority of what had come before. All remains present before their inquisitive gaze—the sure method and faith of scientific investigation. Geiger also appeals to a notion of human autonomy, for spirit exemplifies an individual power unbounded by natural limits of time and space. But spirit delimits an autonomous power that stretches the present to include recollections of the past and images of potential futures. Memory links the present to the past, while imagination opens future worlds. Possessing knowledge is not of the present, but a presence: an attentiveness to the past and openness to the future.

The power of memory displaces the present. Human beings are not restrained, like other natural bodies, by physical limitations. They are embodied, to be sure, but memory transposes the self beyond the present: persons "bear within that which is past." For Geiger, retrieving the past marks a significant category for knowledge on the one hand, and a distinctive quality of human identity on the other. Appealing to memory and imagination offers a strong rebuttal to the autonomy of "the knowing ones" who regard religion as antiquated and naïve. The inner world of spirit links knowledge to memory and imagination. The present no longer stands privileged and independent of its past and future. For Geiger, "the knowing ones" are profoundly ahistorical thinkers. Their knowledge has no history, past, or collective memory. And so the choice of Geiger's title for his lectures: *Judaism and Its History.* World history embodies the principles of an eternal, organic Judaism. In turn, those very principles move history in ever-new configurations that carry a trace of past meanings. Historians like Geiger track *Geist* as the material embodiment of Judaism.

Geiger believes that historical knowledge (*Geist*) exposes the false assumptions behind the claims of the "the knowing ones." Enlightened reason does not overcome a past, but rather understands that past in a clearer light, and through this new understanding persons imaginatively gaze at potential futures. But if his appeal to *Geist* does not satisfy, then Geiger contends that even science proves him right. His discussion of perception offers the scientific corollary to his argument that historical memory displaces the present. The consciousness that I live in the embodied present, and yet I can recall the past and imagine the future, exposes the deceptive act of perception in which, "properly speaking, man sees no distance, the impression made of an object through the medium of ray is fixed within his sense of seeing."[49] Every object appears at the same close distance; depth perception is a habit (*Gewohnheit*) to be acquired rather than an innate feature of human perception. We must learn how to distinguish objects spatially, Geiger argues. Human perception remains flawed because without skill, thought, and habit, it cannot determine appropriate spatial distinctions of perceived objects of knowledge.

I cannot vouch for Geiger's scientific research. But I do want to argue that his account of human perception mirrors his critique of "the knowing ones" who remain stubbornly blind to important distinctions among past, present, and future. "The knowing ones" only consider the present, just as human vision sees objects only at one distance; both reveal a profound lack of depth perception and knowledge. To envision only the present, without distance or history, recalls only a partial record of total perception.

Memory can train moderns to be historical thinkers and can help reveal the historical dimensions of the present. Geiger's account adopts the Kantian claim that persons frame objects of perception through the rational structures of the mind. But that mind, consciousness, or *Geist* in Geiger's argument does not apply a universal grid to each and every historical situation. Consciousness is itself historically conditioned. "I am a child of my time," Geiger confesses; "I suffer myself to be impelled and guided by what my time presents as truth; I am a child of my environment, I am not the creator of myself nor of my own actions."[50] Spirit as historical memory limits knowledge to the conditioned present, even as it broadens those boundaries to include the past and future. Moderns are thus historical beings in two senses: as children of their time, they are guided by a consensus account of truth and proper activity, yet they also retain the memories of how they arrived at this consensus, and thus can imagine a quite different future. Persons both inhabit and surpass the boundaries of their own making. "The knowing ones," like innate perception, offer a very limited and unimaginative sense of human knowledge. And even natural science, according to Geiger, can reveal the constraints of ahistorical thinking.

Geiger's rhetorical use of *Geist* to shore up religious sensibility before Enlightenment critics mirrors Schleiermacher's Christian liberal move to distinguish between science and religious feeling.[51] Rational science maintains its own criteria for truth, separate and distinct from religious concerns. For both liberal thinkers, science cannot undermine religion, as each maintains its separate sphere of influence. Indeed for Geiger, science may even support religious claims—thus his appeal to visionary experience—but in no way can it usurp religious authority. This protective strategy, as one scholar of nineteenth-century religion has called it,[52] undercuts how "the knowing ones" criticize Judaism as a "dark belief" (*dunkles Glauben*) with "hypotheses that cannot be proven."[53] Religion has less to do with faith, according to Geiger, and more with "the consciousness [*Bewußtsein*] of our eminence and lowness; the striving after perfection, coupled with the feeling that we cannot reach the highest plane."[54] Religion is a longing rather than "a system of truths": "[I]t is the jubilation of the soul conscious of its eminence and, at the same time, its humble confession of its finiteness and limitations. Religion is the flight of the spirit after the ideal; the pursuit after the highest notions."[55] This sense of longing captures "the very nature, the very essence of the human," and reveals how Geiger grounds religion in personal identity. Religion is a "searching after truth" rather than ownership of "the whole truth," even as it lives "within man."[56] The nature of religion, then, marks an inner spiritual longing for truth forever protected from scientific scrutiny. It will remain "one of the noblest animating forces"[57] so long as human beings search after truth.

Geiger claims here in the first chapter of his history that Judaism animates this kind of religious longing, and so must be counted among the great religions. But when he compares Judaism to Greek culture and religion, his rhetoric shifts from "inborn longing" to religious moral truths. Religions do not exist on an even playing field—although an appeal to aspirations, feelings, and longings might lead one to think so.[58] Judaism's superiority becomes clear in its higher ethical truths. According to Geiger, only Jews long for the loftiest ideals of moral worth. Like many of his colleagues, Geiger favorably compares Jewish ideals to Greek conceptions.[59] Where Judaism provokes "the inner striving for higher purity, the desire to lay aside human moral defects, and the reliance upon the Divine as the source of all purity," Greek religion remains "imperfect" and "childish" in its conception of the gods. Greek gods exert power, but they also exhibit "moral defects" and "indulge in the most sensual pleasures, break faith and promises, have sexual affairs [*Buhlerei*], dispute and quarrel," and are generally cruel, arbitrary, and envious of human welfare. Even more, the Greek gods remain subject to fate, an amoral doctrine of "mysterious, unconquerable power, before which even the gods must bow."[60] Geiger argues that with such a deformed image of the gods, the Greeks "cannot aspire to true perfection." The spiritual ideal above us, Geiger claims, is too close "to the moral ideal within us for the defects of the former not to make an impression on the latter."[61] By contrast, Judaism offers a picture of ethical purity and holiness: a moral and just God who remains the supreme and only power. Jews seek to realize the "idea in Judaism" in practical life, but in all cases they preserve the pristine moral truths in the various material "vessels." Let the vessels be broken, Geiger asserts, so long as Jews "preserve the precious contents."[62]

Religious Judaism is for Geiger a set of moral truths that stand above historical contingency and progress. One could certainly seek after these truths, even in the sense of a "flight of the spirit after the ideal." But Geiger is less concerned to defend an inborn longing, and worried far more to protect these moral truths from historical contingency. Moral truths have no material history, Geiger argues here, but memories, passions, and spiritual longings do. In particular, these higher truths materialize "vessels" that never fully contain their power. Although he appeals to an inner longing for truth in the first chapter on religion, Geiger adopts Salomon's Kantian approach to ethical perfection when he turns to the substance of Judaism in the second chapter. Recall how Salomon responded to Bauer's critique of "the Jewish question," where Salomon admitted that Jews remain ahistorical actors because they "cling" to a set of eternal moral truths. The historical vessels do indeed change, but the fundamental moral laws remain pure and safe. For Geiger, too, Judaism is *religious* in its moral ideals. Any other kind of Jewish practice would not be religious in Geiger's sense. Religious Judaism means for Geiger a set of moral universal truths that continually reappear in Jewish history.[63] These truths create and move that history, such that Jewish tradition becomes the progressive rediscovery of universal moral ideals.

That Geiger can so quickly move from Hegelian language of historical progress in his response to Bauer, to a Schleiermachean appeal to religious longing, to finally a Kantian safeguarding of eternal Jewish principles reveals the various rhetorical strategies he employs to defend Judaism before its critics. But it also suggests that Geiger feels the force of these criticisms, and his apologetic rejoinders will only comfort those already converted, as it were. Still, he seeks a religious authority that will ground Jewish history, and he finds it in Jewish moral ideals:

> A religion which carries within itself a more powerful idea than it can exhibit in temporal imperfection may, in the course of its development, cast away many a side-shoot, efface many antiquated expressions and produce new ones by its creative ability.[64]

The historian maps out this development with all its various tangents and "antiquated expressions," and helps to create new vessels to harbor universal moral truths.

Geiger redirects historical memories to focus on those moments of ethical perfection in Jewish history, and casts away "many a side-shoot" that undermine moral purity. He seeks an organic, seamless web that stretches the present to include visions of a past and future moral life. He appeals to such a web in his theoretical pieces on Jewish liturgy. In *The Necessity and Extent of a Reform of the Jewish Divine Service* (1861), a programmatic essay on Jewish liturgical reform written only a few years before his lectures on Jewish history, Geiger speaks of a "richly remembered past" to invoke the power of Jewish prayer:

> The power of the religious expression of life lies not merely in individual feelings, but especially in the living relationship of the individual to the community standing upon the same ground: in the firm grasp of a great, richly remembered past, and in the joy of being led from such a past into a new future.[65]

A meaningful past mediates the relation between individuals and the broader community, and in the medium of such rich memories one is displaced from the immediate present (note the passive voice in Geiger's text). Memories not only intensify individual feelings; they also point beyond the self to a community with a shared past and future. Identity is stretched beyond the immediate present and the enclosed self in the joy of public religious worship. In a second essay on Jewish liturgy, published in 1868, Geiger argues that the Jewish prayer service contains "the complete historical past, with all the promises and expectations of the future, and indeed the whole faith of the community."[66] But that faith and history are moral, and the "richly remembered past" weeds out moments of moral rupture. Geiger claims that "every reform is a transition out of the past into a revived future."[67] Reform is not revolution but a moral dialogue with the past in order to link the present with a future "standing upon the same ground." Historical memory effects a productive act of ethical transition.

Yet even as Geiger appeals to historical memory and the power of the past to shape contemporary moral concerns, those very concerns dominate his perception of the past. Is this not a reworked version of "the knowing ones," who claim that autonomy of spirit guides the human search for truth and value? This is how Amos Funkenstein reads Geiger. Funkenstein exposes how historiography and collective memory unite in Geiger's works to support contemporary values and needs.[68] Memory and historiography do not stand, as Yosef Yerushalmi would have it, "in radically different relations to the past": the one closer to myth, the other "a truly new kind of recollection."[69] And the historian is not for Funkenstein what she is for Yerushalmi: the guardian of fact, proof, and evidence who acts against "the agents of oblivion, the shredders of documents, the assassins of memory."[70] Funkenstein's historian acts much like Geiger, who reads the past as a retrospective self firmly committed to the collective memories of the present. Group memories do indeed shape the way in which historians read the past. So even as Geiger appeals to memory in order to displace culturally dominant accounts of common sense ("the knowing ones"), he still reads that past as a mirror to the present. In Geiger's texts, historical memory is a hermeneutical exercise of retrieval that manifests the religious moral spirit. Geiger displaces history as "merely a historical consideration" with the more significant and meaningful account of communal memory. In so doing, he retrieves a religious Judaism that resonates with the moral claims of his liberal Jewish community.

Geiger's hermeneutical question remains how to interpret a remembered and forgotten past to better ground religious Judaism in history. This methodological position recalls the central issue in Assmann's study on Moses. "Mnemohistory," for Assmann, is "concerned not with the past as such, but only with the past as it is remembered." Assmann reminds us that a past retrieved, remembered, or forgotten also functions as a rhetorical strategy for constructing identity. Geiger's *Judaism and Its History* rebuilds the past into an attractive source for modern Jewish moral reflection. Judaism becomes a pristine, ethical source for moderns to draw upon and develop. Geiger constructs a usable past out of eternal moral ideas to better ground the authority of personal meaning. But Geiger's model of a "great world-historical phenomenon" highlights some figures and events just as it represses others. We should expect no less. Geiger's history is not positivist in any sense of the word, and it never pretends to be. Instead, Geiger appeals to a new, meaningful, and ethical past to ground his vision of religious Judaism. Jewish religious authority is rooted in the hermeneutics of historical memory.

Geiger's professional and personal rival, Heinrich Graetz (1817–1891), also appealed to historical memory, even labeling *Wissenschaft des Judentums* a "return of memory" (*Rückerinnerung*).[71] But Graetz's remembered history recalled a far different past than Geiger's, and the disparity between their visions highlights the distinctive ideological focus in Geiger's works. Heinrich Graetz was the most famous and popular of Jewish historical writers in nineteenth-century Germany, and his animosity toward Geiger has become that of legend. Ismar Schorsch considers Graetz's life work as a committed refutation of Geiger's liberal Judaism.[72] Lacking the Jewish and secular education that Geiger had from his very early years, Graetz attained much of his learning on his own, although he studied for three years with the Orthodox rabbi Samson Raphael Hirsch. Graetz came to his teacher's defense after Geiger published a harsh critique of Hirsch's *Nineteen Letters,* and henceforth forged a visceral hatred of Geiger and his movement.

In his magisterial *Geschichte der Juden,* written over a twenty-year period (1853–1874), Graetz blames Geiger for assembling numerous historical errors, for narrowing Judaism into theological categories, and for sowing the seeds for religious schism within Judaism.[73] Geiger's professional shortcomings, however, echoed personal ones as well, for Graetz often reduced "historical trends and intellectual currents to personalities."[74] Graetz embodied dynamic historical conflicts in great personalities, often contrasting Hillel to Shammai, Rabbi Eliezer to Joshua, or Akiba to Ishmael.[75] That great-men theory of history continues in Graetz's attack on Geiger and the defense of his mentor and friend, S. R. Hirsch.

Graetz's hermeneutical focus on historical personalities sharply distinguishes his moral vision of Jewish history from Geiger's own. In the first volume of his *History of the Jews,* Graetz begins with the poetic "on a spring day."[76] This rather appealing opening immediately draws the reader into a story about ancient Jewish history. It helps to situate the wanderings of pastoral tribes in the land of Palestine. But it does something more as well. Graetz's opening sentence offers a sharp contrast to I. M. Jost's earlier *History of the Israelites* (1820–1828). Jost's history was the first to integrate *Wissenschaft* scholarship into Jewish historical studies, and marked a watershed in Jewish historical research.[77] With its sharp critique of rabbinic Judaism and defense of Mosaic monotheism, Jost's work appealed more to the liberal camp than to conservatives like Graetz. Still, in general outline, scope, and length (the structure of the index is remarkably similar), Graetz modeled his history on Jost's example. But the differences prove telling, especially in Graetz's opening sentence in the first volume. For Jost, too, opened his history with a discussion of Palestine, and focused on the minutiae of climate and location of land—even noting its precise longitude and latitude.[78] Graetz detested this "dry, Philistine character" of Jost's history, for he felt that Jost had "torn to shreds the heroic drama of thousands of years."[79] Geiger had a very different assessment of Jost's work. He mentions in a letter dated January 25, 1833, that "the tone [of Jost's history] is dignified and calm, the language understandable and pleasurable, so that one notices a very welcome advance in his achievement."[80] Graetz, however, found little pleasure in Jost's prose, and wanted to infuse a lost brilliance to Jewish history.[81]

When Graetz discusses Palestine in his first volume, he focuses on the *people* of that land, and invigorates their wanderings with poetic flourishes that read more like storytelling than arid historical scholarship. Where Jost self-consciously wrote as a professional historian, identifying himself as a "researcher" in both his 1820 history and in a later scholarly work titled *The History of Judaism* (1857), Graetz reached out to a broader audience of educated Jews who desired a passionate, lively story of Jewish history. Indeed, Graetz discovered *Jews* in history, not Jost's *Israelites.*[82] And if Graetz's popularity is any sign, he did not let his Jews down. For Graetz yearned, above all, to instill a sense of self-respect (*Selbstachtung*) and self-confidence (*Selbstgefühl*) for modern Jewry, even labeling a sub-section of his work on the modern period "The Growth of Self-Confidence."[83] To instill this sense of Jewish accomplishment, Graetz focused on the Jewish people and their advance from humble beginnings to great political, religious, and cultural heights. These were a people modern Jews could be proud of as they identified with the lofty pursuits of great men from their own past.

Graetz italicizes most of the names in his history, marking them off from the institutions and cultures surrounding them.[84] He wants to show how "a people arose out of the night of the grave, the only ones so far that the chronicles of human memory bear witness to."[85] The Jewish people are both singular and central to world history. Even when Graetz discusses the origins of Christianity, he reads that history *within* Jewish history, and describes Jesus as a relatively ignorant but good Jew, and Paul as the great deceiver who abandons Jesus' Jewish teachings for "foreign elements."[86] In reasserting the centrality of Jewish history, Graetz empowers his modern Jewish readership to regain their pride and confidence in Jewish tradition as embodied in great historical figures. This "return of memory" recovers the lost heroics of the past for a present yearning for pride of ownership and place.

To the surprise of many, Geiger welcomed Graetz's first published volume on Jewish history (volume four on early Christianity and rabbinic Judaism).[87] He appreciated Graetz's "fresh air and zealous spirit," together with his "eagerness and passion."[88] But there was much to regret as well, for "the work in no way claims to be a product of careful historical research and writing."[89] Graetz's work contains "stories" (*Geschichten*) held loosely together, but no "history" (*Geschichte*).[90] To be a historical work, Geiger wants "an inner law" that moves history to a determinate end. But Graetz's history has no beginning, and thus no grounding premise to understand historical movements. Geiger is simply baffled by Graetz's decision to begin with his fourth volume that covers the years 70–500 C.E. How could a reader possibly understand the "legal-religious character" of the age, Geiger asks incredulously, if the author withholds the historical background to make sense of rabbinic Judaism? Instead, Graetz trots before his readers an overwhelming array of names from the Tannaitic and Amoraic periods with equal force and weight, such that a reader cannot recognize (much less remember) their importance to Jewish history.[91]

Graetz has merely assembled a cluster of stories and pieced them together, but in so doing has lost the forest for the trees. In focusing on Jews, Graetz has lost Judaism with its "inner law" and development. Geiger, to be sure, finds other details to complain about—Graetz's biased reading of historical figures, and his failure to appreciate the work of other scholars (particularly Geiger's own).[92] But his protest focuses on the "void of ideas" that should have controlled Graetz's history.[93] Without the moral and ideological weight of a driving ideal, Graetz's history remains nothing but a collection of amusing and animating stories about Jews in the past. It simply fails as a historical critique of the highest order. Geiger desires a history of Judaism that reveals the progressive movement of eternal ideas, rather than one that merely studies fascinating Jewish lives. For Geiger, Graetz offers a passionate account of Jews in history, but not a vision of how Judaism moves and determines that history.

Geiger's "return of memory" recalls an ideological development of religious Judaism and its moral ideals. To achieve a higher critique, historical works must uncover latent moral truths, and bring them into full view before the reader. Graetz's history fails on both accounts, argues Geiger. For in the end, modern Jews reconnect with Jewish ideals rather than ancient Jews. Geiger and his liberal Jews require a history of religious Judaism rather than a history of Jews.

Liturgical Reform and Memory

Geiger's works on memory and history are bold attempts to refashion the ways in which Jews think about Judaism as an ideological moral force. Yet constructing religious Judaism was not just a theoretical pursuit performed in lecture halls, but also a practical problem that liberal rabbis like Geiger encountered regularly in their rabbinic duties. Jakob Petuchowski, in his work on Reform liturgy in Europe, has tried to separate Geiger "the liturgical theoretician" from Geiger "the liturgical practitioner." According to Petuchowski, Geiger proved far more traditional in practice than in theory.[94] To take but one example, Geiger criticized the Hamburg Temple reformers in 1842 for failing to produce a more radical liturgical reform, but he adopted some of their conservative practices in his prayer books of 1854 and 1870. One reason for the divergence between theory and practice might be Geiger's wish to appease all members of his community, many of whom would not follow his more liberal ideas.[95] But even in his "theoretical" pieces on liturgical reform, Geiger's moral principles transformed theory into material practices, so that "the house of God does not remain completely closed to the youth on the one hand, but on the other, that they do not drive away the older generation."[96] Geiger believed the prayer service could unify theory and practice: "The most important act of unity of the religious community is its communal worship of God. The individual concentrates entirely on the worship service. In prayer, he creates a unity out of his feelings and the religious principles that had become separated from life."[97] Scholars have good reasons to distinguish practice from theory, or in Meyer's terms, to recognize the tension between Geiger "as scholarly critic and as rabbi."[98] But Geiger believed the prayer service, and particularly his liturgical works, could bridge the gap. Rather than explain incongruities in Geiger's theoretical and practical works, I want to focus instead on how Geiger integrated his moral claims about religious Judaism into practical discussions on Jewish liturgy.

Geiger's history of religious Judaism underlies his two most important pieces on liturgy, his *Nothwendigkeit* (The Necessity and Extent of a Reform of the Jewish Liturgical Service; 1861) and *Unser Gottesdienst* (Our Liturgical Service; 1868), and his two edited prayer books from 1854 and 1870. Geiger seeks a balanced compromise in liturgical reform to better win communal acceptance. He astutely manages a multi-level approach to Jewish history: he leaves powerful recollections intact even as he expunges some more disturbing memories, yet just as often he displaces particular historical moments to the "background" in order to foreground more "spiritual" memories. And in one crucial passage in his two prayer books, Geiger blurs historical memory altogether, effectively opening imaginative space for infusing personal meaning into the prayer. This multi-tiered approach to liturgical reform edits and even eliminates memories from Jewish history. But so too does it preserve, in its very absence, those disquieting memories that challenge the progress of moral ideals. The contemporary student of "mnemohistory" witnesses how Geiger invites, constructs, and often impairs memory to root liberal religious Judaism.

Reimagining modern Jewish identity through prayer-book reform was no easy task, for as Petuchowski astutely warned, the synagogue represented the whole community in Europe, and not (as today) particular segments of Reform, Conservative, or Orthodox Jewry.[99] Political compromise accounted for many of the moderate changes in Jewish liturgy, for prayer-book editors sought a middle ground between completely new prayers and what they regarded as meaningless old ones.[100] Geiger understood the politics of prayer-book reform, and struggled to include multiple generations in the communities he served—Wiesbaden, Breslau, Frankfurt, and Berlin. His desire to reach the entire community could explain why he rejected the leadership of the more radical and private Berlin *Reformgemeinde* in the mid-1840s. The Berlin society had too emphatically distanced itself from the larger Jewish community. Even in 1838, Geiger refused the homiletical and educational roles of rabbinical leadership in Breslau so long as the traditional rabbi Solomon Tiktin still ruled on halakhic issues.[101] Such dual leadership would lead inevitably to conflict and schism, and Geiger wanted complete control over all rabbinic functions.[102] So Geiger had to play the game of political compromise to gain support from his constituency, and though "history had spoken its judgment" on the course of liturgical reform, Geiger could not afford such radical positions. "The future," Geiger admitted, "is still not here," and so "the way of compromise" indicated the only feasible position in prayer-book reform.[103]

Yet political considerations alone did not move Geiger in this more conservative, inclusive direction. Though Geiger had argued at the Frankfurt rabbinical conference (1845) that only German symbolized the true "language of the heart" because it moved him more deeply than Hebrew,[104] he also recognized the power of Hebrew (and the memories associated with it) to maintain strong Jewish commitment:

> Our divine service must and will celebrate in the near future its linguistic rebirth. *But the time has not yet arrived.* There still exist important members in the community who, with utter clarity of spirit and warmth of heart, find their customs and memories of their youth rooted in the time of the established [*altbefestigten*] Hebrew divine service. These men are capable powers within the community, and are the bearers of a profound Jewish sensibility.[105]

The political message was clear: as long as "important members" of the community honored the traditional liturgy, Geiger could hardly pursue more radical changes to Hebrew prayer. The "near future" was still in some distant time. But Geiger also evinced heartfelt respect for the power of Hebrew prayer to carry forward "a profound Jewish sensibility." He had remarked on this before in the preface to his first edited prayer book:

> The prestige of the prayers is not only connected with their contents, but also with the traditional form [*die ganze überkommene Gestalt*], with the word in which they

> have been bequeathed unto us—that is to say, with the Hebrew language. Let it remain, therefore, with a few exceptions, the language of prayer.[106]

More than political compromise had convinced Geiger to include Hebrew liturgical prayers. The Hebrew language evoked intense personal memories that connected Jews to a past, and granted prestige and stability (*altbefestigten*) to the liturgical service. The memories associated with Hebrew prayer transported important Jewish sensibilities through the generations. Geiger's compromise in liturgical reform with the powerful, older members of his community signaled more than a politically prudent act.[107] It also returned Jewish identity to its roots in historical religious Judaism.

Not all historical memories, however, carry equal weight. At one time the notion of a "people of Israel" (*das Volk Israel*) evoked strong national and religious feeling in public worship. But Geiger claims that "it is natural that historical memories [*geschichtlichen Erinnerungen*], in so far as they concern the destiny of a people, no longer have the meaning which they had in the past." Such is the case with *das Volk Israel,* which "no longer lives in the heart and wishes of the present." Better to highlight the idea of a "holy teaching," Geiger continues, rather than stress the character of a chosen people. So too with nations like Amalek or characters like Haman who "no longer arouse the feeling of disgust in our hearts." These historical memories must assume "a more spiritual character and their expression in prayers must be therefore more spiritual." Rather than effacing these recollections altogether, Geiger wants to stress their "spiritual" significance over against their "sensual representation."[108] This too distinguishes Geiger's history of *Judaism* from Graetz's history of the Jews. By foregrounding the *geistige* character of historical memories, Geiger can maintain a strong connection to a past, but one now colored by his modern ethical commitments to religious Judaism rather than by the particular heroes venerated by Graetz's history. Jews can still recall the people Israel, not as the chosen ones, but as the bearers of divine teaching. Amalek and Haman still draw Jews back to a more horrifying past, but only to teach moral and spiritual lessons for the future. Geiger recovers the inner, spiritual meaning of historical persons, and returns "the power of interiority" (*die Kraft der Innerlichkeit*) to public prayer. Jews will practice religious Judaism by reimagining historical memories that privilege spiritual depth.

Like historical memories, not all prayers contain the spiritual "interiority" required for Geiger's liturgical reform. Some prayers, so empty of spiritual significance, should be eliminated altogether from historical memory, and cannot, in Assmann's phrase, be "modeled, invented, reinvented, and reconstructed by the present." In 1861, Geiger had emphasized the spiritual component within Jewish prayer. But by 1868, in writing his *Unser Gottesdienst,* Geiger proved far more critical and severe in assessing the depth of spiritual meaning in the prayer service. When discussing the "outer forms of divine worship" (*das Aeußere des Gottesdienstes*), Geiger desired "a resolution between the past and future." But not so with "the contents of prayer" (*Inhalte der Gebete*) that "do not fulfill our hopes and wishes" and clearly undermine the spiritual values of religious Judaism.[109] Geiger continues this point in the preface to his 1870 prayer book:

> [A]ll respectful retention of Judaism's historical elements, religious *concepts* [*Vorstellungen*] which have had a temporal validity, but which have been displaced by *a progressively purer conception,* must not be retained in a one-sided and sharp accentuation. Rather they must be either totally removed or recast into a form which does not contradict the purer conception [*geläuterten Auffassung*].[110]

Geiger despised prayers that turned worship into a "sacrificial service" (*Opferdienste*). All prayers that reminded Jews of the ancient human sacrifice "must fade completely from the prayer book." The memory (*Erinnerung*) of human and animal sacrifices contained not a "moment of religious edification."[111]

For Geiger, sacrificial worship "was not merely unnecessary, but rather superfluous, and not merely superfluous, but a mistaken view."[112] The most powerful memory of human and animal sacrifice in Jewish liturgy recalled Abraham's trial with his son Isaac. Geiger's attacks against liturgical representations of the *Akedah* border on the hysterical. But they also reveal his passionate insistence that some memories damage Jewish religion and identity.

In Geiger's remembered past, Judaism's battle against human sacrifice represents its first "great feat" in world history.[113] Abraham's greatness lies in his rejection of sacrificial worship. The story of the *Akedah* shows us how Abraham's "pure faith" overcomes sacrificial duty, and thus Abraham begins the Jewish "world historical mission": "This story [of Abraham and Isaac] is and remains for us a confirmation of the fundamental truth of all Judaism: for the abhorrence of every human sacrifice, and for removing every thought that God demands such sacrifice. . . ."[114] *This* memory of Abraham has profound spiritual meaning. But the liturgy reformulates Abraham's faith into Abraham's merit. It is not quite right to say, as one Geiger scholar has argued, that "Geiger considered the biblical story of the binding of Isaac an example of human sacrifice which ought to be eliminated from the liturgy."[115] Geiger has nothing but praise for the *biblical* story, but only scorn for the representation of that story in Jewish liturgy: "Our God is no idol, our piety not callous barbarism. And should we praise this trial of Abraham in prayer as the merit [*das Verdienst*] that he himself acquired, and claimed for us as a treasure of mercy?"[116]

Jewish liturgy, especially in the New Year and Day of Atonement prayer books, has misconfigured the Jewish memory of Abraham. From a biblical story about faith and the overcoming of sacrificial worship, Jews have remembered the *Akedah* as a story about sacrificial merit.

Geiger understands the motives behind this portrayal of Abraham. The liturgical Abraham reveals a "jealous" adoption from another religion, one that stresses "the sacrificial atonement of the son." Geiger is unwavering on this point: if Jews remember Abraham for sacrificing his son, then they appropriate a thoroughly Christian reading of the Hebrew Bible, and undermine "the fundamental principle of Judaism."[117] Jews do not receive merit, grace, or any other kind of atonement from Abraham's act. As a test of and model for faith, Abraham's act remains Jewish to the core. But to interpret it otherwise permits a Christian sacrificial reading. As Susannah Heschel has convincingly argued, Geiger "blamed Christian influence for those elements he rejected within Judaism."[118] So Geiger calls the liturgical account of Abraham a flawed, Christian interpretation of Genesis 22. Defective readings, in this case, damage Geiger's account of religious Judaism as a moral force. "Here," Geiger challenges, "there is no compromise! Either confession in the service to Moloch or the true worship of God!"[119]

Geiger seeks to erase from memory all prayers devoted to Abraham's meritorious sacrifice, together with all other sacrificial worship. Petitioning for the return of sacrificial worship is not only "a lie in our mouths, but even the memory of its former existence has for us no religious value."[120] Geiger's religious Judaism redraws the historical landscape so that Jewish memory only traverses across spiritual domains. The more sensual pursuits of sacrificial worship lie instead in a wasteland of base and uncharted territory. If Geiger could rewrite the liturgy on Abraham entirely, then his merit for future generations would appear utterly foreign and hostile to Jewish tradition. In this sense, Geiger's implicit critique of Jesus as the sacrificial son, while muted, is no less damaging. The Abraham in Jewish liturgy mimics Christian representations of Jesus. He represents *their* savior, Geiger argues, not ours. Religious Judaism must adopt *Jewish* ethical readings of the past.

Geiger's essays contain phrases such as "our present condition," "for us," and "our hopes and wishes." Who is this "we" that Geiger appeals to? The imagined "we" suggests how Geiger reshapes Jewish historical memory. "Our hopes," Geiger shows, should be yours as well. He invites readers to imagine a community secure in its own self-perceptions and memories of the past. But Geiger knew well that German Jewish communities were far more diverse than his enticing "we" suggests. Some members of his Breslau community, for example, were well educated in Jewish texts and interpretations, fluent in Hebrew, and comfortable with the traditional Hebrew liturgy. But others "do not know Hebrew at all, or do not know it sufficiently to find edification in a Hebrew prayer."[121]

In composing his prayer books, Geiger thus recognized how "nowadays a prayer book must make provision for the great number" of Jews unlearned in classical sources and the Hebrew language. The diversity in readership helps explain Geiger's use of Hebrew and German in his two edited prayer books. He left the Hebrew text relatively untouched (especially in the 1854 edition), but the German printed on the same page represented "a completely new *reworking* [*Bearbeitung*]" of the Hebrew prayers. A simple translation, Geiger argued, would not offer "in content and expression" what an estranged Jew demanded. His audience was a German-speaking and -reading public unmoved by traditional Hebrew texts. Unfortunately, those devoted to the Hebrew sacrificial prayer would not criticize its "religious point of view and its form." So politics would play an important role in Geiger's editorial decisions: only in the German would he express "the religious idea which must pervade the prayer."[122] David Ellenson notes that "this tactic—retaining the Hebrew while employing translation as a tool to obviate meanings that were perceived as objectionable—was to become a hallmark of countless numbers of subsequent Liberal liturgies."[123] Even the more conservative Manuel Joël, who replaced Geiger in Breslau, followed him in this practice when he revised Geiger's liturgy.[124] For those Jews still devoted to the Hebrew, Geiger and others could appease their sensibilities while instilling others in their German reworkings.[125]

Geiger embedded his appeals to "us" and "our hopes" in the German texts, for there he could reconfigure Jewish memory for his liberal audience. The imagined "we" represented Jews like Geiger who valued German as the "language of the heart." The loss of traditional Hebrew, Geiger admitted elsewhere, translated into a loss of memory. All for the better, Geiger might argue, regarding the ancient animal sacrifices. He could reshape memories and even discard others entirely in his German reworkings without altering the Hebrew text. The decline in Jewish learning had for Geiger at least one advantage: without the damaging memories that threatened a "true" worship of God, he could appeal to the religious principles that "must" accompany prayer. A new language offered hope for new historical memories more in tune with an ethical religious Judaism.

Geiger's strong editorial hand moves throughout his two prayer books. Liberal principles concerning the unity and spiritual nature of God, ethical monotheism, Jerusalem as "symbol," and messianic ideas are everywhere in force in Geiger's prayer books.[126] In the second benediction to the Amidah prayer, which praises God's ability to resurrect the dead, Geiger's German text reads, "Yes, You are the all powerful one who fulfills the promise to the dead for its salvation in a new eternal life [*neuen ewigen Leben*]."[127] Eternal life, to be sure, but still not a God who revives the dead (as the Hebrew indicates).[128] Or, when returning the Torah to the ark, the congregation asks God (in Hebrew) to "bring us back to you, and we shall return, and renew the days of old." But Geiger's German text requests "ever clearer" knowledge of God, and does not mention a return to the past.[129] While the Hebrew text, especially in 1854, remains close to the traditional prayers, Geiger's German reworkings evoke new meanings and memories.

Given Geiger's view that his German would express "the religious idea which must pervade the prayer," it proves significant that Geiger fails to offer *the* religious meaning regarding one essential historical memory. The passage appears after the last readings from the Torah during the morning Sabbath service. The Kaddish is recited, and the Torah raised for all the community to observe. Upon viewing the Torah, the community makes this declaration in Hebrew: "This is the Torah that Moses placed before the children of Israel, upon the command of Hashem [God], through Moses' hand."[130] Geiger quotes the Hebrew in its traditional form. This in itself is noteworthy, for the more liberal Hamburg prayer book does not include the last phrase, "upon the command of Hashem [God], through Moses' hand."[131] The Hamburg omission raises an important historical problem for liberal Jews: did God actually "command" Moses to write this text? The Hamburg reformers decided to "forget" this historical (and certainly theological) question in its prayer-book reform.

Geiger maintains the Hebrew, but we should note his German reworking: "This teaching [*Lehre*] Moses gave to the children of Israel; it is God's word!"[132] The Hebrew *Torah* becomes the German *Lehre,* and in this rendering the text glosses over how, or even whether, God transfers that teaching to Moses. Compare Geiger's German to a more conservative, but still not traditional translation from his contemporary Michael Sachs: "And that is the teaching [*Lehre*] that Moses presented [*vorgelegt*] to the children of Israel by the command of the Eternal [*auf den Befehl des Ewigen*] through Moses."[133] Sachs struggles, like Geiger, to offer a fitting translation without stating directly that Moses copied God's commands into writing. But there is no commander, command, or hand in Geiger's German text. He conceals these difficult passages, and states only that Moses offers to Israel the word of God.

This absence represents neither an accident nor oversight on Geiger's part, and his response to Manuel Joël's essay on prayer-book reform explains why.[134] Joël was Geiger's rabbinic successor in Breslau, and his 1869 essay, "Toward an Orientation on the Question of the Cultus," marked new liturgical changes that Joël instituted for the Breslau community. Geiger's criticisms of the piece were personal in nature, for here rose a man set to unravel part of what Geiger had promoted in Breslau.[135] Geiger appears most distressed by the dogmatic intent of Joël's essay.[136] With such a dogmatic view of Torah from Sinai, Geiger asks, how could the more Orthodox in the community accept Joël's revisionary stance?[137] Not Joël's account of Torah, but his divisive dogmatism troubled Geiger, for he found it both unnecessary and devastating for a pluralistic community. This kind of overt theological rigidity would only lead to a religious schism.[138] Geiger appeals instead to the freedom of theological inquiry to pursue all questions without fear of religious exile. In this, Geiger echoes the second of the founding pillars of *Wissenschaft des Judentums* that Schorsch has catalogued: the right to absolute free inquiry. So in his own prayer books Geiger remains silent on such charged issues as Torah from Sinai. Indeed, Geiger describes his prayer book in his response to Joël as one that "was a true symbol of unity for the overwhelming number of the community."[139] This would be unity at the price of obscurity and silence, but unity nonetheless.

Geiger's silence on these weighty matters suggests both political compromise and an opening for personal meanings. His Hebrew readers were assuredly committed to the traditional Hebrew phrasing (unlike, for example, many Jews in Hamburg). But the question concerning the Bible's divinity, even the very meaning of divinity, unleashed theological debate and doubt among traditional and liberal Jews alike in nineteenth-century Germany. No wonder, then, that Geiger would leave that debate alone, even in his German texts. Geiger's German raises too many unanswered questions: upon whose authority did Moses give "this" teaching? How do we know it is God's word? Did Moses receive this teaching from God directly? With such diverse and potentially explosive views on the divine source of Torah, Geiger allows his readers, in this one but still significant case, to construct their own historical memories. The fundamental moral truths of his religious Judaism do not rely upon one firm answer to these theological questions.

Here, his strong editorial hand, in force elsewhere, is noticeably absent. Geiger blurs the historical memory of divine authorship and transmission, and thus opens space for "our hopes and wishes," and the memories that speak "to us," to enter into that history. Though Geiger himself could not believe in a divine lawgiver in the language of the traditional Hebrew, he would not force upon his German readers "the religious idea which must pervade the prayer." It was enough that Moses had given "God's word" to Israel. To state "what really happened," or how that history should be remembered, was better left to personal discovery and significance.

Geiger's German reworkings of Hebrew prayers do not answer "what really happened," but instead offer new religious memories of the past. For Geiger, spiritual Jewish history trumps a Judaism as "merely a historical consideration." His history and liturgy are retrospective, recalling only a "great world-historical phenomenon" because only that Judaism has contemporary moral significance. He understands that historical memories are powerful sources for modern religious observance and worship. Perhaps God did command Moses on Sinai, and Moses really did transfer those commands into writing. Yet these religious positions *make claims* about history, and Geiger has effectively withdrawn the historical question (what really happened?). In its place, Geiger offers a new one: what meaningful past could command an ethically sensitive Jewish religious practice? In answering this question of mnemohistory, Geiger utilizes different rhetorical devices—Hegelian appeals to Spirit, Schleiermachean language of inner longing, Kantian claims to moral truths—to better position religious Judaism at the center of Jewish history. Geiger displaces history as it really happened with a focus upon *how* religious Judaism rediscovers moral truths in Jewish history.

Contemporary Jews reading Geiger might well recoil from his appeal to moral truth, even as they recognize the power of memory to inform religious practice. American Jews, in particular, might speak the "first language" of individualism, even if their second language of community underscores much of their beliefs and practices.[140] By embedding religious Judaism within historical memory, Geiger can help resituate that individualism within communal patterns of remembering the past. For there is some evidence to suggest, as I argue in the conclusion to this book, that contemporary Jews, despite the power of their first language, really do yearn for, and are deeply informed by, strong memories of the past.[141] If Geiger's moral sources no longer command, perhaps his appeal to historical memories, and their weight upon the present, still do.

Yet by employing moral language to describe such a complex social and cultural phenomenon as religion, Geiger narrowly channels historical writing and memory. Moral ideas in history prove far more compelling to Geiger than historical actors—a preference far at odds with Graetz's sweeping account of Jewish lives in his history. Not that Geiger dismissed the ancient rabbis altogether, for he wrote important critical works about them and their medieval followers. Indeed, his most important biblical study, the *Urschrift* (1857), offers trenchant historical analysis of rabbinic figures—a major concern of the following chapter. But all too often these historical actors mediate important religious truths, and they do not by themselves enliven and command modern Jewish practice. As his liberal colleague Samuel Hirsch once argued, the thoughts of Abraham and Moses prove significant, but not their historical personalities.[142] There is much in this claim that fits Geiger's account of Abraham and sacrificial worship, for Geiger had neglected the commanding authority of ancestors upon modern Jewish allegiance. Note, too, that in his *Judaism and Its History,* Geiger appeals to Judaism's moral justice and urgency, comparing it favorably to the debased and chaotic Greek religion. He tethers the higher historical critique of Judaism and Greek religion to the development of an "inner law" that moves history to a desired goal. Only Judaism manifests this inner driving force, and Greek religion succumbs to the indiscriminate weight of fate. The spiritual ideal above, Geiger had argued there, delimits the moral ideal within. Greeks cannot become truly moral persons so long as they worship such "childish" and sensual gods. Liturgical services embody moral ideals, and so worshipping the true God in the right way informs and cultivates the ethical life. Geiger unites historical writing with moral urgency, but disengages contemporary Jews from their ancestors.

In this sense, Geiger's essays on liturgical reform are ethical works tied directly to his historical accounts, for they too focus on ethical memories rather than commanding personalities. For if Geiger reimagines Jewish history to embody the ethical norms of religious Judaism, then his edited prayer books echo that moral history in ritual practice. The "theoretical" and "practical" Geiger coalesce in a moral religious spirit of ritual acts. Writing history and reforming liturgical worship enact this religious agenda, and root the moral thrust of Geiger's liberal Judaism. So Geiger's Abraham recalls a "pure faith" and the "fundamental truth of all Judaism." The historical and liturgical Abraham conforms to a new moral standard for recalling the past. Historical memory, in Geiger's account of religious Judaism, is an ethical act of divine service.

Yerushalmi reminds us that memory implies the notion of forgetting. The historian often recalls events long forgotten or repressed. But acts of retrieval also expose how forgetting is a motivated practice in its own right. If Geiger recalls a history of moral significance, then he too easily forgets the actors who embody those ideals. This is, to be sure, the central point of Assmann's work on "mnemohistory." The significance of the past appears "only in the light of later readings. Mnemohistory is reception theory applied to history."[143] Assmann reveals how a past, remembered or forgotten, helps to fashion liberal Judaism as it offers new grounds for religious authority. Geiger's discussion of history and liturgy clearly follows this pattern. These works tell us more about Geiger's understanding of Jewish religion than Jewish history, remembered or forgotten. The significance of Geiger's works discussed in this chapter lies not so much in the conflation of memory and history (Funkenstein's point), but rather in how moral ideas transform historical memories, and how those memories inform religious practice. Memory functions in Geiger's texts to instill a modern, ethical, and meaningful identity for contemporary Jews. To be effective, Geiger's history and liturgy had to replace a past "in its radical form of positivism" with a very different kind of Judaism, one tethered to moral truths rather than Graetz's Jewish heroes. But Geiger's history, for all its concern with nineteenth-century religious polemics, still offers contemporary Jews a provocative challenge: Jewish history must be a meaningful one to count as religious authority, or it will all too easily succumb to "merely a historical consideration." The liberal's search for religious authority is rooted not in fact but in meaning, not in history but in memory, not in the past as such but in an ethical presence that bridges that past with contemporary moral aspirations.

The Practice of Hermeneutical Authority

2

Like many of his young colleagues and friends at university, Geiger recoiled from the Talmudic legalism of the ancient rabbis and their "hairsplitting" readings of the biblical text. Yet even before entering his studies in Heidelberg and Bonn, the young Geiger recognized how "the spirit [*Geist*] of the Talmud is so thoroughly different from that of the Bible."[1] Even more, strong differences arise in Mishnaic and Talmudic interpretations of biblical law, and these suggest very different methodological interests and concerns among the rabbinic readers of early Judaism.[2] Geiger blamed much of this divergence on Christian influence.[3] To rectify the abuse of Talmudic readings, he began his commentary on the Mishnah, together with his Mishnaic dictionary and grammar book, in July 1827.[4] Geiger's interest in the Mishnah and biblical interpretation, as Susannah Heschel has rightly noted, would motivate his lifelong study of religious authority.[5] He sought to curb the abuse of biblical misreadings as reflected in Christian arrogance, on the one hand, and Jewish parochialism, on the other. Reading the Bible well, so Geiger believed, grounded a liberal Jewish practice in textual authority.

But rarely was Geiger consistent in his early readings of the Bible. Recall Bruno Bauer's infamous pamphlet "The Jewish Question," in which he lamented the Jewish theological move toward a "Mosaic religion" that would triumph over a debilitating rabbinism. The Mosaic law, so many of these Jewish thinkers argued, comprised "the most pure ethical teaching." But to Bauer such a pristine time, if it ever existed, was in the unrecoverable past. Jewish theologians could not simply revive the past in order to firm up the unconditional value of liberal Jewish religion in the present. Their *Mosaismus* was an imagined purity dictated by the complexity of Enlightenment and emancipation politics. History proved unyielding, Bauer had argued with force, and the Mosaic constitution, when purified of all its priestly privilege and sacrificial rites, would appear as nothing but rabbinic Judaism in all its degrading and illusory existence. Indeed, world history had moved far beyond the biblical Mosaic faith, and so any attempt to recapture it would immediately condemn Judaism to an ahistorical life.[6] Geiger, as we have seen, responded to Bauer's article point for point, and even adopted Bauer's own Hegelian language to defend the historicity of the Jewish people and its religion.[7] In rejecting Bauer's static conception of Judaism, Geiger instead offered a grand, historical sweep of Jewish texts and life, painting a dynamic picture of Jewish history that undercut all claims to a pristine, Mosaic faith.

Yet in the very same journal in which his *Bruno Bauer und die Juden* appeared, Geiger published *Das Verhältniss des naturlichen Schriftsinnes zur thalmudischen Schriftdeutung* (The Relationship of the Natural Sense of Scripture to Talmudic

Scriptural Interpretation), a profoundly influential essay[8] that defended the "natural sense" of Scripture against the turgid and "unnatural" readings of the rabbis.[9] In appealing to a "natural sense," Geiger had reproduced the hermeneutical moves of those Jewish theologians who defended a pristine Mosaic faith. For the Mosaists as well as for Geiger, the biblical text provided a clear blueprint for an inner religious life that the rabbis then abandoned and tragically redirected to support a barren, public worship. Here Geiger's religious idealism resurfaced in his appeal to a prophetic moral core at the heart of historical Jewish thought and practice. He defended a static, natural reading of the text that challenged the contingent, messy, and to Geiger, blatantly absurd exegetical creations of the Talmudic rabbis. He did so even as he rejected a static conception of Judaism in the Bauer essay of the very same journal.

That Geiger could be so unclear about biblical hermeneutics in the early 1840s only highlights the remarkable exegetical breakthrough in his study of the Bible and rabbinic exegesis some fifteen years later in his *Urschrift* (1857).[10] Many scholars have failed to recognize that the thoroughly historical critique in the *Urschrift* marks a decisive shift away from his earlier appeals to a "natural sense." In place of a pristine, natural reading stands a text forever reworked and rewritten by redactors and readers who project into it all that they hope to get out of it: this is hermeneutical authority through revolution, a creation of meaning through radical revision. Where the young Geiger mocked Talmudic exegesis and the hairsplitting readings of the rabbis, the more mature Geiger now recognizes their hermeneutical creativity. Geiger abandons claims to a "natural" or even "unnatural" sense to Scripture, and instead promotes interpretive reworkings that produce new meanings, and in some cases, new texts as well. Jews—even rabbinic Jews—discovered personal meaning by reading it into and within the biblical text.

The full title of Geiger's most prodigious work, *The Original Text and Translations of the Bible in Its Dependence on the Inner Development of Judaism,* is itself ironic, for he subverts the notion of an "original text" by the many translations and revisions it undergoes throughout Jewish (and non-Jewish) interpretations. The inner development of Judaism reveals a fractious history of competing political and social readers, each claiming the Bible as his or her own authoritative source. Jewish readers created a sacred authority by making the Bible an *Urschrift.* In doing so, they transformed a reading practice into a personal search for religious authority.

Scholars often obscure these issues because they believe Geiger's *Urschrift* merely continues the agenda of his "Natural Sense" article,[11] and so they fail to see the important differences between these works.[12] Readers have also narrowly focused on Geiger's thesis concerning the Sadducees and Pharisees—in part, I believe, because his claims most interested the Christian scholars of his day, and moved Geiger to write an essay solely devoted to this issue five years after his *Urschrift.*[13] But one Geiger contemporary and colleague, in his review of the *Urschrift,* correctly identified Geiger's motivating concerns. When Geiger claimed the Bible "is and was an eternal living word for all time," Leopold Löw stressed that "these words express in short the content and tendency of the entire book."[14] Geiger's *Urschrift* uncovered a text shot through with revisionary readings that would turn an "original text" into the "eternal living word." Somewhat later, Felix Perles would argue that for Geiger, "the history of the text would be understood as part of the history of religion, and the history of religion would develop from the testimony of textual history."[15] A more recent critic, Susannah Heschel, notes as well this radical hermeneutic. For the Geiger of the *Urschrift,* "there was no fixed and absolute text; revisions and interpretations were not *of* the text, but were the text itself—a remarkably modern, if not postmodern, hermeneutic."[16] It is a hermeneutic, I want to argue, that reveals how Jewish readers convert a text into an authoritative source of personal meaning.

Readers of the *Urschrift* witness this exchange in Geiger's analysis of the early biblical translations (the *Targumim* and Septuagint, among others). Geiger argues that differences in translation suggest alternative original wordings. The Aramaic translations, for example, developed out of a very different text than the Masoretic Bible. This means, for Geiger, that the biblical text itself had been altered and reworked before it became fixed and canonical. At a time when the canon is not yet assured, the translations can point to older variants. The *Urschrift,* in other words, precedes the Bible as we know it today. But even when the biblical text achieves canonical status, the translations expose how revisions through creative interpretation produced new meanings for the now sacred words. If readers cannot alter the words on the page, then they must change their meanings to fit new social and political landscapes. The Pharisees and Talmudic rabbis took up this revisionary approach by converting translation into productive and meaningful exegesis. These translations mediate and therefore establish biblical authority, and force the "original" text to speak in a different language—in a new voice that reflects contemporary debates and concerns. For Geiger, textual interpretation mirrors the movements of religious history and polemics. This history reflects the contours, dynamics, and cultural dimensions of religious traditions that impose authority on a text through transformative readings. In Geiger's *Urschrift,* the search for origins produces the authority of personal meaning as hermeneutical practice.

The Natural Sense of Scripture

In his very early writings, Geiger had shown a keen interest in Talmudic and Mishnaic readings of Scripture. In 1836, he published a short article on the order of the Mishnah, and there proposed the simple but valuable insight that the editor arranged the tractates within a single order (*Seder*) according to size.[17] In the same journal, Geiger reviewed a number of works on Karaite history and interpretation, noting the interpretive similarities in Sadducean and Karaite readings of the Bible.[18] When he finally turned to a fuller account of rabbinic exegesis in 1844, his appeal to a natural and unnatural sense of scriptural reading became a widely borrowed trope in rabbinic studies.[19]

Geiger's *Das Verhältniss des naturlichen Schriftsinnes zur thalmudischen Schriftdeutung* is a caustic, biting, and all-together absorbing critique of the "turbid exegetical sense" of rabbinic exegesis. The Mishnah begins what the Gemara takes to the extreme, such that "it is possible to find everything in the Bible."[20] Talmudic rabbis interpreted the Bible in ways that obscured its natural sense. When Geiger published his *Urschrift* some fifteen years later (1857), he reclaimed those rabbinic interpretations as the most "natural" device for revising a text to fit contemporary sensibilities. The rabbis practiced creative exegesis to maintain their allegiance to a sacred work. For the Geiger of the *Urschrift,* the text does not reveal a sacred order to the reader, but is made to do so. Yet Geiger arrived at this view a good while after his essay on *The Natural Sense of Scripture.* When writing this essay in 1841 or 1842 (the text was not published until 1844), he believed instead that such blatant reworking of the text was nothing but creativity gone mad: an unnatural and perverse rendering of biblical meaning. In the early 1840s, Geiger still maintained that one could easily recognize the natural sense of Scripture, and clearly distinguish that sense from absurd rabbinic exegesis. A return to the biblical natural sense, Geiger suggested, would reinvigorate and purify a modern Judaism still moored in the turbid readings of its rabbinic past.

When Geiger speaks of a "natural sense of Scripture," he does not always mean *peshat,* or the plain sense.[21] At times the "natural sense" renders the *peshat* reading, but more often it yields a very different meaning. This becomes a bit clearer when Geiger answers the two basic questions that open his essay: 1) what is the relationship between Talmudic exegesis and the exegetical process that derives laws from the Bible; and 2) how did these Talmudic readings cohere with the natural interpretation of the Bible?[22] Geiger contends that the post-Mishnaic rabbis grounded all rabbinic norms and laws in Scripture. Their exegesis became increasingly "muddied" and unhealthy the more they rooted extrabiblical laws, conditioned in a different time and place, in the Bible itself. Rabbinic exegesis did not produce the laws (or at least in most cases it did not), but once the laws emerged the rabbis supported their legal authority in the biblical text (as if the biblical text really had been the source and basis of the law).[23] So the rabbis had violated the "natural" sense of Scripture by forcing the text to yield an authoritative ground for extrabiblical laws.

But violate they must, continues Geiger, because the Mishnah had already suppressed the "natural" sense of Scripture proclaimed by the prophets as the "inner secret of man and his relation to God." The Mishnah transformed that "inner life" into the "outer" life of law; "the inner religious way of viewing the world" had given way to everything "outer" (*äußerlich*).[24] Geiger distinguishes all that remains inner, spiritual, and prophetic from that which is outer, material, and rabbinic. The exegetical turn from inner prophetic religion to outer rabbinic law signals a move away from the "natural" sense, both in terms of a proper scriptural reading and a true religious understanding. This hermeneutic also mirrors Geiger's religious idealism—for here too an inner, eternal core surfaces as a historical, temporal practice. Geiger's "natural sense" reveals an inwardness that rabbinic readers then submerge and stifle in order to draw attention to external acts of law. The rabbinic "expansion of biblical law" and its "new apparatus" signify unnatural movements of religious spirit away from prophetic interiority.[25] The rabbis transport an inner, natural religion into a public, legal, "muddied," and contrived realm of religious experience.

In many passages, Geiger translates *peshat* as the natural sense or the "*einfache Erklärung*"—the simple explanation.[26] But in these cases, the meaning is always conditional; *peshat* could yield the natural sense, but only if it conforms to the inner spirituality of prophetic Judaism. In the main, however, *peshat* lies far closer to the "muddied" and "turbid" meanings of *derash* (as a kind of rabbinic "development" of *peshat*) than it does to a clearer sense of the natural meaning.[27] Inner spirituality (the "natural sense") marks an ordered, peaceful, and personal relationship with God. By translating this hiddenness into a public rite of obligatory acts, the rabbis forced the most absurd and arbitrary form (*Unregelmäßigkeit*) of scriptural exegesis. To overcome this rabbinic heritage, Geiger supported a natural religion that would remove the stiffness of rabbinic Judaism.[28] Only a return to the "natural sense of Scripture" could do that, so Geiger believed. He would recover a Jewish naturalism through the prophetic sense of an inner moral relation to God.

The Original Text and Its Translations

Yet for all his appeal to a "natural sense," Geiger never questioned whether the biblical text actually contained such a meaning. He merely assumed it did. This critical lapse is striking, for the notion of a natural sense to Scripture in his 1844 text is entirely missing from his analysis of biblical exegesis in 1857. Geiger's *Urschrift* has nothing to say about a prophetic, inner spirituality, or the natural meaning of Scripture, or even the turbid and unwholesome process of rabbinic exegesis. Gone is the acerbic critique and mocking scorn of rabbinic practice. In its place, one finds instead a seasoned, careful scholar wholly absorbed in a new and engaging project. Geiger appears utterly enthralled by his discovery of an old and new *halakhah*,[29] and by the intricate relations between political and social forces. He reveals the competing factions and temperaments of Sadducees and Pharisees, uncovers new biblical readings to fit altered sensibilities, and explains how translations function as interpretive works.[30] Both the tone and content of the *Urschrift* mark a decisive turn away from Geiger's earlier account of rabbinic exegesis and moral idealism.

This shift is dramatic, even if scholars like Ismar Schorsch admit that the origins of the *Urschrift* are "difficult to recover." Schorsch notes that in his *Natural Sense of Scripture,* Geiger proposed a further investigation into early biblical translations (*Targumim*) which, he adds, "is exactly what he [Geiger] did in the *Urschrift*."[31] Yet Geiger abandons entirely the methodological approach of his early essay, and it seems forced to suggest that he would pick up a thread some fifteen years later. But Schorsch and Susannah Heschel offer another theory, and this one remains far more plausible and, I will argue, can be supported by claims in the *Urschrift* itself.[32] Two years before publishing the *Urschrift,* Geiger wrote to the Christian Semiticist Theodor Nöldeke that his book had developed from his studies on the Karaites and their works from the eighth century onward.[33] The Karaites had rejected rabbinic readings of the text but they did not, Geiger makes clear in the *Urschrift,* merely return to the "literal" meaning of the Bible. Instead, they recovered an older *halakhah* that later rabbis supplanted with a newer one. This older law offered markedly different readings than what would become normative rabbinic Judaism.

The insight electrified Geiger, and helped to establish his theory that the older reading corresponded to the Sadducean political and social ideology, while the "newer" *halakhah* represented Pharisaic Judaism. Through the Karaites, Geiger could appreciate the political, social, and religious forces that overwhelmed and informed biblical exegesis. There were no longer "natural" senses to Scripture, but competing political and social forces that desired control over biblical meanings. Indeed, the biblical text proved remarkably open to such forces, and was at times radically altered to fit new cultural movements. Even more, Geiger could reimagine the rabbis as creative political readers because he understood the text as a battlefield of competing social claims for religious authority. The biblical text reflected a history, with all its political intrigue, social forces, and religious reforms. The text had changed for Geiger, and so too his account of biblical translation and interpretation.

In the introduction to his *Urschrift,* Geiger reviews the history of Jewish exegesis and biblical critique. The Masorites, who in the seventh and eighth centuries transformed the Jewish Bible into what it is today, followed the traditional focus on individual words (and even letters) in the text. They sought to protect the spoken quality of the canon, and left others (like Saadia Gaon in the ninth and tenth centuries) to decipher its grammatical structure. Yet this narrow focus on grammar and wording neglected how strikingly dissimilar translations expose hidden cultural features. The Septuagint, for example, deviates from the Masoretic text, and the various Greek translations are markedly at odds with each other. The Syriac, too, differs from both the Septuagint and Masoretic versions, and Geiger believes it derived from a very different source. The various Aramaic translations (Onkelos and pseudo-Jonathan, together with other fragments) do not fully agree in their renditions, and even the Talmud deviates from the Masoretic version.[34] Geiger certainly did not discover these discrepancies, for older sources had previously commented on the differences among Greek, Aramaic, and Latin biblical translations. But he argues that these differences reflect a fractious world of political and social relations.

Yet scholars rarely discussed these cultural forces, according to Geiger, until Asariah de' Rossi (sixteenth century) argued that the Septuagint was based on an older Chaldean translation, and many of its variations could be traced to that ancient source. More important to Geiger, however, was de' Rossi's claim that the Septuagint did not stand alone but within a historical context that reflected local needs and concerns. Geiger learned from de' Rossi how to read biblical translations within a cultural setting.[35] He could then criticize scholars who viewed the Septuagint only as an ill-informed reading of the Hebrew Bible, as Geiger argued

Zacharias Frankel had done.[36] Frankel attributed variations within the Septuagint to authorial ignorance: the editors simply did not understand biblical Hebrew well enough to translate it correctly. To Geiger, however, Frankel had simply missed de' Rossi's larger point, for he failed to appreciate the *Sitz im Leben* of the Greek translation. How could the translators make such colossal blunders, Geiger asked sarcastically, errors that had been completely overlooked until Frankel's reading?[37] De' Rossi suggested a more productive approach: translations rarely succumb to blatant ignorance, but instead reveal a historical life. To understand the politics of translation, scholars must situate texts within cultural history.[38]

Geiger's *Urschrift* uncovers the cultural life behind the biblical text—the life that made such a text, grammar, and vocalization possible. If Frankel would only turn his critical lens to biblical translations and commentaries,[39] Geiger would search for a material *biblical* history. He recovers "traces" (*Spuren*) that reveal cultural struggles for biblical authority. This "inner development of Judaism" is "the history of the biblical text and the translations."[40] The text lives as part of a community and embodies dominant cultural meanings.[41] Geiger marks an important distinction here between the biblical text (*Bibeltext*) and the original one (*Urschrift*). The history, culture, and politics of the latter (*Urschrift*) produce the former (*Bibeltext*), as the German title of his work suggests. The *Urschrift und Übersetzungen der Bibel* reveals Geiger's emerging understanding of the Bible as a communal, historical work, and its translations as windows into the cultural polemics and political ideologies of Jewish history.

The biblical texts expose local historical concerns and dilemmas. Geiger discusses, for example, the fear of foreigners and the problem of intermarriage. He notes Solomon's marriage to Pharaoh's daughter and her travels with him to David's city (1 Kings 3:1–2). Solomon, it appears, maintained an insatiable attraction to non-Israelite women. But in Second Chronicles 8:11, a later text that revises much of the kingship history, one reads a rather confusing account of Pharaoh's daughter, and a very different story, one in which Solomon brings her *out* of the city because "the places are holy." To Geiger, the Chronicles text reveals concerns and fears unknown in First Kings.[42] The author of Chronicles expresses a clear discomfort with Solomon's marriage to an Egyptian, for it suggests that a foreign wife lives with him in the holy city. In Geiger's telling, the Chronicles redactor *must* reread Kings in order to fit Solomon within contemporary cultural perceptions of holiness and pollution. First Kings captures meaningful history only if the author of Chronicles can make it so. Biblical revision remains a feature of the Bible, and highlights shifting cultural sensibilities and historical conflicts.

Geiger reads "against the text," as Heinrich Graetz once observed (but in a rather critical tone).[43] He notes the various passages that discuss Israel's eternal hate and struggle against Ammon and Moab. Yet Geiger contends that, at an earlier moment, the Ammonites, Moabites, and Israelites were once close and friendly neighbors. Only a suitor spurned, it would seem, could generate such aversion. Where other biblical texts fiercely abhor the Moabites and Ammonites, Deuteronomy 2:18–29, for example, remains quite mild in its portrayal, and even the conclusion of Deuteronomy recounts Moses' death and burial in Moab. Geiger reads the story of Ruth the Moabite in terms far more congenial than other, more ominous accounts. For in Deuteronomy 23:3–4, the text condemns the Ammonites and Moabites as eternal foreigners to God's community. In Geiger's reading, passages such as Deuteronomy 23 suggest a fear of personal relations with non-Israelites, and reveal a time when the Israelites desired national independence. The restoration of "the young state," soon after the return from Babylonia, appears to be the likely date of composition.[44] Geiger turns as well to the prophetic texts, especially Jeremiah 48–49, where he reads conflicting accounts of Moabites and Ammonites. Again, national jealousy accounts for the various discrepancies. All this suggests that "meaning remains in the memory of a later time."[45]

Riddled with conflicting accounts, the Bible reflects a torn history that lies behind and informs the written text. Since "the Bible is and was for all time an eternal living word, and not a dead book," Geiger reads "against" it in order to uncover "traces" of cultural memory and conflict.[46] He need not determine whether the Moabites or Ammonites, or even Solomon's wives, remain insiders or outsiders to the Israelite community. That would merely be a game of citing the relevant texts, and cleverly rereading or hiding more inconvenient ones. Geiger's interests lie not in fixing Moabite identity, but in recovering the cultural history that shapes it; not in a self-revealing text, but one transformed into a sacred authority. Creating authority through textual rereadings justifies a social and political life. The biblical text now contains the significance and power to further and support a cultural history. Geiger uncovers these cultural and political "traces," for only there can the biblical text reveal an *Urschrift.*

As Geiger's Moab example suggests, the Bible had once been open to textual emendation. Where Midrash refashioned the meaning of a fixed and received text, a far more powerful medium to revise biblical meaning had been to alter the very words on the page:

> The eternal word does not belong to a particular time, it could not be dependent upon the time of its writing down, and could just as little dispense with what would become new truths and knowledge. So each and every time, direction of thought and individuality brings to the Bible its own point of view [*Auffassung*]; thus we have expansions, clarifications, typological and symbolic explanatory schemes. Every effort and demand for an objective point of view [*Auffassung*] will, as such, be unsuccessful, for even the unbeliever brings to the text his own antipathy in his explanatory efforts. . . . What still in a later time had taken place on the ground of exegesis, must take place in an earlier time through revision [*Ueberarbeitung*] because the Bible had not yet been firmly closed and sealed.[47]

Cultural modes of reading absorb contemporary beliefs and practices, and expand the text to fit new sensibilities. Such writing, according to Geiger, can occur in two modes: through exegesis or through deliberate emendations of the text. The former occurs with already fixed and established sacred texts, but the latter proves far more valuable when the text has yet to acquire an authoritative and fixed status. In his discussion of intermarriage and foreigners noted above, together with many similar examples, Geiger points to "the character of a later revision [*Bearbeitung*]" and "the hand of revision [*die Hand des Ueberarbeiters*]"—German terms that suggest a working over, a strong rereading, and revising of previous work.[48] These textual variations suggest reworkings that conform to dominant cultural meanings of the text. Geiger also checks if these revisions find their way into biblical translations. When the Septuagint or Aramaic *Targumim* fails to translate a biblical phrase, this gap often suggests to Geiger a later addition to and emendation of the Bible. In this way, Geiger employs early biblical translations to show the revisionary phases within the text. So the Septuagint did not get it wrong, as Frankel would have it; rather, the biblical text had been altered sometime after the Greek translation.[49] Divergences in early translations reveal both the cultural location of their authors, and, even more, the flexibility of the biblical text as *Urschrift*.

Geiger understands that some biblical texts were accepted as canonical quite late (Kohelet, Esther), and some not at all (Ben Sira). But to drive his point home about textual expansion and elasticity, he turns to a number of telling examples in the Pentateuch. Note the puzzling passage in Gen. 33:18, in which Jacob enters the city of Shechem. The sentence includes a somewhat awkward reference to "Shalem" (שלם), another name for the city of Jerusalem, and reads, "And Jacob came to Shalem, a city of Shechem." Geiger argues that the term שלם is a textual addition to mark Jacob's arrival in Jerusalem. The editor seeks to undermine any sense that Jacob first enters Shechem, a city holy to the Samaritans (but not to the Israelites). Geiger notes other textual revisions that highlight Jerusalem, and claims that the editor reworked the text to better foreground the central site of Temple worship. For Jerusalem is the center of Israelite cultic practices, and priestly lineage and power derive from them.[50] But if Jacob had first entered Shechem, it would mean he erected an alter in the Samaritan holy city rather than in the center of Israelite worship. So the Israelite editor altered the biblical text to read, "Jacob entered Jerusalem, a city of Shechem." Geiger notes that the Septuagint, Vulgate, and Syriac translations all include a reference to Shalem. But the Samaritan Bible leaves it out—replacing the term *Shalem* with *Shalom*—and so their Bible reads, "Jacob entered the city of Shechem in peace." In highlighting its own "rival holy city," the Samaritan Bible remains "true to its system."[51] Geiger reveals just how fluid and elastic the "original" text could be for rival communities and cultic centers.[52]

Alterations in the text also surface in the ways in which the rabbis refashioned early Hebrew grammar.[53] This is particularly clear in feminine and masculine Hebrew nouns, where Talmudic Hebrew feminizes masculine biblical nouns, and the later rabbis often added feminine endings and articles to words that had been masculine in early Hebrew (Geiger notes cases, for example, in which editors attribute the articles הוא or היא to the opposite gendered noun).[54] Hebrew language too has a history, and Geiger traces its development to these scribal emendations that expose a more developed Hebrew replacing an earlier grammar.[55]

When Geiger lectured on philology in the early 1870s,[56] he claimed that the development of Hebrew opened the spiritual channels of Jewish history. One can trace the Jewish spiritual presence through the variations in Hebrew grammar and practice. Yet one cannot find such religious idealism in the *Urschrift.* Geiger does not recover a spiritual essence that works through the various forms of Hebrew grammar. Neither does he map out a "natural" continuity or a core moral source. Instead, he positions Hebrew language as the site of cultural struggle for sacred meanings. Altering the text—either through grammatical or substantive revisions—controls textual meaning and authority. The *Urschrift* is a material product of these cultural engagements, and reveals the political and social practice of hermeneutical authority.

All these examples (and many others not mentioned here) suggest to Geiger that if contemporary readers seek textual purity, they simply will not find it in the Bible. The care and attention to a received text reflects modern concerns about authenticity and authority. Earlier textual emendations had been far more "arbitrary" (*willkürliche* and *eigenmächtigen*).[57] Geiger quotes from a well-known text in the Babylonian Talmud (Nedarim 37b/38a) that lists several biblical passages in which one should read unwritten words, and others where one remains silent before written words, to better make sense of the biblical text. Even the Talmudic rabbis understood, says Geiger, that variations and deviations abound in the biblical text: some due to scribal errors, others because of variations in language, and to Geiger, others still that reveal older texts unknown to both the early biblical translations and to the Masorites.[58] But the rabbis did not situate the text within cultural struggles, as Geiger would do. For him, terms have been altered, texts reworked, names for God revised, all because the "received" text had not adequately reflected the concerns and beliefs of a particular time. This "inner history," as Geiger calls it, reflects a struggle for cultural meaning and authority.

The two opposing Jewish parties, the Sadducees and Pharisees, initiated and animated this struggle for cultural control of the biblical text. Geiger believes the hereditary character and purity of the priesthood during the first Temple period helps explain numerous biblical passages and conflicts. There existed two main "houses" during this early time—David and the high priest Zadok—and to this latter family Geiger traces the Sadducean lineage of power and political aristocracy. This priestly aristocracy continued during the second Temple period after the Babylonian exile, and Ezra, Nehemiah, and Chronicles give it much prominence. Geiger argues forcefully that these and other post-exilic texts reflect motivated reports that foreground priestly concerns and activities.[59] To be sure, Geiger's thesis on the origin of the name *Sadducees* as an Aramaic variation of the term *Zadokites* is far too circumstantial, and is often refuted by his critics.[60] But his principal conviction that the Sadducees represented an exclusive and closed aristocracy, one opposed to the more democratic and populist Pharisees, has been immensely influential, even if, in the end, scholars have emended or thoroughly rejected it.[61]

In Geiger's social schema, the Sadducees included members of the high priesthood—the Levites and noble families—all born of privilege and ruling as an aristocracy. The Pharisees, by contrast, reflected the party of "*das Volk.*" National and democratic, the Pharisees projected a grassroots appeal and harnessed popular resentment against the aristocratic Sadducees. The two parties offered opposing social views, and often differed in their reading of rabbinic law. But these religious debates remained complex and subtle, defying easy categorical distinction. The Sadducees, for example, placed greater weight on racial purity to protect their noble heritage, but both they and the Pharisees supported the Levite tax, even though the tax benefited the ruling priestly elite (one would expect the Pharisees to oppose the tax).[62] The Sadducees differed *sociologically and politically* from the Pharisees (the one aristocratic and priestly, the other democratic and populist), but in theology and law they were at odds only in degrees.[63] The major religious differences appeared much later, after the fall of the Temple in 70 C.E. and the rise of Christianity. Social class and position determine the nature of religious conflict between Sadducee and Pharisee, and so too the cultural revisions within the biblical text.

Old and New *Halakhah*

The social and political battles that make up an *Urschrift* also inform early biblical translations, now recognized by Geiger as transparent rereadings of older meanings.[64] The early Aramaic translations (*Targumim*) inform Geiger's understanding of the *Urschrift* in two ways. The *Targumim* often suggest a very different original wording. Geiger believes that the biblical text, as we have it from the Masorites, is not the same text cited by early Aramaic, Greek, and Latin translators. So the rediscovered *Urschrift* looks markedly different from *die heilige Schrift.* But just as often the translators confront a text that, in a new historical and social climate, stands rather aloof from their more immediate concerns. They delicately, but no less clearly, alter the meaning of the text to fit contemporary sensibilities. The translators interpret in order to relegate older meanings old. Geiger believes the early Aramaic translations reveal an "old" *halakhah* covered over and eventually repressed by a "new" one. But the "old" is no less revolutionary in its revision of past meanings:

> This translation [the Palestinian *Targum*] was in Palestine, in the middle of the Jewish spiritual movement, in the center of halakhic and aggadic development [*Fortbildung*], and was not a naked word-for-word reproduction [*nicht eine nackte wörtliche Wiedergabe*]. The translation was even more an explanation, a widening, an adjusted reading and warning directed to the present, and thus not rarely even a reshaping [*Umgestaltung*], and so represented completely the standpoint of the older halakhah and aggadah.[65]

The early biblical translations reveal an "inner history" too, and this history reflects social and political forces in which *halakhah* and *aggadah* represent creative, active rereadings. Just as rabbinic theology and legal rulings shaped the biblical text, so too early Aramaic translations reconfigured the Bible in a new historical context. In so doing, the translators recover an older *halakhah* and *aggadah* that challenge prevailing norms transmitted through the biblical text. Recovery of silenced textual layers becomes a weapon for religious renewal.

Geiger appears utterly fascinated by his discovery of both old and new laws. He radiates genuine enthusiasm and scholarly delight in recovering these repressed fragments, and publishes a number of short articles after the *Urschrift* to further justify his claims. In one such essay published in 1871, Geiger discusses the laws of ritual slaughter, and cites a baraita in the Talmud (Menachot 29a) that reveals this tension between new and old *halakhah.*[66] The laws under review focused on priestly privilege and cultic Temple purity. According to Geiger, with the fall of the Temple in 70 C.E., and the loss of priestly power that came with it, the Pharisees usurped the priestly sacrificial meal for their own enjoyment, and democratized it for everyday consumption. The new, Pharisaic law had overcome and repressed the older, Sadducean rulings. But Geiger recovers the older law in order to show how the Pharisees struggled "against the arrogance and the conceit of holiness of the Sadducean party."[67] In working against the "priestly Sadducees,"[68] the Pharisees undermined aristocratic power, politics, and privilege. Geiger highlights the social and political stakes in the tension between old and new ritual laws.

Geiger is similarly preoccupied with the recovery of lost *halakhic* fragments in the *Urschrift.* He appreciates, for example, the Jerusalem Talmud and older Palestinian *Midrashim* (*Mechilta, Sifre, Sifra*) because they better suit his agenda to reconstruct an earlier time when older fragments of *halakhah* and *aggadah* achieved authoritative status. The Babylonian texts, in contrast, stand too far removed and often obscure this earlier material.[69] Jay Harris has argued that Geiger favors the *Sifra* to the *Mechilta* and *Sifre* because the former (*Sifra*) represents the school of Akiba and his new, progressive movement in halakhic reform, while the latter texts (*Mechilta* and *Sifre*) characterize the work of Rabbi Ishmael and his far more conservative view of Jewish practice. Harris argues that Geiger "saw an inextricable link between the natural sense of Scripture and the stultifying conservatism of a portion of the rabbinic elite of the second century."[70] But this is not so, at least for the Geiger of the *Urschrift.*[71] Geiger states explicitly that he favors the *Mechilta* and *Sifre* because they contain "*alter Elemente*" (older elements), and these texts recover appeals to "old" (Ishmael) *halakhah.*[72] Even more, the *Mechilta* and *Sifre* offer versions and explanations that agree with the older translations "against" the received Masoretic Bible, and so provide more evidence of an *Urschrift* underlying the canonical text.[73]

Of course, by appealing to Palestinian rather than Babylonian texts, Geiger undermined a rabbinic heritage that has closely followed the Babylonian tradition. The myth of Sephardic Judaism enraptured Geiger's generation because, in part, it offered a history less embarrassing to the reformers.[74] So too the Palestinian texts, for they produced lost fragments that could revitalize the perceived sterility of Ashkenazic Judaism. Geiger cites these older Palestinian texts not to side with Akiba, nor to champion the more progressive *halakhah,* and even less to contest a "natural sense." Rather, these texts show how older traditions, represented by Ishmael and his school, have been reworked by Akiba and his followers.[75] The very notion that sources reflect conservative or progressive tendencies contradicts Geiger's claim that texts reveal the consciousness of an age, and in that sense are *always* progressive because they reshape older meanings to fit new cultural sensibilities. Recall that the Aramaic *Targumim* in Palestine developed "in the middle of the Jewish spiritual movement, in the center of halakhic and aggadic development, and was not a naked word-for-word reproduction. The translation was even more an explanation, a widening, an adjusted reading. . . ."[76] Indeed, on this fundamental point, Harris and I agree: "As Geiger saw matters in 1857, the creative power in Judaism had always been expressed by controlling the text of Scripture, with different groups, upon achieving power, changing the names and words of the text to suit their preferred reading of history."[77] That the *Sifra* and Akiba's school undercut the received, "older" *halakhah* in order to fashion a new one only proves Geiger's point that the text embodies a religious battleground of competing interpretations and revisions.

Geiger's delight in the *Mechilta* and *Sifre* also reflects his original interest in the Karaites and their reading of Scripture. Like these rabbinic texts, Karaite literature cites "older" halakhic views.[78] For Geiger, the *Mechilta* and *Sifre* offer resources for understanding the Karaites in a new light. The Karaites do not read the biblical text literally, nor reject entirely the rabbinic tradition, but instead reshape, like their rabbinic predecessors, received biblical readings in favor of "older" variants.[79] They too, like their Sadducean predecessors,[80] want to own the text, as much, if not more so than their rabbinic opponents.

Perhaps we can now imagine more clearly Geiger's fascination with these older fragments (*Trümmer*), and the originating impulses for writing the *Urschrift*. As he tells us in his letter to Theodor Nöldeke, Geiger desired to write a history of the Karaites. But his research moved in an unexpected direction: "I came upon the Sadducees, and I began to understand their being and development; and moving upwards and downwards, it was revealed to me now the method for biblical critique and the development of *halakhah*. From a completely different standpoint I came to the aims which I neither actively worked toward nor which I fully expected."[81]

The originating impulse to study the Karaites had evolved into what would become the *Urschrift*. From the Karaites, Geiger learned of an "older" *halakhah*, though in the spirit of scientific discovery, he acknowledges this in a reflexive construction ("it was revealed to me"—*enthüllte sich mir*). Geiger then turned to the Sadducees as representatives of this forgotten tradition, and discovered texts such as the *Mechilta* and *Sifre*, as well as the Aramaic biblical translations, that revealed active revisions of canonical texts. From there, Geiger built a thesis of biblical hermeneutics and halakhic reform, one that recovered the "inner history" of the received Masoretic text. And so the *Urschrift*.

Sadducees and Pharisees

Geiger stresses the inner history of old and new *halakhah*, as well as the social and political underpinnings of Sadducean and Pharisaic conflict, for two reasons: to undermine the accounts reported by Josephus, the New Testament, and rabbinic writings, and to distance his own readings from the Tübingen school. Josephus cataloged the ideological differences between Sadducees and Pharisees in this way: 1) the Sadducees believed in complete free will without immortality, while the Pharisees defended a free will still dependent upon God and, closely connected to this claim, believed in immortality; 2) the Sadducees rejected many oral traditions and considered only the written words of Moses, but the Pharisees followed the oral law; 3) and finally, in methods of punishment, the Sadducees were far more severe than the Pharisees.

Geiger, in the end, rejects all of Josephus's conclusions, considering them either far too general or simply misguided. He doubts the Sadducees denied the resurrection, for if such were the case we would surely find far more evidence in the rabbinic texts, and Geiger dismisses the Christian reports as overtly polemical pieces. Certainly differences surfaced between Sadducees and Pharisees, but they reflect differences in degree rather than in kind. Geiger even praises the Sadducean "practical piety" which, in good Kantian fashion, pursued duty for its own sake without recourse to future recompense.[82] The Pharisees, it turns out, proved far more fanatical, and they grounded their belief in resurrection in "hot-blooded national hopes."[83] Geiger is equally troubled by Josephus's claim that the Sadducees jettisoned the oral tradition. The Talmud, says Geiger, certainly recognizes individual Sadducean deviations, but nowhere does it suggest that the Sadducees relied merely on the written text while the Pharisees followed the oral law, and only later did the rabbis identify the Karaites (who appealed far more regularly to the written text) with the Sadducees. Indeed, the opposite may very well be true, for the Sadducees held fast to the old norms, *halakhah,* and tradition, and the Pharisees would turn to the written text if it suited their political views.[84] Appeals to the oral or written law fail to explain the primary distinctions between Sadducees and Pharisees. Geiger instead highlights the Sadducean focus on persons and families, in contrast to the Pharisaic critique of priestly office and its functions. He foregrounds the social and political claims that root Sadducean and Pharisaic views of Temple purity; the aristocratic family stresses personal integrity and priestly lineage, but the democratic party highlights the nature and function of priestly office regardless of the persons who hold it. When Geiger turns, finally, to Josephus's third distinction, he stresses how the Pharisees could be just as harsh, if not more so, in rules of punishment. Differences stem from historical factors and particular cases rather than strong ideological disagreement.[85]

The Sadducees are, to Geiger, the priestly, aristocratic family thoroughly opposed to the "national and religious middle class." And the discrepancies between old and new *halakhah,* Geiger argues, bear this out. This appeal to class reflects Geiger's fundamental belief that "the differences touch more upon political and party standpoints than upon diverging religious principles."[86] Sadducean power rested with the Temple and the independent state. With the destruction of both, the Sadducees had lost their prestige and power. Hillel and his family, together with Jochanan ben Zakkai, moved decisively against the Sadducees in order to renew Pharisaic Judaism. But the religious differences that would mark Hillel's victory over Sadducean dominance were further developments of original and more powerful social and political forces: "The profound difference between Sadducees and Pharisees was, as we have recognized, not religious, but much more political and social, and with the fading of political independence even this in general had to come to an end."[87]

More than a disagreement with Josephus, however, underlies Geiger's defense of biblical "inner history" and competing social factions. Most critical works on the *Urschrift* document the profound influence of the Tübingen school on Geiger's account of sacred texts. Heinrich Ewald, in an early review of Geiger's work, was the first to note how "all this reminds us, above all, only of the way in which the Tübingen folks treat the New Testament: and unfortunately the author agrees word for word with these people in that he seeks and finds *tendencies* [*Tendenzen*] everywhere." By depending so thoroughly on the Tübingen method of reading scriptures, Geiger's work "remains completely groundless."[88] Ewald despised the Tübingen school, in part because its leading figure, Ferdinand Christian Baur, strongly influenced the course of liberal Protestant research of New Testament history and theology.[89] As the leading conservative professor at Göttingen, Ewald would have none of this.[90]

But later scholars would all agree with Ewald that Baur's theories heavily influenced Geiger's understanding of biblical studies.[91] One can readily see this in Schorsch's claim that Geiger's oppositional approach to the Sadducees and Pharisees is "quite analogous to the struggle [described by Baur] between Pauline and Jewish Christians during the first two centuries of Christianity."[92] Baur interprets early Christianity as an ideological struggle between two parties, "in which the diverging views must necessarily come into conflict with each other." If one studies the debate over circumcision in the New Testament, for example, two parties emerge: Peter and his "Judaic" focus and Paul with his universal, gentile approach. Baur calls each of these views a "*Tendenz*," the one reactionary, the other progressive, and he traces these tendencies throughout the New Testament period.[93] To be sure, as Heschel notes correctly, Geiger distanced his views from Baur's anti-Judaic bias, even though he recognized how the Tübingen school historicized Jesus' "new spiritual system," and so debunked much of his uniqueness and genius.[94] But Heschel, too, believes that "Geiger's affinities with Baur remain clear."[95]

Yet Baur, as Peter Hodgson has astutely observed, treated the New Testament materials "as products of literary-theological tendencies."[96] For the Tübingen school, the battles fought between the two Christian parties in the New Testament period were *ideological* ones that reflected a particular *Tendenz*.[97] But for Geiger, the battles between Sadducees and Pharisees were primarily *sociological* and *political,* and only much later did they become *ideological* disputes. Indeed, Geiger sharply criticized Josephus for describing overarching tendencies in Pharisaic and Sadducean approaches to religion.[98] Geiger did speak of general tendencies when describing the Sadducees, Pharisees, and Essenes in an early work published in 1835, and one published much later in 1866.[99] But in the 1857 *Urschrift,* Geiger consistently argues that social class and political views remain central to Pharisaic and Sadducean religious disputes.

Thus Geiger's *Urschrift* challenges rather than conforms to the work of the Tübingen school. If Baur and his followers search and find "*tendencies* everywhere," as Ewald would have it, Geiger dismisses those tendencies in favor of an "inner history" that uncovers the social and political tensions inscribed in the biblical text. Geiger criticizes Josephus for distinguishing tendencies between religious parties, when those two approaches better reflect social struggles for power and authority. An *Urschrift* does not reveal general ideological tendencies, but hidden histories and sociological parties.

Contemporary scholars have too often decoded the *Urschrift* through a reading of a later essay, *Sadducäer und Pharisäer* (1863), in which Geiger is far more apologetic, blatantly ideological, and far closer to the Tübingen school. The *Urschrift* succeeds, Geiger tells us in this later essay, because it shows the reader how the Bible develops through a lengthy spiritual process of internal polemic. The Pharisees and Sadducees remain the central players in this struggle for religious authority.[100] The *Sifre, Mechilta,* and the later *Targumim* all contain fragments of an older law that had been rendered so by more contemporary readings. In repressing these older fragments, however, the Pharisees move Judaism in a more progressive direction.

When Geiger published his essay on the Sadducees and Pharisees, he targeted his article to a select group of Christian scholars. He reviewed a number of Christian readings of his *Urschrift* (Ewald among them). These Christian readers focused primarily on his account of the Pharisees and Sadducees, in part because they feared the implications of Geiger's research. For many, Christianity had resolutely overcome the deadening logic and legalism of rabbinic Judaism. But now Geiger had claimed a renewed sense of interpretive freedom, and had opened a dynamic interplay of social and political forces to understand early Jewish history. In *Sadducäer und Pharisäer,* Geiger transforms his textual research in the *Urschrift* into an apologetic defense of Pharisaic Judaism.

In terms quite foreign to his *Urschrift,* Geiger now discusses the general "direction" (*Richtung*) of each party, echoing Bauer's notion of "tendencies," and he altogether sidesteps the social and political distinctions between Sadducee and Pharisee.[101] Geiger also moves beyond his original research, and traces ideological developments in New Testament literature to better reveal the similarity between Jesus and other progressive Pharisees like Hillel. In a lengthy supplement to the essay, Geiger compares Hillel quite favorably to Jesus, even if, in the end, Jesus turns out to be a traditional Pharisee himself![102] "Enough," Geiger announces; "Jesus stands upon Pharisaic ground, and fights with Pharisaic weapons against Pharisaic half-measures."[103]

No surprise this, because Geiger portrays the Pharisees as the leaders of an ideal, "Protestant" sect of progressive Judaism. The Pharisees subordinate theory to practice without undermining the text or Jewish law, and they represent "the people" and "religious development." They are the democratic reformers of Judaism, and Protestant Christianity portrays "the complete mirror-image of Pharisaism."[104] The Sadducees, enslaved to past traditions and a fixed reading of the text, become the precursors to Roman Catholicism. In defending such wildly absurd claims, Geiger hopes to rehabilitate the Pharisees among Christian scholars (in this, as Susannah Heschel has argued, he failed miserably). Pharisaism marks "a term of honor" and symbolizes the principle of "progressive development."[105] When modern persons fight against hypocrisy and aristocracy, they return to the Pharisees and their ancient struggles. True, progressive religion is Pharisaic Judaism.

Such religious ideology, while certainly present in the *Urschrift,* is surprisingly muted and comes in softer tones. Geiger is careful to avoid sweeping statements about the Sadducees, and blames Saadia Gaon, among others, for too easily identifying the Sadducees with the great opponents of rabbinic Judaism—the Karaites.[106] Surely Geiger does this too, but only *after* the writing of his *Urschrift.* In an essay published in 1861 (just a few years before the Sadducees and Pharisees article), Geiger speaks of the "Sadducean-Karaitic view" as "puritanical."[107] But in a letter written in 1853, four years before the *Urschrift* appeared in print, Geiger admits that "in general, the fate of the Karaites is incomprehensible to me."[108] Geiger certainly recognized significant correlations between Karaites and Sadducees, and he discusses them in the *Urschrift.* But they are not of the kind found in his later writings in the early to mid-1860s, in which the Pharisees strongly oppose the "Sadducean-Karaitic view."[109]

Much of Geiger's later essay *Sadducäer und Pharisäer* has been read into the *Urschrift,* in part because the *Urschrift* has proved so foundational for Geiger's understanding of biblical and rabbinic Judaism. In the same letter to Nöldeke in which he describes the genesis of his work, Geiger himself admits that his *Urschrift* is "the final objective of my endeavors."[110] He carefully follows how well the *Urschrift* sells, and appears generally smitten when he receives letters of praise from those he calls "Geigerians."[111] Yet he remains bitter and angry that his Christian colleagues take so little notice of his work, and believes that "had the book not come from a Jew, and had not been accomplished with Jewish learning, it surely would have found a far larger following."[112] That larger following, I submit, would come with his later essay on the Sadducees and Pharisees. There he reached out to his Christian audience, hoping that, if only Jews profited from his *Urschrift,* at least Christians could now learn something about Jesus and his relation to Pharisaic Judaism. His son and biographer, Ludwig Geiger, not only regarded the *Urschrift* as "the principal work of his life," but also argued that his father considered all his later studies as further elaborations of the thesis proposed in the *Urschrift.*[113] If Abraham Geiger did believe this, as surely as his critics did, then he prized that Christian audience far too much. He, too, fell victim to reading the present into the past. His *Sadducäer und Pharisäer* essay of 1863 quickly turned into a restated thesis of the *Urschrift.* Meaning really does reside in the memory of a later time.

Yet toward the end of that "principal work" called the *Urschrift,* Geiger summarized the "aims" that came so unexpectedly to him. The Pharisees and Sadducees must have thrived during the second Temple period, Geiger concludes, because their views dramatically fashioned the shape of that history. Theirs was a class struggle "with religious and political colors." With the end of the Bar-Kochba revolt in the second century of the common era, Sadducean views suffered complete defeat before new religious practices, and the Pharisees revised their work from the ground up. Thus the older traditions were suppressed or revised, but "fragments" of the older tradition remained inchoate in the text, and Geiger labors to make them speak, if only to show how readers struggled to revise and repress them.[114] The gradual "fixity" of the Bible, Geiger summarizes, "must have been influenced by the views of the time, and so too the various recensions."[115]

In the end, Heinrich Graetz was right: Geiger does indeed read "against" the text, but he does so to reveal the "inner history of the time"[116] obscured by layers of interpretive revisions. In many ways, Geiger's interests lie in what remains repressed and unstated. The fragments of a different way of thinking and reading help to locate obscured memories, and Geiger as biblical scholar becomes the archaeologist of memory. The *Urschrift* is a text about repressed memories, lost meanings, and recovered possibilities. It tells us that the Jewish tradition has always been, and continues to be, a contest for the interpretive meaning of its sacred scriptures and religious practices. In this, it remains a work far different from what his son, biographer, and later scholars have wanted it to be. In this, too, the *Urschrift* has become a material witness to the authority of personal meaning.

Religion, Politics, and Samuel Holdheim

To understand the nature of an *Urschrift,* Geiger recovered the intricate relations among social, religious, and political forces. The biblical text produced a site of contested cultural struggles within complex social relations. Clearly, Geiger's notion of textual origins and conflict mirrors his contemporary battles with reform and emancipation. For many early Jewish academic scholars, critical studies of Jewish history would support political and social acceptance of Jews within Europe. *Wissenschaft des Judentums* rekindled Jewish religious politics, and its practitioners employed their disciplinary skill to battle social prejudice and religious intolerance. Religious discourse carried political meaning and weight. When Geiger reconfigured the biblical text as a battleground for competing social and political views, he thereby grounded his religious reform in the Jewish academic study of origins. The *Urschrift* became, in his hands, a template to understand contemporary emancipation politics. If Hillel and Akiba once struggled to overcome the old law to make room for the new, so too Geiger in his day battled the "old" school that maintained loyal ties to traditional practice and textual reading. In Geiger's view, readers manipulate the text to better align it with contemporary social pressures and political movements. Interpretation is reform, Geiger argues, because readers employ texts for cultural ends.

The old school, in Geiger's thinking, imagined a biblical text free from cultural constraints and interpretive prejudice. But it would be misleading to believe that he only had the traditionalists in mind when he argued against a "pure" reading of the Bible. More radical reformers than Geiger held this vision too. Bruno Bauer had already provided some clues for sniffing out those who appealed to a pristine Mosaic religion. In a search for sacred origins, liberal Jewish thinkers imagined the moral purity of a Bible unencumbered by political turmoil. Yet as Bauer concluded, Jewish theologians who defended a pure biblical faith were still fully embedded in contemporary politics, even if they sought to protect religious texts from the disarray of social emancipation. These Jewish thinkers believed that if life proved messy, at least the Mosaic religion as "the more pure ethical teaching" could stand alone above the fray.

Samuel Holdheim (1806–1860), Geiger's more radical reform colleague, appealed to a pure, uncontaminated biblical text, even as he recognized the ways in which political forces inform biblical interpretation. Like Geiger's old-school traditionalists and the liberal "Mosaists," Holdheim defended a revealed text severed from all political and interpretive claims. The text stands, in itself, pure and holy, but becomes enmeshed in political discourse as soon as readers interpret it. Holdheim resolutely separated religion (the biblical text) from politics (interpretation), but in so doing revealed the politics of biblical reading practices. He demonstrated a keen sense of his contemporary political environment, and respected the power of religious discourse to inform political debates.[117] Indeed, Holdheim's concern over marriage law in Jewish practice witnessed to the significance of religious politics for his thought. Even as he shielded religion from political intrigue, Holdheim still maintained a strong political interest in protecting religion from historical contingency and human desires.[118]

If Holdheim's appeal to a pure biblical text unravels in his own reading, as I will argue it does, then he offers, surely despite himself, a productive study of how Geiger's *Urschrift* acts as an authority for personal meaning. In his *Urschrift,* Geiger claims that political and social interests pervade the text itself and are not merely, as Holdheim would have it, secondary readings of a primary, pristine text. For Geiger, one cannot simply disengage religion from politics without diminishing the cultural vibrancy that undergirds the Bible. But Holdheim desperately sheltered the Bible from such political encroachment. All biblical analysis yields sullied political readings, but the Bible remains pure. Only the *reading* of it counts as a political act. The pure text, in other words, reveals itself as motivated political acts of reading. But Holdheim's distinction between a pure, religious text and a motivated, political reading makes no sense. For an unread text cannot plausibly retain the weight of religious authority that Holdheim places upon it. Yet unraveling Holdheim's argument goes a long way to strengthen Geiger's claim that the biblical text remains a site for social and political struggle. In staking this claim for a religious politics, the *Urschrift* performs it as well.

Holdheim's political voice comes to the fore when he distinguishes between religious and political realms of thought and activity. Scholars have already made much of this distinction in Holdheim,[119] leading one to quickly sum up: "In short, the absolute and pure *religious* elements of the revealed Mosaic legislation remain eternally binding; the rest no longer applies."[120] But this does not push far enough into the political significance of those *religious* elements. Holdheim erects a protective barrier to thwart religious critique and interpretation. His protective strategy[121] shields religious ideals from the turmoil and complexity of political discourse and action. Indeed, Holdheim's biblical exegesis reveals a severely constricted view of religion as a necessary and eternal promise by God to all human beings, and a view of politics as the realm of human free response to this covenantal promise. But this means, for Holdheim, that all biblical interpretation is political. To put this another way, there cannot be religious interpretation in Holdheim's schema.

For in that schema, the human interpretive act is always a political one because it remains this-worldly, material, and historical. By contrast, religion contains only divine, universal, and necessary truths, and one cannot interpret truths so much as recognize them. Jews do not make the biblical text into a religious authority; rather, they accept it as such. The strange consequence of this position is that one cannot produce a religious interpretation of the Bible, for all readings would yield a political meaning that pollutes the integrity of religious truth. Geiger agrees that biblical readings do represent motivated political and social acts. But he believes as well that they go all the way down to the biblical text itself. Geiger's work aggressively challenges an appeal to the purity and innocence of textual meaning. If for Holdheim the Bible communicates textual authority in its very purity, then for Geiger the Bible becomes a religious authority by virtue of the political and social conflicts already embedded there.

Holdheim struggles to keep those conflicts at bay, and relegates them to purely political acts within civic society. This is the clear intent of his *Rabbinic Autonomy and the Principle of Jewish Marriage* (1843).[122] As the title suggests, Holdheim limits the juridical civic capacity of rabbis in order to firmly place all marriages within the public, political sphere of civic law. To defend such a claim, Holdheim classifies proper religious autonomy and authority, and in so doing separates national or political concerns from religious ones. Although his argument begins with an appeal to the contemporary situation in which Jews simply desire a national identity within their country of residence, it becomes increasingly clear that his target is Jewish tradition and its representatives.

Holdheim turns to sources within the Jewish tradition that suggest a strong contrast between religious and political goods; he wants to discover the "religious moment in Judaism," and return it to its "natural borders or limits."[123] By restricting this religious moment to God's relation to humanity, Holdheim integrates human encounters within the wider public space of civic community. One enters the province of the state from a "pure human capacity" rather than from a religious standpoint or concern. This sharp division between private and public virtue, identity, and space suggests that altogether different relations exist in the two spheres.

It is as if one could live a private, religious life in the confines of home and God, but then check that baggage at the door as one enters professional and communal spaces.

Holdheim marks this separation in the forward to his *Rabbinic Autonomy:* the religious contains "that which is eternal and unchanging," while the national and political "has to be considered according to its essence as that which is transient."[124] The religious stands for all that is universal, ever-present, and unmoving (in short, *being*), while the political signifies all that the religious is not: particular, ephemeral, and changing (in short, *becoming*). These categorical distinctions sharpen in his *Lectures on the Mosaic Religion for Thinking Israelites* (1844), a text published a year after *Rabbinic Autonomy.*[125] In these popular sermons, Holdheim distinguishes "the Mosaic religion" as "the revelation of divine Providence" from "the Mosaic state" as a "worldly government." All states, together with their laws and orders, "are transient as everything else that is human," but religion, by contrast, "can alone eternally remain unchangeably itself."[126] Bauer's critique of the Mosaists applies equally well to Holdheim. Human activity, Holdheim claims here, is as ephemeral as the state within which it acts. But Mosaic religion remains eternal and beyond the limits of historical contingency.

Witness Holdheim's reading of Kiddushin 37a, a text in which the Gemara distinguishes obligations to the body (גוף) from those to the land (קרקע). Rashi notes those obligations to the body (including Sabbath, circumcision, and tefillin) as well as to the land (laws, for example, concerning the mixing of different fruits and the growth at the end of fields). In the Gemara, Rabbi Yehuda claims that all obligations to the body are duties for both those inside and outside the Holy Land, while obligations to the land pertain only to those in Palestine. Holdheim offers this reading of the Gemara and Rashi:

> The subject of obligation is and can be at all times only the person, that is, his moral personality. The object of obligation is either his own body or something other outside of it. Obligations to the land [חובת קרקע] can only have the sense that the land or its products are the object of obligation, and if obligations to the body [חובת הגוף] should make up the other category, then it can similarly have no other meaning than the human body is the object of obligation.[127]

Note how Holdheim reduces obligations, to land as well as to body, to objects of duty. The moral personality remains duty's proper subject. So one has a duty toward the body and those things outside of it, but one should distinguish these obligations from the person actually performing or intending to perform those duties. There exists an immense gulf between human acts and the persons or personalities who perform them. This is why Kant argues that we can never know a moral act when we see one, because we can never be completely sure of an actor's intentions (is she preventing him from drowning to save a life or to steal his wallet?). For Kant as for Holdheim, morality has more to do with human intentions (what Holdheim here calls the "moral personality") than it does with external acts.

And it is not difficult to understand why. For if morality were to reside in external acts, then it becomes as ephemeral and contingent as all historical and material bodies. And if a good many Jewish commandments concern objects of obligations (body and land) but not their subjects (the moral personality), then they too become as fleeting and temporary as material bodies and land, and therefore cannot be *religious* obligations at all, but only political ones. What Holdheim has done in his reading of Kiddushin 37a is quite radical: he has turned apparent religious duties into political ones by exposing their focus on objects rather than human subjects. Religion has to do with faith and ethics—the stuff of the moral personality. Jewish *mitzvot* concern material objects, and so too the political laws of civic life.

Holdheim has removed the religious sphere from historical and human development. Indeed, human relations to God lie outside of religious discourse because they signify human rather than divine movements: "Religion itself, as a being of divine origins, is not capable of being perfected, educated, or developed. It is as its author, as perfect as God is perfect. But the *relationship* of human beings—as more limited and imperfect beings—to religion is indeed capable of progress and perfection."[128] Holdheim here again contrasts eternal and unmoved religious truths to all other relations that remain outside this pristine domain. Persons relate to religion, but never embody it. Religion, like God, is monotheistic, and excludes all other challengers to its eternal authority. Holdheim has severely curtailed the content and nature of the religious so that it conforms to the pristine purity of a perfect God. Every religious idea stands aloof to human response, activity, ritual, and textual interpretation. Religion has no history or culture.[129]

The Bible, says Holdheim, contains "the active seed for the many-faceted designs and expressions of religious life," for it remains "the unchanging divine expression for human beings." The biblical text exists as a "holy text," in Holdheim's view, because it truly manifests, in material form, the eternal divinity of religious truth. The Bible is unchanging, but not the way in which readers interpret it: "The *use* and *application* of the Bible covers only a *particular time.* Religious instruction, in its most all-encompassing meaning, always searches and draws out of the Bible the most fitting expression for a particular period and formation of religious life."[130] If history conditions biblical *reading,* then what claim does a divine, unread, and unusable text have upon the reader? The biblical text, untouched by human hands, embodies religious truth. But once sullied by human touch, read and "used," it becomes a feature of a particular time and of various religious needs. Religion is not religion, Holdheim claims, "when it allows itself to be degraded as the handmaid of the times and its needs."[131] So, then, what is it?

Geiger's answer, as we have seen in his *Urschrift,* is that religion encompasses the cultural and political struggles that inform it. Geiger essentially adopts Holdheim's political vision and inscribes it within the biblical text. The Bible really is the handmaid of the times and its needs. Geiger reveals the political interpretations *within* the text, and readers simply reenact, in their own very different cultural settings, the very movements embodied therein. Holdheim's forced separation between religion and politics distances readers from sacred texts. They confront a pure text too removed from their own limited, historical practice. Geiger, however, bridges this gap, for cultural struggles *within* the Bible re-emerge in cultural readings *of* the Bible. Geiger's readers come to recognize their own political and social concerns in those of the text. The authority of personal meaning works, in Geiger's case, because political and social claims in the text mirror the religious life outside it. In and through the politics of religion, modern readers discover religious authority in sacred texts.

Andreas Gotzmann has persuasively argued that the politics of nineteenth-century German emancipation formed the background to German-Jewish accounts of religion and authority.[132] There were real goods to be had in public life, and Holdheim, for one, desired them for their universal and human value. But to enter into the uncharted waters of social and political life, not as a Jew but as an equal German citizen, Holdheim required an anchor to moor his Jewish identity. If public life represented progress with uncertainty, politics with intrigue and power, and history with competing visions and goals, then religion supplied the unchanging authoritative ground for purity, eternity, and identity. There the Jew was always and forever a Jew stamped by the eternal covenant of divine promise. No political deceit or human error could overturn that bedrock. Eat their food, marry their daughters and sons, live among them and prosper. God's promise is eternal, and so too Jewish identity founded upon it.

The price Holdheim must pay for this purified vision is high, and certainly too high for a thinker like Geiger who recovers the political from within religious practice. The past, says Geiger, worked with a very different notion of religion, one in which readers could easily, and without guilty conscience, rewrite a sacred text with "layers upon layers" to better control contemporary political debates.[133] The words on the page were malleable and soft enough to alter when new social, political, and religious issues required words with more powerful meanings. And when those words dried and hardened on the page, more creative hermeneutical efforts were enlisted to produce a sacred text infused with religious authority. Translations became interpretations, and, so Geiger believes, their authors and readers understood them as such. Geiger at times recoiled from this practice of authority, and often criticized its lack of methodological rigor. But he also seemed genuinely moved by, if not nostalgic for this lost sense of interpretive freedom: for a time when interpretive play, and not enslavement to a text, became the source for a meaningful religious life. The sacred does indeed bind, but it should not shackle modern freedom, as Geiger believed it did in his own time but not in the distant past. Geiger understood he could not return to that more innocent age. But he need not do so. He recognized that textual readers perform this act of making sacred through *practicing* authority—through creatively rereading texts and their translations. A sacred text does not arrive *a priori,* but is actively made by readers to appear so.

Geiger's *Urschrift* performs this act of making and controlling authority, and reveals the modern Jewish discovery of personal meaning in sacred texts. Recall

Geiger's discussion of Genesis 33:18, in which Jacob enters "Shalem, the city of Shechem." The priestly editor, so Geiger claims, supplied the word "Shalem" so that Jacob would enter the cultic center for Israelite worship rather than the Samaritan holy city. Editors, as much as, if not more so than translators, emend "original" texts to yield religious meaning. But Geiger's *Urschrift* does much the same. Note that Geiger distinguishes between creative translation and textual emendation, where the one rhythmically furnishes new meanings, while the other actively manipulates words or phrases. Perhaps the "original" text contained the word "Shalem," and the Samaritan Bible altered that word to read "Shalom" ("Jacob entered the city of Shechem in peace"). But how does Geiger know when the one translates and the other emends? In this particular case, Geiger argues that "the demands of the times" forced the editor to change the text. In other occasions, Geiger speaks of the text's "shocking" nature and the need for creative translation.[134]

It is Geiger's need as well, for his *Urschrift* selectively configures the Bible to reflect cultural struggles that resonate in his own time. Jerusalem is, in Geiger's reading of Genesis 33:18, a cultic center for sacrificial worship. The editor must alter the text and force it to justify Jerusalem as that center. The conflicts within the Bible, then, resonate with those outside it. But the Temple stands no longer, destroying with it the base of priestly control and prestige. If Jews need not enter Jerusalem to worship there, they might very well do better at home in Germany and work, as Geiger does, to build a vibrant liberal Jewish life. And if the editor can rework the text, then so too can contemporary Jews reread it. Geiger's *Urschrift* performs the authority of personal meaning by making the Bible a precedent and source for contemporary cultural patterns and debates.

Like the editors and translators before him, Geiger reworks the text to speak to "the demands of the times." He recovers a Bible that now speaks with authority. In a letter to his son Ludwig in 1866, he admits: "if the Bible were written only by Moses, it remains incomprehensible, it becomes a monstrosity. Only as a mirror to the entire centuries-long development of a people does it become clear, comprehensible, but still worthy of veneration."[135] To be a sacred authority rather than an embarrassing monstrosity, the biblical text must mirror the cultural expectations of its own time in order to do so again for contemporary readers. Geiger too needs an *Urschrift* to venerate, as do the modern Jews who follow him. Contemporary Jews discover the authority of personal meaning in much the same way as did Geiger. The practice of that authority lies in reading the Bible as an *Urschrift*—as a text of competing cultural pressures that inform the struggle for Jewish identity, then and now.

The Gendered Politics of Authority

3

Geiger's wife Emilie died in Berlin at the age of 51 on December 6, 1860. She had been ill since the birth of their last child some ten years earlier.[1] Geiger recalled those painful moments in a letter written to his friend Joseph Derenbourg a bit more than a year after her death:

> She suffered cruelly during the last few years, and she bore it with dignity. Early in 1860 she underwent a painful operation in Berlin. On her sickbed, which seemed to be a couch of convalescence, she was quite cheerful; she had loving care and devoted friends.

When she finally succumbed to her illness, Geiger made a pledge to "go on living, true to my children, to my office and to scholarship." Yet even as Geiger redoubled his efforts at work, he admitted to Derenbourg that "the painful void remains forever new; my home is and remains empty." Recalling that painful loss, Geiger remembered his wife as one who "remained beautiful to the very last; her womanly dignity and grace grew as time went by." Even today, Geiger admitted, "she still lives within me."[2]

These personal reflections of loss expose the undercurrents of Geiger's emotional life. But they also reveal something more in that they reflect bourgeois sensibilities of refinement and space. To Geiger, Emilie remains the dignified, honorable, and pleasant mother and wife, devoted to her children's welfare and her husband's profession—a portrait that her son Ludwig, in his biography of his father, admires as well.[3] She still "lives within" Geiger because she cultivated all that he associates with home and the inner life. His world is one of scholarship and labor; her duty resided, as Geiger tells it, in "understanding and sympathy for all my work and all my endeavors." Through her sympathy and support, Emilie enabled Geiger, both in her life and death, to dedicate his passions to "one idea," and to "labor faithfully in its cause."[4] The home was indeed empty, but the power of Geiger's reform would carry forward. In writing about that "one idea," and the virtuous feminine support of it, Geiger reproduced bourgeois gendered assumptions of feminine interior space and male public labor. At home and "within," Emilie could support Geiger's public world of religion and political reform. The tropes of personal loss, however deeply and honestly felt, reveal Geiger's sense of gendered space, and the fitting work to be done within and beyond the self.

Geiger sought to translate this inner, feminine, yet ever-present spiritual sensibility—one that he associated with his wife Emilie—into more public, communal spaces. Doing so could help him channel the inner life into the sphere of ritual performance; it could turn Emilie's personal support into a more engaged and worldly religious reform. This public expression of inner piety represents Geiger's commitment to a religious idealism that discovers eternal spiritual ideas in material forms. We have already witnessed this idealist practice in Geiger's historical works. There, he appealed to a moral core that continually reappears in progressive Jewish history. Geiger models his ritual reform on a theory of religious idealism: rituals that no longer convey the eternal, spiritual ideals should give way to new material practices that more concretely expose those ideals. The authority of ritual reform lies in how well religious practice translates the inner core of spiritual sensibility into material acts.

This inner-outer movement in ritual practice mimics bourgeois sensibilities of proper feminine virtue and male public virility. But it also explains Geiger's gendered reading of Jewish texts. Geiger reads inner religious virtue and public political morality into the biblical texts in order to read out of them an authoritative precedent for bourgeois Jewish practice and identity. The texts, through Geiger's interpretive skill, define virtue as private and female, but label political morality as public and male. Biblical women such as Rebecca, Miriam, and Deborah are domestic, private persons cultivated in virtues that reflect aesthetic beauty. Yet Geiger highlights the strong ethical principles and noble grandeur, the political savvy and moral rectitude of such diverse male figures as Abraham, Hillel, and Honi. Figuring biblical women as modest and virtuous enablers is certainly not peculiar to Geiger, for he shares this image with many of his contemporaries. Amos Funkenstein is surely right when he argues that Geiger, and not only he, imagined a past that reflected the "liberal-bourgeois ideology" of the time.[5] Derenbourg, for one, could sympathize with Geiger's portrait of Emilie's devotion and care, in part because she expressed bourgeois traits of elegance and fidelity.

But in reflecting that ideology, Geiger also helped to produce modern bourgeois standards of taste and refinement. As progressive Jews like Geiger entered the middle-class society and culture of Western Europe, they adopted a male civic society dependent on gendered configurations of the private sphere.[6] When Geiger rereads the Jewish biblical heritage to support bourgeois values of female domesticity and public male power, he produces the very discourse that justifies ritual reform as a male authoritative practice.

Geiger's liberal Judaism is a gendered politics that situates religious authority within the public realm of male activity and ritual performance, but it is one modeled on gender constructions that enact this very authority. His politics, like his idealism, moves from the inner world of virtue to the public sphere of ethical life. Convictions arise from within, but develop into real claims only in public forms that adequately translate private ideas and beliefs. The public, male space becomes the expressive arena for rituals that correspond to the interiority of faith—a pure and refined sphere that Geiger associates with the feminine. Only public ritual performances that embody private virtue fully express domestic female piety. By encoding female modesty as a private, interior sensibility, and modeling male virility on public acts of courage and moral integrity, Geiger embodies his religious idealism by transforming feminine spiritual sensibility into male religious ritual performance. Ritual reform translates feminine interiority into male exteriority, and in so doing both silences and undermines female power and authority.

This silencing of female power is a response to the cultural anxiety before a more provocative, "feminized" religion. Where traditional Judaism prized textual study in male domains of learning outside the home, modern Judaism now focused on inner spirituality, refinement, family integrity, and personal experience *in* the home.[7] Indeed, the home is precisely where Geiger locates his spiritual Judaism, and he, like his bourgeois contemporaries, engenders that space as feminine. To be sure, the home had always been a feminine space in traditional Judaism, and liberal thinkers such as Geiger accepted the separate domains of religious practice. But now women controlled and had access to the religious goods of modern Judaism, because much of modern religious practice occurred in the home and within the self. Judaism as a modern religion appropriated the traditional feminine home by withdrawing religious authority from the synagogue, and directing it to more private spaces. Yet in privileging the inner life with its spiritual potential, Geiger also fears the loss of male Jewish power. His religious idealism seeks to return that inner religiosity to public domains of male authority. By translating feminine interiority into male exteriority, Geiger yearns to regain male power through ritual reform.[8] His modern Judaism would be one that still upholds male religious authority.

Geiger reinscribes his religious idealism into the biblical text in order to justify male ritual practice in the public sphere. But I want to argue as well that Geiger's gendered analysis, in the end, undermines his idealist revisionism. Instead of justifying the reform of ritual practice, Geiger's account of feminine interiority and male public activity undercuts his religious idealism. For his gendered analysis does not empower feminine spirituality to ground the variety of public ritual acts; instead, those public acts determine the nature and content of the spiritual interior realm. Though Geiger argues as if spiritual ideals justify ritual reform, it is instead ritual performance that delimits and defines the meaning of religious ideals. In other words, the authority of personal meaning is decidedly male, and is worked out and determined in the public space of ritual practice. A "feminized" Judaism becomes so only after the work of male public actors.

A critical reading of Geiger's gendered account of ritual, as I offer here, turns Geiger's idealism on its head to reveal a more pragmatic, performance theory of ritual. This deconstructive reading exposes the relations between gender and authority in Geiger's liberal Judaism. If religion had become feminized (internal, spiritual, domestic) according to the cultural assumptions of the time, then Geiger sought to win back control of the religious sphere for men, usurping the feminine and relabeling it as masculine. He is responding to an anxiety felt by the possibilities (real and imagined) of women's power and control in German society. But in translating spiritual interiority into expressive public acts, Geiger redirects his idealist rhetoric to support a performance theory of ritual in which the ritual act itself determines the meaning and content of spiritual ideals. As the female image is reconfigured within male bodies and authority, so too the spiritual ideas become ever more subservient to, and transformed by material practices.

Figuring Biblical Women

In the fourth chapter of *Judaism and Its History* (1864–65)—those popular lectures on Jewish history offered in Frankfurt and Berlin—Geiger compares the shallow familial life of Hellenism to the prominence of "domestic life" in Judaism. He chastises the Greek nation for undervaluing "the sanctity of matrimonial life" and "the intimacy [*Innigkeit*] of the family." Indeed, "a woman's worth according to her true being [*wahren Wesen*] has not been properly highlighted in Hellenism."[9] Like many of his contemporaries, Geiger compares Judaism to the Greek nation of antiquity. He has much to say about a woman's character, and believes Judaism offers the most robust and true picture of it.

In this remarkable chapter that reflects upon, among other things, nationality, slavery, and the status of women (*Stellung der Frauen*), Geiger situates a woman's place within the private, virtuous space of familial integrity. He notes the biblical injunction to leave father and mother in order to become "an essential unity" with one's wife. This is, for Geiger, a male responsibility, for the son leaves his parents to join his wife who, Geiger adds, "follows her husband." Though the couple live in full equality, a woman's desire remains steadfast for her husband alone, for in Geiger's view, "he rules over you [*er soll über Dich herrschen*]."[10] The value of domestic harmony drives Geiger's notion of gender equality. A son abandons his father and mother to establish "domestic life." Within the serene confinement of the private home, the husband recognizes "a woman's worth according to her true character." Both husband and wife "become one being, one house," and "full equality" prevails within Geiger's invented private sphere of domestic contentment. This picture constructs the woman with "familial" virtues of desire, reverence, loyalty, and humble subservience to her husband. She is the virtuous matriarch, the enabler of family fortune and public praise, the simple and honorable wife, and the mother of noble males. Her "true character" is one of inner purity and domestic tranquility.

Geiger's portrayal of Jewish domestic life actively constructs the "cult of domesticity." This bourgeois model "called upon women to create a peaceful domestic environment free from the stresses of the larger society and devoted to the preservation and transmission of traditional morality, while men assumed the burden of earning a living and governing society."[11] Public political life was hard and demanding, even degrading for many Jewish males who desired the status and wealth of middle-class culture and society. Middle-class society for Western European Jews marked an entry into the wider public realm. Jews left the ghetto not for labor-intensive work but for the status and wealth that accompanied middle-class culture.[12] But Jewish males were not always successful in attaining the wealth, status, and prestige of bourgeois society, and so many imagined a home far more welcoming and secure. The family could provide the easy comforts that still remained elusive in the public sphere.

The Jewish woman as wife and mother would console, nurture, and strengthen her husband in the private sphere so that he could return to the more demanding requirements of public life:

> Middle-class men reacted to the stresses of this new and maddening industrialized world in part by expecting wives to provide islands of tranquility. . . . The image of the family as a haven became an integral component of bourgeois class consciousness, even if actually achieved only by some. The family was the place where men were to be loved, consoled, and refreshed (usually by wives whom they had married for financial and status reasons).[13]

Familial bliss, for many middle-class families in Western Europe, served political ends. A harmonious and loving home offered the father and husband "a sheltering environment ideally free from stress"[14] so that he could once again do battle in that "maddening industrialized world." The *Hausfrau* would play her political role by cultivating domestic virtues in order to secure a peaceful home for her husband. She would be "domestic, weak, modest, dependent, self-denying, emotional, religious, and virtuous."[15]

Geiger's account of domestic Jewish women is rooted in this image of the "cult of domesticity" that had developed in Europe and played out elsewhere, though in varied and often more radical forms.[16] He figures the Jewish wife as humble and subservient, and she cultivates a serene and amiable home. Jewish domestic life, in this picture, remains free from the stresses of middle-class conflict and impersonal market forces. There is unity and tranquility in the Jewish domestic world, and this because Jewish women exhibit the virtues and discipline that mark the bourgeois "cult of domesticity."

The image of the domestic and supportive *Hausfrau* is not, however, a nineteenth-century ideological invention. As Isabel Hull reveals in her important work on sexuality and civil society in Germany, the notion of family contentment that subordinates female desires for male happiness in civil society has roots in Enlightenment philosophy, and especially in eighteenth-century cameralist thought. One of the more influential cameralist thinkers, Johann Heinrich Gottlob von Justi (1720–1771), argued that women should subordinate their interests for men's happiness to better promote the goals of civil society. Hull quotes Justi at some length, for he argues forcefully and with typical candor that "it is without question disadvantageous to the republic for men to be hindered in [doing] the business of the state by domestic conflict, for them to be made unfit [*untüchtig*] for [state business] by consuming worries and depression and to be pushed prematurely into the grave."[17] Justi's text reveals two crucial assumptions: 1) civil society is predominantly male, and 2) those males are married. The domestic sphere of family life serves the interests of male civil society; but even more, family life grounds the status of male political action and rights. Hull shows how notions of gender, sex, and family undergird the male project for constructing civil society. The "cult of domesticity," in turn, does more than mark women as familial enablers of male public virility. It also serves to reinforce the public space of male performance, and grounds that authority in the household and family.

So even as Geiger imagines a marriage of equality and contentment, the male husband "rules over" his domestic spouse. In representing women as domestic, Geiger shows them as subservient to male authority and power *within* the family. As Hull reminds us, Justi's married males receive the rights of civil society only as dominating husbands and fathers.[18] Geiger's constructed images of domestic bliss and contentment serve to widen male authority in the private and public spheres. He defines the "status of women" only in relation to a male authority rooted in and dominating over the private sphere.

Yet Geiger still fantasizes that servile and privately modest women wish to be so, and he discovers these virtuous women throughout Jewish literature. In the Bible, Rebecca appears as a "maiden of innocence, friendly and kindhearted toward the stranger, readily complying with his request for water to drink, and caring even for his camels."[19] Geiger emphasizes Rebecca's "maidenly blush" and her sexual purity when she first encounters Isaac. She is for Geiger a picture of female nobility: kind, innocent, modest, and sexually pure. And in "readily complying" to Abraham's servant's request, Rebecca actively desires and conforms to the enabling role of spouse.

This sense of chosen modesty and female subservience to male actors underscores a dominant motif in Enlightenment and nineteenth-century images of familial duties. In Fichte's influential view, marriage involves "the unlimited subjection of the woman to the will of the husband." But her minor status is not willed but desired: "Woman is not subjected to her husband, so that her husband should have a *right of compulsion* over her; she is subjected through her own continuous necessary wish—a wish which is the condition of her morality." As Hull comments on this passage, "the moment a women [*sic*] chooses to lead a moral life, she has also chosen to disappear from society."[20]

This chosen hiddenness manifests the "domestic" virtues that transform Rebecca into the guardian of traditional piety and goodness. Indeed, Isaac loves her for precisely those qualities. Miriam too is always pure, like "a fresh source of water," and fiercely loyal with "the intimacy [*Innigkeit*] of a woman's heart." After citing a well-known midrash that praises the Israelite women for the communal deliverance from Egypt, Geiger asks rhetorically: "Who guarded their homes, who attended to the pure moral sense [*reinen Sinn*] of their children, who protected the hearth fires of ethical life [*das Feuer der Sittlichkeit*]?" Since men labored outside the home in Egypt and, not far from Geiger's view, in Europe too, his answer was surely commonplace: "It was the mothers in Israel who attended to those matters."[21] Rebecca and Miriam were not exceptional in their private virtue. Israelite women protected Jewish domestic life in their purity and chastity, in Egypt and modern Europe, while men labored in the public sphere. This depiction represents more than a social image; it also naturalizes female desires so that Rebecca and Miriam yearn for the very modesty and silence they come to represent. Geiger inscribes the virtuous, compliant, and innocent spouse as a "woman's *natural* purpose"[22] both within the familial economy of civil society and the biblical Exodus story.

The association of virtuous Jewish women with private contentment, virtue, and purity continues even in Geiger's account of more politically astute figures such as Deborah, Hannah, and Ruth. Note Geiger's ambiguous praise of Deborah as a "beautiful" figure (*eine schöne Gestalt*), prophetess, and judge, "a bold and courageous woman, an enthusiastic leader, yet one fully conscious of her womanhood." Deborah's public courage and bravery, together with her mastery of religious politics, express little of her feminine virtues. Even Deborah recognizes this, according to Geiger. She is reluctant to enter battle because, as she tells Barak, victory should not be a woman's. Yet Barak insists she accompany him and so, as Geiger tells it here, she grudgingly consents and gains the victory.[23]

Geiger's reading draws together texts in Judges 4: 4–10. As the biblical text has it, Deborah forcefully encourages Barak to enter battle, but he desires her assistance. She then agrees with Barak's request, adding only that the honor will be less for Barak now that God will hand over Sisera to a woman (and, as it turns out, Sisera does succumb to a woman, but her name is Yael). Geiger, however, discovers only Deborah's timid deference and reluctance to enter into the public fray, and she appears more concerned about Barak's glory than her own prowess. She is a strong and public figure in the Book of Judges, and so Geiger must stress her private and more feminine virtues. Deborah desires neither the spoils of war nor praise for her own courage. Instead she recognizes her womanhood, "and announces the victory in enthusiastic words, chastising and praising like a true prophetess of God."[24] However public and courageous, Deborah embraces her femininity—in enthusiastic words, but not public heroic deeds—even as she enters male space. Geiger can only praise her political boldness as he notes her more graceful, beautiful figure. Courage, leadership, and bravery are truly male virtues, and so Geiger must defend Deborah's womanhood. One might think it bold that such a courageous woman arose in Israel. But we need not fear her triumph, for she is fully conscious of her "place" even in the public sphere.

Hannah not only recognizes her place within this gendered economy; her very identity integrally relates to it. Geiger introduces her to his readers as "Hannah, the mother of Samuel," and her fervent desire for a child marks her as a "complete woman." Her identity, in Geiger's reading, is as mother "who laments that children are denied her," and, while standing "*in Innigkeit,*" she prays to her God for a son from "the depths of her heart."[25] Her husband Elkanah comforts her by claiming that he alone is far more valuable to Hannah than even ten sons. Elkanah's response to Hannah, I would think, is a rather poor excuse for male insensitivity. But Geiger thinks otherwise and claims, "what intimacy [*Innigkeit*] those few words express!"[26] Elkanah is, for Geiger, the devoted husband who requires only domestic bliss from his wife. To see her weeping and in such sorrow disturbs that private peace, and so he asks Hannah to focus on the husband she loves rather than on the son she will never bear. And in the Fichtean image now transplanted into biblical history, Hannah should want this too. But Geiger praises Hannah's sense of self as intimately related to a child rather than to her husband. Here we have, in Geiger's image, a man at the center ("am I not better to you than ten sons?"), and a childless woman who follows not her husband but her natural desire for a son.

At one stroke, Geiger subordinates Hannah to her husband's rule within marriage and the family, even as he naturalizes and praises her feminine needs for motherhood. She must desire the very thing (a son) that marks and continues male dominance and inheritance. Even Ruth is only worthy in Geiger's eyes "to be the ancestress of David." This is so because Ruth cares unselfishly for Naomi: she follows Naomi "as an obedient child, remains her daughter, lovingly cares for her and is her devoted companion."[27] Geiger praises Ruth's adoring and innocent qualities of feminine beauty (*eine liebliche Gestalt*), and her value as bearer of future male leaders. Husbands all but disappear in Geiger's account of Ruth, as they do, no less, in the biblical text. He marks the home of children and fellowship as a feminine site of modesty and innocence, but one *always in the service of* the male political and civil sphere. The "cult of domesticity" is women's desired work as enablers of the male public sphere. The private sphere of family life, in Geiger's biblical readings, serves the male role as public actor.

Figuring women in the service of civil society revealed how men, so concerned with social power and legitimate inheritance, imagined familial life and marriage. Even as legal rulings protected family life from state coercion and enforcement, the requirements of civil society determined and legitimated private life. In this sense, the private sphere became a male domain in the service of male public interests. Marriage extended the private sphere, according to Hull, but the male's "position as private dominator qualified him to participate in the wider, public sphere of equals, in civil society." Geiger's image of female biblical figures evokes one of Hull's most central and provocative claims:

> Men's autonomy (and therefore fitness for the new public of civil society) rested upon their presocial, private individuality, reckoned independently of society, whereas women's dependence derived precisely from the social, "public" reckoning used to define their "nature." From the standpoint of determination, men were private, women, public. The institutional location of this intellectual dichotomy was the family, which reformed civil law constituted as the sphere of male domination over women, beyond the purview of state intervention.[28]

If a woman's private status relies upon her "public" determination, then the protected and inner world of private life is always caught up in its public representations. The private exists to help further the goals of the public, and "the practitioners of civil society" delimit and figure the private sphere in the service of male political and social power.

This political move, in which public interests create and determine private space, reflects Geiger's reading of feminine biblical characters. For they, too, represent a desired familial modesty to better support male heirs and social goods. Indeed, those male actors justify their social status through their roles as dominating husbands, fathers, and householders in the private sphere. As Geiger associates women with an inner spiritual sensibility, and men with public actors of ritual material performance, Hull's reversal of the common private-public and female-male dichotomies becomes ever more significant. For just as women are determined by public concerns, so too the eternal (feminine) spiritual idea is shaped by material (male) bodily expressions.

As we shall see, the religious idealism that underwrites Geiger's challenge to traditional ritual unravels in this gendered economy. The public, material world of male ritual performance actively reworks the spiritual ideals imagined to underlie it. Here too, public concerns shape private interests. The religious inner spirit is not the cause, but the effect of public ritual acts. As Hull eloquently states, "though women read, they did not publish."[29] Women became for men the passive constructions of their dominating husbands. And, Fichte might add, they liked it like that.

The passive women readers in Geiger's biblical text are all beautiful people. They represent affectionate, lovely, caring, selfless, obedient, and devoted women who maintain domestic and reproductive bliss for their male companions. This portrayal of the woman of valor glorifies the site of private virtue, even as it hides from view the male center of family life. For Geiger, feminine value lies in character, not moral strength, in beauty and charm, not boldness, in tranquility and comfort, not political tenacity. Geiger even praises the biblical accounts of female heroes as "told with childlike simplicity, without embellishing pomp, because it is so deep in the nature of Israel."[30] That very simplicity continues in Geiger's reading of the Song of Songs, a "feminine" book that retains fresh, natural, emotional, and sensual qualities. Exclusively devoted to the meaning of a "fine, pure love," the Song of Songs remains aloof to the more combative historical narratives of Israel.

But the world of romantic love also reveals the political stories of Israel's history that promote and shape "pure love." Religion and history belong to the public realm of male dominance; yet they also determine the private sphere as shapers of it. Women are beautiful, pure, and private characters who enable and make possible public history and religion. But these women do not enjoy public identities in Geiger's biblical exegesis, even as they serve and are defined by the public sphere.

This sense of service and devotion to public goods arises in Geiger's tribute to the woman of valor in Proverbs 31. Observant Jewish husbands recite this text to their wives every Sabbath—a text that praises women's "devotion to their families as expressed in tireless work and domestic productivity."[31] Geiger highlights this central theme toward the end of Proverbs 31: "Her children arise and call her blessed, her husband also, and he praises her." That praise and blessing mark the honorable woman as mother and wife, and so Geiger joyfully concludes his chapter on Jewish women by declaring that "the pure estimation of woman, the moral eminence of matrimonial life, remain the fundamental principle."[32] Within the sphere of "a noble family life,"[33] women find their most honorable and moral place. Familial bliss serves the historical and religious practices that belong to male power and activity.

A good many of Geiger's colleagues share his views of women and the public sphere. Witness the account offered by Geiger's contemporary and rival, Heinrich Graetz, in his *History of the Jews*. Deborah's heroic strength, for Graetz, lies in her "gentle whispers of poetic loftiness" rather than in "mannish woman acts" (*durch mannweibische Bluttbaten*). She is a poet and singer, and her gifts in song and word mark and enliven her prophetic call. Barak still represents the popular battle general and director, and Deborah remains the people's spiritual leader. But Deborah leads only in song and through poetic movements, as Barak commands through heroic deeds in battle.[34] Deborah's spiritual inwardness, one that motivates and encourages grand public acts by male leaders, dominates Graetz's depiction of Deborah in an earlier text as well. In his *Structure of Jewish History* (1846), he described Deborah as a model for "the religious factor" because her own courage "was brought about by God's all-powerful arm. The poetess Deborah does not sing of Barak's acts of heroism but of God's wonderful help." Deborah, in the end, represents Judaism as "the religion of the spirit [*Geistesreligion*]."[35]

As either spiritual leader or deferential subject to God's intentions, Graetz's Deborah transfers her personal agency onto public actors. So too for Geiger, for whom Deborah remains the crooning cheerleader for Barak's public battles. Geiger stretches the biblical text to project Deborah's "womanhood" and her preferred life of the home. Though public and political, Deborah still remains acquiescent and gracious. Both Geiger and Graetz weave domestic feminine values into Deborah's prophetic character. For the reformer and the historian, Deborah expresses all the virtues of a private life in the service of male public actors.

This is no less true for Geiger's one-time mentor and friend, the modern Orthodox rabbi Samson Raphael Hirsch (1808–1888).[36] In his commentaries on the Bible, Hirsch speaks of Deborah as "borne up by the Spirit of God, fired through and through with enthusiasm for His Word, who put the men to shame, who, with her 'flaming words' inflamed their courage and steeled their powers of action." Like Graetz, Hirsch commends Deborah's heroism in words only but not deeds: "not the sword of Barak, the spirit of Deborah, the words of Deborah, won the victory."[37] Hirsch evades Deborah's public acts and dealings with Barak. Deborah's spiritual words enable men to conquer and control the political world. For, as Hirsch comments elsewhere in his *The Jewish Woman:*

> By excusing the female sex from the hard labour of subduing and mastering the earth, he [God] left it [the female] free to be devoted to the higher and more humanistic task of employing the products of the man's labour for the ethical purposes of building up a house and family. . . .[38]

Women encourage public males to subdue the earth, and reap the benefits of a private, virtuous home from male public work. Note too how Hirsch speaks of Hannah as "the prayerful [*gotterfüllte*] mother of our Samuel."[39] She offers a picture of endurance and hope, and in her despair for her child she still maintains her modesty before her husband Elkanah: "she nevertheless did every thing possible to make this [sadness] unobtrusive and kept in the background." Hannah becomes the decent, faithful mother who "simply wants just a human child on whom to exercise her maternal duties."[40] Those duties, of course, express natural female desires for "house and family" in Hirsch's schema.

Hirsch even limits the political realm for women *to* women. If Deborah supports male aggression in the public sphere, Miriam can only inform other women.[41] In his commentary on Exodus 15:20, a text that describes Miriam as "the prophetess, sister of Aaron," Hirsch decisively focuses on the phrase "sister of Aaron" and adds: "amongst the women she occupied the position that Aaron held amongst the men. As Aaron spread amongst the men the Word that was revealed to Moses, so did Miriam amongst the women." In regulating Miriam's prophetic voice, Hirsch reduces her political power to a silent community. Where Rashi notes how Miriam recited her song to women in Exodus 15:21 (and Moses crooned to men only),[42] Hirsch claims that "Moses and Israel sang, Miriam and the women responded,"[43] an uncanny reminder of Hull's phrase, "though women read, they did not publish." Deborah's public words of encouragement seem all the more daring and radical in light of the passive and modest figures of Miriam and Hannah. Hirsch, like so many other Jewish thinkers of the period, absorbs and reinscribes bourgeois views of women and the political sphere. When one reads Hirsch on Rebecca, for example, as a "modest, morally pure, innocent girl" who maintains "a spiritual beauty of the face, an impression of grace, indicating character,"[44] one could cite any number of Geiger's contemporaries who share this view. Geiger's portrayal of female biblical characters is, indeed, so commonplace that one could easily mistake Hirsch's comment on the woman of valor for Geiger's own: "Where is the European woman of the nineteenth century who would not be stirred with an ardent longing [*mit begeistertem Verlangen*] by this picture from the oldest Jewish past [of Proverbs 31]."[45]

To be sure, Geiger shares gendered images of female piety with Hirsch, Graetz, and many others. But to belabor this would miss the point of Geiger's gendered politics. For the central and most compelling issue is the way in which gender works to undermine Geiger's ritual reform. In Geiger's idealist view, the inner kernel of spiritual truth becomes manifest in successive temporal husks of material expression. Yet that inner spiritual core never loses itself completely, as it were, in material practices. The purity of truth can manifest itself in various forms without sacrificing the power and wholeness of its truth content. So if a particular ritual act no longer illuminates the spiritual truth that justifies it, another more adequate ritual should replace the outmoded one. This is the idealist logic that underlies Geiger's principle of reforming ritual. But if bodily ritual acts shape and determine the kernel of spiritual truth—just as public male desires fashion domestic feminine virtues—then the idealist logic breaks down, undermining Geiger's reforming principle. For ritual does not express religious truths so much as determine them. And in that determination, ritual intimately incorporates and produces religious meaning.

Religious Idealism

By highlighting this performative aspect of ritual activity—in which material acts produce religious meaning—I am not suggesting that Geiger himself held this view. Quite the opposite, in fact. Geiger's theory of ritual reform does not advance a performative model, but rather an idealist one in which inner meaning or truth is realized in public ritual acts. He defends a religious idealism modeled upon an inner-outer movement from spiritual essence to embodied religious practices. But I do want to argue that a critical, gendered analysis reveals how the text works against Geiger's intentions, such that his idealist views are turned on their head to support a performative model of ritual performance. I find this pragmatic, materialist model of ritual a productive resource for understanding contemporary Jewish practice—a claim I will return to in the conclusion to this book. Here, I focus on Geiger's idealist philosophy to better position the critical move I want to make from idealism to material performance.

One can begin to recognize Geiger's idealist program in his response to Bruno Bauer's *Die Judenfrage* (1842), a text discussed in the previous two chapters. Bauer had ridiculed Judaism as an unhistorical religion, and Geiger in response had co-opted Hegelian terms to position Judaism at the center of historical progress. As a feature of this historical argument, Geiger claimed that the idea of religion must, according to its very nature, make this movement from inner content to outer public forms:

> The idea of religion, as the consciousness of a holy source for community life and individual duties, must determine itself through a form, must choose for itself a narrow vessel to individualize and limit as soon as it enters into the world of appearances, so that it moves with this holy source in an ever closer connection.[46]

Only Judaism recognizes that universal ideas appear in constricted forms, and only public actions as "ceremonies" could adequately express such inner content. Certainly no one form reveals the robustness of "the idea," but this only points to the superiority of Judaism as *the* historical religion that reveals the progressive movements of religious forms.[47]

For Geiger, the inner spiritual sensibility perfects itself in a material presence. Compare this to the religious idealism of his reform colleague Samuel Hirsch (1815–1889).[48] Hirsch laments the fallen necessity and loss of purity in the movement from spiritual content to material form.[49] The human essence reveals the basic conflict that while "free of nature, nothing however can be free of nature."[50] This sense of entrapment in nature rarely surfaces in Geiger's account: the material form intensifies and realizes what still remains inchoate. Even if limited, the material forms "individualize" the religious idea so that rituals move "ever closer" to that original spiritual source. For Geiger, the spiritual becomes a practicing religious life when inner content expresses itself in material forms. One does not escape material presence so much as work in and through it. In that working through, human subjects invest material forms with spiritual depth.

But the "narrowness" in form points to the progressive thrust of the religious idea, for spirit always requires more adequate representations that move "in an ever closer connection" to the spiritual core. Geiger builds into the notion of reform the very idea of religious history—one that describes how rituals express, or fail to express, eternal religious ideas. In the Hegelian language that Geiger adopts in his response to Bauer, the religious spirit manifests itself in a limited determination of form. So religious ritual would become the central site of spiritual practice and, it was then clear, the focal point of religious controversy.

Note Geiger's well-known letter to Leopold Zunz (1794–1886) in March 1845 concerning the practice of laying tefillin and following kosher dietary laws. For Geiger as for many in his generation, Zunz's work provided the model for scholarly studies of Jewish history. His *Die gottesdienstlichen Vorträge der Juden* (The Homiletic Literature of the Jews; 1832) marked a watershed in Jewish scholarship by offering a unified Jewish history that organically develops in time. His command of the sources and inspiring message provoked one modern commentator to claim that "Zunz had provided his bewildered generation with an astonishing display of the power of *Wissenschaft* to steer Judaism through the shoals and rapids of emancipation. A meticulous and unprejudiced study of the past could become a force for revitalisation."[51] In the early period of liberal Judaism from 1819 to 1824, Zunz "stood in the forefront" of a small group who sought to reform Berlin Jewry.[52] Geiger revered Zunz, sought his scholarly approval for a good number of his published articles, and maintained a close friendship through the many letters that passed between them.

All the more astonished was Geiger, then, when he read Zunz's edifying article on laying tefillin (1843), and later overheard a rumor that Zunz was now observing the kosher dietary laws.[53] Both Zunz and Geiger had written often to each other—many of their letters express warmth and admiration, and both comfortably discuss personal matters at length. So even as Geiger hesitantly notes Zunz's article, and warns that he harbors no ill will, he nonetheless cannot understand how someone so progressive as Zunz could practice what, for Geiger, appeared as a groundless religious practice to bind (through a leather housing and straps) biblical texts close to the heart and mind.[54]

But Geiger's letter reveals that at issue were the underlying principles for Zunz's ritual observance. Geiger seeks only "the grounds" (*Gründe*) upon which Zunz justifies his practice. All "ceremonies" warrant a deeper meaning—a noted reminder that for Geiger, commanded observance (*mitzvot*) had now become a vehicle for personal fulfillment (*Ceremonie*). But could laying tefillin, based "on a false explanation of biblical passages," and one "so completely foreign to our entire way of thinking, to our own cultural and aesthetic sense," could *this* ritual performance truly edify and enlighten?[55] The question's rhetorical force highlights the distance between the ritual act and the justificatory grounds that underlie it. Geiger presumes that Zunz inhabits his world of cultural and aesthetic refinement, and so both should recognize the religious gap between sensibility and performance. For Geiger, "what is dead remains dead; the spirit, which earlier existed therein, continues to have an effect in other ways and under other forms."[56]

Geiger cannot relive a past and reawaken a sensibility so out of touch with his modern world. He suggests that even as Jews discover meaning in laying tefillin, none can be found there, for the practice lies in notions of "charms" and faulty biblical exegesis. But the real stumbling block for Geiger centers on Zunz's character. How could someone like *Zunz* practice such a rite? As Geiger admits later in this letter, if Zunz himself could discover spiritual meaning in tefillin, then "even the most vigorous of minds could close itself off at a certain time."[57] Geiger questions how "a man like *Zunz*" could plausibly practice what he knows cannot be grounded in reasonable exegesis or an enlightened view of Jewish history. A man like Zunz should know better. If unenlightened Jews habitually lay tefillin, one can understand the power of nostalgia to comfort those who continue the ancient traditions. But the author of *Die gottesdienstlichen Vorträge der Juden* should recognize the principled view that material practices embody a rational or spiritual ground.

So when Geiger hears of Zunz's observance of kosher dietary laws, his shock reveals a good deal about his religious idealism:

> I honor those considerations that one has to observe in life. And I would find in it nothing strange if you had considered keeping kosher suitable under the circumstances of your position as head of a seminary. But it has been said that you did this out of principle [*prinzipiell*] and not according to the necessity of your position. . . . I admit that I cannot come to terms with that at all. Just these dietary laws are so thoroughly lacking in spirit [*Geistloses*].[58]

When Ismar Schorsch reads Geiger's letter, he claims that the "controversy centered on what should be the decisive force in shaping contemporary Judaism, the cultural level of the present or the legacy of the past?"[59] Zunz had surely privileged the "norms" of the past, and Geiger the cultural and aesthetic tastes of modernity. But this misses entirely the ideological battle that resides at the heart of Geiger's critique. For despite the "cultural level of the present," even Geiger could understand Zunz's dietary habits as leader of a Jewish community. Indeed, at the very end of his letter Geiger hints at his own observance of Jewish dietary laws, for he admits that "our kosher lunches and dinners taste delicious."[60] Surely the observance is not at issue, but rather the "ground" that lies behind and within it. Geiger criticizes Zunz's observance of the kosher dietary laws "out of principle" when no such "spirit" can be found there.

To Zunz, Geiger admits that reform carries little worth if it merely "clears away" and does not stimulate "the higher, vigorous meaning that refers to the idea." Reform practice always signifies the higher idea that underlies it. If religious reform sweeps away practices, it does so because those practices no longer cling to that idea. Zunz, by contrast, seeks to establish "norms" built upon ancient ideas and upon an earlier consciousness.[61] But what is dead is dead, according to Geiger, and the dietary and tefillin laws speak to an outmoded and superseded past.

Geiger's religious idealism evokes the image of an eternal religious sensibility that continually seeks out more adequate ritual practices. Tracking the movement from an inner spiritual idea to an outer material world underwrites Geiger's reforming practice, and grounds his critique in the 1845 letter. In Zunz, Geiger has lost more than a liberal Jewish colleague.[62] He confronts an enlightened scholar who acts from commitments hostile to Geiger's own idealist principles. Geiger energetically defends those principles in his letter to Zunz, even at the cost of personal offense and friendship. If Geiger cannot come to terms with Zunz's religious observance, it is because he so thoroughly presumes that eternal ideas ground the meaning of all ritual practices.

Feminine Interiority and Male Authority

The religious idealism that underwrites Geiger's critique of Zunz is also one that links inner spirituality with feminine innocence, and outer public ritual acts with masculine virility. As spirit moves from the inner halls of religious sensibility and truth to the worldly material sphere of bodily expression, so too does the feminine migrate from its familial modesty to male social acts. Geiger's idealist appeal to a feminine interiority that becomes fully expressive in public ritual is the focus of his early essay on women entitled "The Status of the Female Sex in the Judaism of our Time."[63] Though the focus clearly remains women in contemporary Judaism, the text reads as a lengthy defense for women in Jewish history. One reviewer of Geiger's article complained it was too apologetic in tone and substance—Geiger simply retrieved biblical and rabbinic texts that supported women's encouraging status in Judaism.[64] Geiger noted the "bitter attack" by D. Caro's review,[65] but the critique stands nonetheless, at least in regard to Geiger's biblical reading. For even as biblical texts often subordinate women under their father's or husband's rule, so that "a woman's independence and the personal rights that derive from it were not granted," Geiger still claims that Israelites regarded women highly, particularly in comparison to other cultures of the time.

Certainly "clever" women (like the judge Deborah and the prophetess Huldah) influenced public life and religious practice, and they engaged in public worship.[66] Even more, a woman's status had much improved even in the Talmudic period. Some degree of freedom had now been sanctioned—though Geiger mentions the one great exception of divorce, an issue he returns to in many of his essays on religious reform. But Geiger still criticizes the Talmudic legal category of women as slaves and children, and he admits that "even the support of a spiritual life for women was considered dangerous."[67] If women had made significant advances in personal autonomy, much of that had been undercut by the Talmudic texts. The Bible, Geiger argues, paints a far more congenial picture of women's rights and responsibilities.

Geiger also turns to the cultural landscape outside the text to argue that, inside the text, the rabbis remain out of step with developments in women's lives. Surely women participated in "the truest expression of the spiritual movement of the people," but one would not think so from reading the Talmud. Geiger appeals yet again to women "with the most beautiful, most sublime virtues and love of the highest devotion."[68] But such virtue and "view of life" stood at odds with rabbinic law. The Talmud resolves this tension between law and life by suppressing female piety, forcing Judaism to suffocate the female "receptive sense for religiosity." Women had been "released" from public worship and thereafter denied "the most nourishing food of religious interiority." They watched to the side as men worshipped "in a foreign language."

The inner virtue that Geiger associates with female piety had been locked out and made foreign by the male usurpation of public space. Yet piecemeal initiatives that grant women a few obligatory commandments, or support new schools for both sexes, cannot undo the repression of the inner feminine spirit. The structural problems remain intact: female inner virtue and higher devotion remain stifled without any means for public religious expression. This is all too clear in the marriage ceremony where men "buy" their women. Although Jewish men treat their spouses as proper subjects rather than acquired objects, the symbolic power of the marriage ceremony undercuts female religiosity.[69] The notion of a woman as acquired property silences female religious activity and expression.

But Geiger believes a pragmatic remedy still exists: rabbinic scholars should grant equal covenantal obligations to men and women, allow women full participation in public worship, and reject entirely the notion that they are spiritually underage.[70] In this way, "both Jewish girls and Jewish women, practiced in faith, will live with interiority in faith."[71] Geiger associates notions of interiority, virtue, and aesthetic beauty with female bodies. And he never once challenges the claim that rabbinic leaders should control and determine the limits of female expression and identity. Rabbis do and should control and define; they just presently do so in the wrong way. In a later essay, Geiger even defends the acquisition of the bride in marriage without her public spoken acceptance. The husband gives, the bride merely accepts, and this appropriately mirrors the domestic order. Though he claims to support equality between men and women, Geiger subordinates female place and power to male agency. The male voice and judgments are decisive. A "virtuous" woman, Geiger concludes, should remain silent when receiving the marriage ring because this replicates the natural order of male dominance and the fitting acquiescence of private virtue.[72]

Geiger's essay on the status of women, together with his later discussion of the marriage ceremony, suggest that even as the inner feminine spirit should blossom in ritual expression, only men act in the social world of ritual performance. Though women are "practiced in faith," Geiger focuses on how women "live with interiority in faith." Even more, male rabbis like Geiger determine and limit the scope of both private and public activity. So even as Geiger demands the full material expression of inner feminine piety, that expression must manifest itself in male bodily forms.

But if the male social actors configure the capacities and borders of the private sphere, then ritual performance as a male activity also constitutes the content of feminine spirituality. Rituals reconfigure the spiritual truths that Geiger claims underlie religious performance. His religious idealism evolves into a claim for male authority in ritual practice. For spiritual truths neither underlie nor are they expressed in material ritual acts; instead, those very acts determine the sense and meaning of spiritual truths. The religious spirit (read *the feminine*) is not the cause, but the effect of ritual acts (read *the masculine*). If women read but do not publish, then spirit is discovered and configured by ritual acts.

We can see this in Geiger's reading of male biblical and rabbinic characters. Unlike the females, Geiger's male actors are public and worldly. In Geiger's discussion of David's sexual adventures, for example, male relations with concubines denote political acts of acquisition and authority. Female concubines function as commodities in the public sphere, and find themselves trapped within the sexual politics of Absalom and David. Although at the center of these politics, women move as passive players in the political world of male activity.[73] Religious and political struggles belong within the gendered space of male activity alone.

Recall how Geiger described Abraham's struggle against sacrificial worship as a world-historical battle to overcome barbarism. Abraham's religious devotion represented Judaism's first "great feat" in world, and not merely Jewish, history.[74] Indeed, Abraham's faith resonates within the public space of religious meaning. His act functions as a test of and model for faith: a faith that is universal, public, and encoded as male. The Jewish world-historical mission embodies this true devotion to God, a model of and for males because it remains public, social, and political.

Abraham poses as a strong counterimage to Geiger's female biblical characters who represent private virtue. Devoted to an ethical principle that resonates within the world of public morality, Abraham's private virtue remains secluded and trivial. Geiger values Jewish males who manifest Abraham's quality of principled moral engagement in worldly affairs, but he must apologize for such activity, even label it idiosyncratic, when women enter the public arena. We remember females for their aesthetic domestic practice, but males for their political morality. Geiger admires, for example, Honi the Circle Drawer (a miracle worker and folk hero of the Second Temple period) for his love of peace and political compromise. In Geiger's retelling, when asked by the Pharisees to pray for their victory over the Sadducees, Honi instead recognizes both parties as God's children, and implores God to ignore their request. Honi signifies, in Geiger's phrase, "the fruit of the true Jewish spirit" because, "inspired by the love of man and country," he remains "faithful" to the Jewish world-historical mission that pursues a moral ideal undeterred by internal religious polemics.[75] Geiger does not tell his readers that Honi, at least in one version, was stoned to death after making his plea. More significant is Honi's devotion to moral principles as the ground of his "noble" martyrdom. Those principles reside in the public arena of political intrigue and religious conflict, rather than within the private, serene, and beautiful home of feminine virtue.

If Abraham and Honi represent social morality, and Rebecca and Hannah signify enabling virtue, then Hillel the rabbinic reformer appropriates the domestic virtues in the service of his public life. He thereby embodies the feminine as enabling spirit within his male political body. The modest dispositions of female character are more than determined by the social; those virtues become fully integrated into Hillel's public identity. In so doing, Geiger's Hillel represents the ideal and true reformer.

In strong contrast to his depiction of Abraham and Honi, Geiger stresses Hillel's virtues, especially his meekness, simplicity, refinement, and kindness. Compare Hillel's humble virtues to those of his great rival Shammai, who is rude, quick to anger, eccentric, dismissive, and callous.[76] Hillel possesses all the traits Geiger had earlier inscribed upon biblical women, as well as the principled (but always pragmatic) desire for justice:

> He [Hillel] accepted what could not be changed by him, but he was the very man who carried on the contest against the priests with all possible determination and narrowed down the limits of their prerogatives most closely. His presentation of the foundation and essence of Judaism fully discloses the sentiment of the man [*seiner Sinnesart*]; the essence of Judaism consists in love of human beings and mutual recognition, in the respect of the dignity and equality for all. That is the foundation and root of Judaism: the rest is commentary.[77]

The virtues of feminine love, respect, and harmonious relations fuse together with "the contest against the priests" to embody private virtue and public moral engagement in one male body. Hillel battles the priests in the public arena, but his message remains dignified, comforting, modest (the rest is commentary). The "essence of Judaism," in other words, is meek, simple, kind, loving, and sincere. It transposes Rebecca and Ruth's biblical feminism upon the social and political spheres. This translation of an inner spirituality ("the foundation and root of Judaism") to a political material presence is then mediated and eventually appropriated by a male body. It seems natural, then, that Geiger calls Hillel "a man, a sound, whole human being."[78]

Geiger's image of male appropriation hints at perceived struggles within middle-class German Jewish life. Shulamit Magnes, in her study of Pauline Wengeroff, argues that Jewish men demanded access and control over areas that had once been the province of female authority. Wengeroff, a nineteenth-century mother and, more to the point here, wife to an aspiring middle-class husband, desired a modicum of control over the household, and especially her kitchen. But her husband Chonon, who coveted above all economic success and social respectability, encroached on her domain. He did so, Wengeroff believes, because he found so little success in the hostile and competitive market economy, and so sought to regain his lost pride and power by dominating "his own family circle." At least in this area, "he wanted to be a total master and he was, too, in the fullest sense." Rejected by non-Jews, Chonon, and other such husbands like him, "saw their homes and wives as one area they could dominate."[79]

Women "were losing status, function, and power" in the home.[80] But those like Wengeroff could lose that power only because it was never really theirs from the beginning. Chonon and other husbands could grasp "total" power because their public place in civil society demanded—indeed required—that they do so. Even

Wengeroff complies, however reluctantly, to the limiting of her familial space. The male practitioners of civil society had determined female "status, function, and power," and in so giving could easily take away. The male appropriation of female power, then, really masks a recovery of masculine agency and authority.

This program of recovery informs Geiger's religious politics. For Geiger portrays Hillel as the great public Jewish figure who maintains both a powerful social presence and adopts the virtues of toleration, kindness, and refinement into his public character. Those "feminine" virtues now find their fitting home within a male public body, dislodged and refigured, as it were, from the private space of female power and identity. If not all can imitate the great Hillel, at least some, like Chonon, can earn their status within political life by reclaiming their rightful and unchallenged domination closer to home. Indeed, one senses that the "total master" in the home learns the skills to access and wield that authority outside of it.

Hillel is Geiger's total master. Geiger claims "he is born for action and the earth [*Erde*] is the theater of his activity." When Geiger writes "earth" he really means public life, as he states a few pages later, but the slip instructs nonetheless.[81] The public arena of action, struggle, morality, and politics *is* reality, where important issues and decisions are made and won. Geiger labels Hillel a "genuine reformer" because he engages only what really matters: the moral and political life of religious communities. If Hillel possesses all the virtues that Geiger associates with biblical women, then he also exercises those virtues within the public arena, and only for the sake of furthering and enabling Israel's mission. Private life and domestic tranquility become vital goods only when translated into public space. The public sphere of male political action is real life: "He [Hillel] had no respect for hermitical piety—he was a man of public life, and he invigorated and elevated the life of Judaism in every way."[82] Geiger's Hillel understands "the life of Judaism" only within the public realm of male activity. As the virtuous and political Jewish male, Hillel becomes the model for modern reformers like Geiger who seek a public, political Judaism still anchored in Jewish piety and virtue. Hillel as the "sound, whole human being" integrates private female virtue within public male virility. So too, Geiger hopes, will future Jewish reformers.

Through Hillel, Geiger confers ritual authority upon male social actors. Feminine interiority—always accessible to male reconfigurations—is now reappropriated by males; Wengeroff must give up what she recognizes as most her own. This mirrors Geiger's idealism when viewed critically through gender. For the religious spirit resides always ready to be appropriated by a material presence, but in this taking up, spirit loses any separate existence or identity. Like Fichte's understanding of the female partner, spirit "does not belong to herself, but to the man."[83] The feminine must be masculinized to achieve religious maturity—and so the male figure Hillel. The public activity of male performance underwrites Hillel's authority for modern Jewish practice.

Though feminine spirituality ideally transforms itself into material religious acts, it can do so only in paradigmatic male figures. In this, Geiger belies his own anxiety of feminine authority in ritual performance. So much of Geiger's religious idealism drives women into the public sphere, and his articles on the status of women in Judaism even compel such reforms. But his reformist idealism unravels when confronted by the possible loss of male religious authority. To restore that authority in the wake of possible feminine incursions, Geiger genders his idealism in figuring the spirit as feminine and its material ritual expression as masculine. In so doing, he reaffirms male authority in the public sphere, even as he delimits the private in service to it. Even Geiger's claim of commitment to equal status, in ritual and liturgy, owes less to the notions of equality and justice, and more to the power of feminine "interiority." Female piety and virtue, for Geiger's liberal Judaism, must be embodied in public ritual acts, yet women remain fundamentally closed to those social performances. Geiger's reform calls for public displays of female piety grounded in "the most beautiful, most sublime virtues" of female devotion. But that public display must be personified in male bodies like Hillel. Geiger encodes his reforms to solidify male authority in public ritual performance.

One can surely imagine a gendered politics, fashioned on notions of female interiority, transforming women's status and identity within liberal Judaism. Indeed, there had been movement in this direction in the early stages of Reform history.[84] But such progress was ineffective and fleeting. Riv-Ellen Prell has argued that Jewish reformers transformed the *legal* status of women, but failed to challenge the gendered *cultural* practices in which men still dominated.[85] Geiger's account of gender and ritual reform bears this out; even as his religious idealism propels female piety into public displays of religious ritual, that ideology also serves to reinforce the female place within domestic subservience. His liberal Judaism translates private virtue into public expressions of male religious commitment and identity, and in so doing confers a powerful sense of male authority upon those public rituals. Religious authority lies not in the feminized inner content, but in the ways in which the inner spiritual power manifests itself in meaningful—and so male—expressive forms.

Gender constructions unravel the tension between female religious piety as an inner spiritual content, and male political activity as its public material translation. For women to become full participants in Geiger's liberal Judaism, they must be engendered as males. Marion Kaplan has argued that Jewish women confronted a double dilemma: "they could reach for new goals opened up by Jewish emancipation and integration into bourgeois society, and they could strive beyond boundaries that once limited women. Yet they still suffered from double discrimination based on gender and religion."[86] Geiger's ideology encouraged these new social goals, but only men could take advantage of them. And where some male Jews did succeed within the cultured world of the German middle class, many did not, and they returned home weakened and demoralized, seeking recompense from their spouses by asserting domestic power.

Geiger's religious politics closed off women from public debate and ritual performance. Though he encodes inner spirituality as female, only males convey the formal or material expression of that spirituality. Ritual, then, doubles back upon the inner life to reshape Jewish spirituality. Reform leaders like Hillel transform female piety into normative ritual practice open only to Jewish males. Geiger's religious politics, in the end, translates feminine spiritual content into masculine religious norms, and in so doing effaces feminine power and religious expression.

For Geiger, authority resides in the public sphere and not the home, in morality but not virtue, in male activity rather than female modesty. By encoding ritual acts as male material bodies, and inner spirituality as feminine enabling virtues, Geiger turns his progressive idealism into a defense for male religious authority. If that authority derives from practice, then only Hillel and his followers determine and judge fitting behavior. Women all but disappear in Geiger's public sphere, and maintain only a serene, welcoming presence in the private home. But that home, and especially the kitchen, have been restrained and figured by male power and control. Women cannot leave their private space to secure public identities in Geiger's schema, even as that interior life becomes less and less their domain. If Jewish husbands like Chonon fail to dominate the capital market economy, then they will surely find other avenues, closer to home, to secure their authority. The public world of social activity expands inward by determining the limits of the private sphere. Public space, with its ritual actors and authority, is *the* space of Jewish life and practice.

Scholars of nineteenth-century liberal Judaism have too often focused on the substantive changes in ideology and thought. New conceptions of self, rationality, and universal ends had moved these German reformers to imagine Judaism as a "spiritual" religion. To be sure, Geiger himself adopted and promoted Enlightenment principles of toleration, reasoned discourse, and human rights, and together these values challenged the traditional Judaism that Geiger knew well from his childhood. But to focus on Reform ideology alone would miss the gendered politics of authority discussed in this chapter. It would also miss how a performative theory of ritual can enliven debate on contemporary Jewish practice. In Geiger's view, the problem of religious authority resides not in the inner spiritual content, but instead in its public expressive forms. It is certainly true that he assumes the vitality and essential power of an inner spiritual sensibility. But public religious ritual determines and even creates the religious power of this latent spirituality. It is Jewish *practice* that produces spiritual reflection and generates religious authority. This was true in Geiger's nineteenth-century Germany, and is even more so today. The authority of personal meaning will be found in ritual performance, and in the public practice of human agency.

Rabbinic Authority

4

As a teenager, Geiger wrote in his diaries about friends, family, and his prodigious studies as a young man. He recalls a moment when, at age eleven, he began to doubt the veracity of the biblical narratives and Moses' teachings:

> Is it possible, I thought, that Moses might well have ascribed his teachings to Jehova, as Minos did to Jupiter, Lykurgus to Apollo and Numa Pompilius to Egeria? Pfui! what sins, called out a voice empowered by eleven years; such thoughts should come to the mind of the son of a rabbi, to a true-believing Jew [*einem rechtgläubigen Juden*]?! Should doubts stir against the holiness and prophetic witness of the divine Moses? The thought went away and I fell asleep.[1]

But Geiger awoke the next day, and so too did those disturbing thoughts about religious authority. Indeed, Susannah Heschel suggests that Geiger moved from "questioning pieties to investigating the suppositions of rabbinic authority" soon after writing these reflections in 1826.[2] Yet the link between religious and rabbinic authority can already be teased out from these diary notes. Geiger's father had died in the spring of 1823—three years before this diary page, and some two years after the recalled moment of doubt at age eleven. Although Geiger does not share his reactions to his father's death in the diaries, the event released a more profound loss of trust in the Jewish tradition. Geiger is the son of a rabbi in two senses: the son of his father, and the inheritor of a tradition passed down by Moses. The death of his father may have "empowered" a stifled voice within him that not only suspected Moses' teachings, but that of the "divine Moses" as well. Rabbinic authority for Geiger is deeply personal in ways that link received instruction to the persons who transmit it. Geiger's diary reveals how a young, "true-believing Jew" associates the holiness of teaching with the purity of character.

Geiger was not the only youth of his generation to raise these issues concerning rabbinic authority. A young man studying for the rabbinate published a paper in the *Allgemeine Zeitung des Judenthums* in 1845 on the differences between "spiritual leaders" (*Geistlichen*) and the laity in Judaism.[3] For a young scholar entering the rabbinic profession, those differences loomed large, as they did for the many liberal rabbis who gathered yearly (from 1844 to 1846) to discuss major issues facing modern Judaism. After reviewing the biblical and rabbinic material on authority and leadership, especially in connection to the priesthood, the candidate M. Dreifuß offered his own reasoned appraisal:

> When the sacrificial cult had disappeared along with the destruction of the Temple, the great meaning of the priesthood, which was intimately connected to the sacrificial service, naturally disappeared as well. Here marks the point in time

> in which the difference between laity and priest [*Priester*] or spiritual leaders [*Geistlichen*] was abolished, and in its stead the community now recognized individual spiritual superiority . . . as alone justifying a prominent position within the community of faith.[4]

Dreifuß concluded that "only the authorized scholar [*Gelehrte*] could be considered a spiritual leader [*Geistlicher*] in the full sense of the word."[5] The priest, like the Temple that grounded his authority, had been dislodged by communities in need of new leaders who would respond to their "faith."

Geiger's journal entry, and this short article by Dreifuß, clearly and to my mind quite astutely raise the problem of rabbinic authority for modern Judaism. By gently linking the cultic priest to modern spiritual leaders, Dreifuß undermined the authority placed in office alone, and instead transferred that authority to scholars who possess the learning and "spiritual superiority" now demanded by the laity. Knowledge alone conferred religious superiority, and justified "in the full sense of the word" a commanding authority upon communal religious matters. Geiger linked this authority to personal authenticity and to the persons who transmit the Jewish teachings from one generation to the next. Privilege and communal standing would no longer be a matter of lineage but of religious learning and character.

To fully appreciate the contentious debates then raging over rabbinic authority, scholars have often turned to Geiger's struggle against the more traditional rabbi Solomon Tiktin in Breslau during the early 1840s.[6] Tiktin embodied the traditional rabbi who prized rabbinic literature over university education, Jewish law over edifying sermons, and a protected Jewish community over one open to modern culture. Geiger's sermons in German, his ethical and critical studies, his charismatic leadership, together with his university education, all challenged Tiktin's authority as communal rabbi.

The fight in Breslau that ensued between the traditional and modern camps proved ugly and fierce. Nine European Orthodox rabbis defended Tiktin by slandering Geiger's reputation and denouncing his scholarship. Geiger was a "Torah denier," belonging more "to the circle of Sadducees and Karaites" than "the circle of Judaism."[7] They savaged his article on the "Natural Sense of Scripture"—yet another indication that Geiger distributed copies well before its 1844 publication date. To these Orthodox rabbis, Geiger showed no desire to understand the tradition, and far worse, considered the traditional law a mere "empty fabrication and human creation." The Breslau community desired a rabbi with "Talmudic learning" and "strong religiosity," not an "ignorant" Karaite who "breaks the chains of tradition."[8] Tiktin, along with his traditional colleagues, would, in the end, fight a losing battle against the emergence of the modern rabbinate, with Geiger at the fore. But even in defeat, they revealed the anxious predicament of rabbinic leadership and authority.

That predicament, moreover, was subject to legal and official pressures imposed by the various German states. Government policy, within the confines of partial emancipation, sought to limit and control the scope of rabbinic authority.

The strategies were by no means uniform, but two basic models predominated: the Bavarian policy that enforced state examinations for rabbinic education, and the Prussian course of action, which sought to undermine rabbinic authority and "deny the rabbinate any opportunity to recast its image by appropriating terminology from the Christian ministry." Where the Bavarian government intervened to incorporate the rabbinate within state policy, the Prussian ministry actively distanced the rabbinate from any political or clerical status, and thereby undermined their "spiritual" character and function.[9] The Prussian government wanted to increase the sense of public alienation from those like Tiktin, but its policy actually reinvigorated Jewish efforts to realign the rabbinate along the Protestant model, where the doctorate certified competence and authority, and where ministry, preaching, and moral leadership conferred authenticity.[10] Views of rabbinic character and scholarship, voiced by Geiger and Dreifuß and their many colleagues, react to this cultural moment of legal and state policy toward rabbinic authority.

Geiger and his liberal colleagues understood this crisis in leadership and their place within it. Their own work did much to undermine rabbinic authority as well. Scholars such as Geiger belittled the older generation for their enslavement to Talmudic scriptural readings, and ridiculed their utter lack of a historical sense and scientific study (*Wissenschaft*). Indeed, this persistent sense of anticlericalism fueled the Prussian policy to undermine rabbinic authority.[11] The damage had been done. As Geiger and his peers became rabbis themselves, they could no longer rely on the reputation of office alone to exercise religious authority over their communities. But that, of course, was the point: rabbis, now transformed into "spiritual leaders," represented less their communities (as the priests did of old), and instead guided them more in religious practice.[12] I employ the term *guide* in this case to expose how ambiguous rabbinic authority had become by the mid-1840s. To be sure, the rabbis knew it, and this helps to explain the impetus for the three rabbinical conferences from 1844 to 1846. Ismar Schorsch has argued that the conferences "amounted to a rabbinic counter-attack [against radical Jewish groups] to reclaim exclusive authority to speak on religious matters."[13] The rabbis certainly failed in that endeavor, as Steven Lowenstein has powerfully argued in his study of reform changes in German-Jewish communities during this period.[14] The "concrete innovations" introduced during the 1840s reveal that "despite the increase in Reform activity and the increased radicalisation of both word and practice, the Reformers were still far from imposing their programme on most communities."[15] Indeed, whatever reform there was varied from area to area. This divergence in practice reflects the opening debates of the first conference in Brunswick, where the rabbis themselves questioned the legitimacy of the conference and, by extension, their own authority to decide religious issues.

Geiger took part in all three conferences, but his view of rabbinic authority stands at odds with the general tendency there. He agreed with many who criticized the conference rabbis for enacting broad "resolutions" for the entire German-Jewish community. Geiger, too, sought more tentative guidelines and approaches from the assembled group. He believed that only rabbis engaged in local and particular Jewish communities could fully respond to personal authority. A convening rabbinic body so distanced from local concerns would have little practical force and authority. In this, Geiger agreed with the prominent critic of those conferences, Zacharias Frankel. But he did not appeal, as Frankel had done, to the religious authority of *das Volk;* nor did he assert, as his liberal colleague Samuel Holdheim had resolutely demanded, fundamental principles of religious observance.

Geiger called for a modern rabbinate fully immersed in local politics, one that prepared and motivated communities to engage larger social and cultural issues. He too challenged the Prussian policy to undermine rabbinic authority. Neither dismissing the rabbinic office as a legacy of a priestly hierarchy, nor uncritically adopting communal "sensibilities," Geiger sought to negotiate between Holdheim and Frankel—between authority vested in principled resolutions and authority grounded in *das Volk.* That middle ground could be had, so Geiger argued, by reinventing the notion of the rabbinic scholar who passionately addresses local concerns through a committed engagement with the Jewish past. Merging Jewish *Wissenschaft* with rabbinic immersion in communal life could recoup a more limited notion of rabbinic authority that still would motivate and command communal assent and respect. Geiger recognized, as did so many of his colleagues, that rabbinic authority could no longer be flatly asserted but had to be justified through an appeal to personal meaning from within the very communities these rabbis served and advanced.

Communal Authority and the Rabbinical Conferences

The first rabbinical conference in Brunswick, during eight days in June 1844, rose to notoriety for its decisions concerning mixed marriages. The rabbis condoned such marriages only if the children could be raised as Jews—a qualification that effectively ruled out its possibility since no states in Germany allowed for it.[16] The issue evolved from a lengthy discussion on the French Sanhedrin. In 1807, an assembly of French rabbis provided Napoleon with general (and in some cases, purposely vague) answers to his twelve questions. Ludwig Philippson wished the Brunswick conference to endorse those answers, and the full response by the French Sanhedrin appears at the end of the published protocols.[17] For the rabbis in Brunswick, the third question concerning mixed marriages provoked the most intense and heated debate. A commission comprised of Samuel Holdheim, Gotthold Salomon, and Naphtali Frankfurter had initially been charged to review the French Sanhedrin's answers to Napoleon and to offer their own critique. The twenty-five participating rabbis at the conference on June 18 would then discuss the commission's response.

That the conference devoted so much attention to the French Sanhedrin, and published the Sanhedrin's responses to Napoleon in an appendix to the conference protocols, suggests how the rabbinic assembly modeled itself on an authoritative precedent. In his published account of the first conference, Salomon not only appeals to the French Sanhedrin model, but also to second-century Judaism, and concludes that this Brunswick conference represents "nothing new under the sun."[18] The liberal rabbis like Salomon hoped to achieve the recognition that, in their day, the French Sanhedrin and rabbinic Judaism had already acquired. This Brunswick conference, Philippson and Salomon had suggested, would be the recognized inheritor of the French Sanhedrin with all its stature and authority.[19]

Yet both Holdheim and Salomon understood, too, that inheriting the Sanhedrin's authority also burdened the Brunswick conference with more pressing, current problems. Holdheim would be forever remembered for his infamous phrase about rabbinic authority:

> The Men of the Great Assembly [אנשי כנ"ה"ג] have authority only for *their time;* what they ordered was *current or up-to-date* [*zeitgemäß*], and upon that the sanction of their ordinances rested. We have *the same* authority for our time if we speak for the consciousness of our time.[20]

When he expressed these views on authority, Holdheim addressed the problem of liturgical reform, and especially the use of Hebrew. He did not reiterate these issues as a member of the commission to review the French Sanhedrin. But he did agree to this formulation concerning the Sanhedrin and the question of polygamy:

> Every resolution of a synod (which the Sanhedrin cites) could never have won the commitment of the general community if European practices and morals, to which Judaism resolutely follows, had not already recognized that polygamy was something that harmed the life of civilized people and therefore was considered inadmissible.[21]

For Holdheim, the Brunswick assembly appropriated the exalted stature of the Sanhedrin "if we speak for the consciousness of our time," for in both cases, authority resides in the prevailing norms and morals of European society.

Only when rabbinic ordinances are "current," or reflect the consciousness of the age, will they obtain the necessary authority to determine Jewish commitment and practice. Holdheim makes the point clear and, characteristically, succinct: "We say only this: that which contradicts the present religious consciousness according to unbiased, careful critique, has no authority."[22] Salomon agrees: "no synod of the people can enforce something that does not lie in the consciousness of the people."[23] The rabbis at Brunswick expressed comparable views to Salomon and Holdheim when they deliberated upon the Sanhedrin's responses. To be recognized as the successor to the French Sanhedrin required rabbinic ordinances in tune with the consciousness of the age and the Jewish people. But once in tune, Holdheim and others concluded, those rabbinic ordinances would acquire the authoritative weight to transform German-Jewish practice.

The tension between rabbinic ordinances and their communal authority surfaced in the very first days of the Brunswick conference, and only came into full view by the time the rabbis discussed the French Sanhedrin on June 18, the seventh day of their eight-day conference. The conference opened with a discussion of formal matters: they would adopt statutes, choose officers, maintain written protocols, and arrive at decisions through majority vote. As Michael Meyer has noted, the conference "began to appear more like a legislature that had given itself the right to determine religious laws for German Jewry."[24] But one of those statutes concerned the very nature of those "laws," and elicited intense debate on their binding character.

The discussion revolved around the wording of one particular statute that mentioned "the resolutions [*Beschlüsse*] of the assembly."[25] Were the decisions of the rabbinical conferences truly binding resolutions (*Beschlüsse*), or instead "free statements of opinion" (*freie Meinungsäußerung*) that carry far less authoritative weight?[26] The initial phrasing suggested that rabbinic resolutions carry a "moral obligation," but many of the rabbis at Brunswick believed that *Beschlüsse* demand far more than a moral commitment—for a moral assent is not quite a religious requirement to act. Thus from the outset, the rabbis discussed the function and scope of the conference, and were clearly anxious about their own authority to enact binding resolutions or decisions. They seemed very uncertain about their status and role in Brunswick. Most of the rabbis there would concur with Levi Herzfeld that the authority of *Beschlüsse* "is the most important of all,"[27] not because the rabbis must respond to the laity, but because the laity must yield to rabbinic authority.

There surfaced clear divisions among the rabbis concerning the status of rabbinic decisions in Brunswick. Holdheim admits that their conference had little "synodal justification" (in the sense that it could pass binding resolutions obligating the broader Jewish community), but he still collapsed the authority of the Brunswick gathering with all previous rabbinic assemblies. Yet again, the authority of any conference resides in "the confidence of the congregations" that the rabbis remain learned and adept in matters of law.[28] Although he concedes that "moral obligation" does not go quite far enough in describing the weight of rabbinic decisions, Holdheim believes "we could hardly find a better expression." Their resolutions do not obligate, in the sense of command, but they do more than advise.

Samuel Hirsch, on the other hand, considers that "the obligation of the assembly resolutions is for individuals only." Hirsch phrases the issue in practical terms, notably anxious about returning to his community with new resolutions in hand:

> Our assembly must have a moral consciousness and must express that it has this, so that a rabbi, who has voted with the majority can rely upon the resolutions [*Beschlüsse*] of this assembly. He must be able to say: although this or that is against a paragraph of the *Schulchan Aruch,* I still teach or do it, and I can rely upon the many rabbis who have voted with me.[29]

Hirsch seeks to justify the new enactments to a diverse body of Jewish congregants. The authority for those decisions resides in the "moral consciousness" of the assembly and in the power of numbers. When challenges arise, rabbis can turn to their peers for support and appeal to the moral integrity of the rabbinic proceedings. Surely, the question of enforcement, or the binding nature of these resolutions, troubled many of the rabbis in Brunswick. Both L. Bodenheimer and J. Jolowicz, for example, believed in the power of words alone to advance "the good." Ludwig Philippson, for one, could not quite appreciate his colleagues' anxiety, and felt that they feebly haggled over mere wording.

Mendel Hess, however, stated the issue correctly when he suggested that the question should not concern "the compulsion of conscience" but rather "what is our assembly? In what relationship do our resolutions stand to the conviction of the individual?"[30] Hess proposed a new version of the statute, one that secured general acceptance among the rabbis there: "the discussions and resolutions of the assembly have indeed no binding force upon individuals; however, we expect that everyone whose conviction is in agreement with the resolutions of the rabbinic assembly will strive even more to adopt those resolutions in life."[31] The awkward phrasing and meaning of Hess's version, with all its expectations and resolutions without real commanding presence, reveal the general uneasiness with which the rabbis discussed rabbinic authority. They conceded that the authority of communal "consciousness" would trump any advance claim on their part to rabbinic leadership. Authority lies in personal conviction alone. What authority the rabbis did have would be decided by the response of the Jewish community to their deliberations.

The rabbis in Brunswick would not have to wait long for that communal response.[32] It arrived from the Berlin Jewish community in an open appeal published in various newspapers, together with a separate letter addressed to the rabbis at the second rabbinical conference in Frankfurt. A small group of about thirty educated Jews in Berlin, including the accomplished writers Aron Bernstein (1812–1884) and Sigismund Stern (1812–1867), gathered together in March 1845 to discuss Jewish religious issues. This radical Jewish group by no means represented the broad spectrum of the Berlin laity, but in its published piece, "Appeal to our German Coreligionists,"[33] they expressed the growing sense among many lay Jews of the conflict between "our inner life and faith and the external life, the given law."[34]

Although the Appeal speaks to "German brothers of faith" (*deutsche Glaubensbrüder*), its critique centers on the present rabbinic leadership. Even as "our scholars and teachers" attempt to reconcile the inner and outer life, the essay reflects a burning frustration with the process and lack of results. For these German Jews, "life has superseded science [*Wissenschaft*]" to such an extent that scholars still engage issues of law long abandoned by the laity.[35] The Berlin group calls for an "elect" who will promote a new direction in scholarship, and establish a synod "that corresponds with our age and the sentiments of our heart."[36] So a change there must be, not of lay practice but of scholarly leadership and commitment. The "age and the sentiments of our heart," so to speak, have got it right, and the scholars need to get in line. The Appeal reflects less a call for changed practice than a challenge to rabbinic authority. The rabbi, as leader and scholar of the Jewish community, should establish grounding principles that justify and authorize the changes already taking place in the German-Jewish community. He should neither guide nor challenge communal practice, but instead provide the textual support for it.

An even stronger statement concerning the role of the laity to determine and authorize Jewish practice can be found in the Berlin Reform community letter delivered to the second rabbinical conference in July 1845 in Frankfurt. The *Denkschrift* (Memorandum) was read aloud before the assembled rabbis on the first day, July 15, and printed in full in the published text.[37] The protocols for the first day, however, summarize only the introduction and conclusion to the letter, and skip entirely the middle section. No oversight this, for the letter begins with lavish praise for the rabbinical conferences, and ends with full understanding that both the Berlin society and the rabbinic leadership work toward the same goals. But amid this praise and hope lie far more trenchant critique and disillusionment with rabbinic authority.

Here in the middle section one reads of an assembly altogether removed and distanced from the laity.[38] The laity, in turn, must "take up for itself direct participation in the progress of Judaism," for "there is a sphere of religious life and religious development in which the community must lead the way for the rabbi."[39] Throughout this essay, the authors appeal to the "community" and its independence from rabbinic authority. This reflects, in part, an apologetic defense for the radical lay group in Berlin. But when the *Denkschrift* speaks of its "free and independent movement" with its own "consciousness" and "needs," it both echoes and directly assaults the already shaky rabbinic authority to determine lay practice and policy. One reporter of the proceedings even recalled the rumor that "should the Synod not agree with its (the Reform Association's) views, the latter would independently pursue its own course."[40] The Berlin community appreciates rabbinic learning and knowledge only "so that our desires and yearnings find their realization."[41]

The authority of personal meaning, of personal "consciousness" and "needs," demands respect and autonomy as it summarily dismisses claims to rabbinic authority. Rabbinic resolutions justify meaningful lay practice, and their authority resides not in assemblies but in active Jewish communities. It is not so much that practice determines theory, but that practice *grounds* theory, such that theoretical claims are rooted in established meaningful practices. In the end, the Berlin community "desires not only your [rabbinic] recognition; we desire to gain also your advice and energetic support for our project."[42] The rabbis have become educated cheerleaders for their practicing communities, mere "representatives of the Science of Judaism,"[43] and nothing more. Authority lies in meaningful communal practice and not in rabbinic resolutions, moral or otherwise.

The rabbis in Frankfurt supported the Berlin community in their courteous response. They overlooked entirely the more critical comments and challenges to their authority as rabbinic leaders. Yet the Berlin community only reintroduced the very same questions that had plagued the liberal rabbis in Brunswick a year earlier. If the rabbis themselves were unsure of their own leadership and command over their communities, one could hardly expect those communities to accept what the rabbis were not prepared to give.

Geiger, Frankel, and Rabbinic Leadership

Geiger was not present for the initial debates in Brunswick, nor did he take part in the deliberations on the French Sanhedrin. He participated fully in the Frankfurt conference, and one suspects that he listened with some sympathy to the Berlin *Denkschrift*. For Geiger's own Breslau community had issued a statement as well in 1845, and had won his endorsement for reform.[44] Even more, in Geiger's support of Hebrew and German prayers, he recognized only the "advice" and "consideration" of the rabbinic assembly, and did not consider their "recommendations" binding upon the Jewish community. He supported, as did the Berlin community, the individual needs and practices of local communities:

> The application of these suggestions [concerning liturgical reform] must still depend upon the individuality of singular communities, for just as little as I myself could commit my community to introduce all that the commission has suggested concerning the German language, so too I could not blame another community if they should decide to move in another direction.[45]

Geiger shares much with the radical Berliners. Rather than appeal to rabbinic ordinances that mirror the consciousness of an age (as did Holdheim), he supports local communities and their cultural practices. He recognizes diversity in communal discipline, and defends it in the face of rabbinic resolutions.

Geiger's loyalty to distinctive communities reflects pragmatic no less than ideological concerns. He admits as much in an essay published much later, in 1870, when he considers the differences between European and American communities.[46] European communities are "spatial" in the sense that their members belong by proximity rather than by shared faith or practice. But in America the communities remain voluntary, and so there exists fundamental agreement and similar sensibilities toward religious reform. Religious development and change prove far more difficult in Europe where so many local obstacles prevail—chief among them local differences and practices.[47] In America one can build from the ground up, as it were, while Europe is weighed down by "old communities in which institutions long cultivated and maintained over hundreds of years have been firmly rooted." America really is "the new world."[48] But in the old world of the German-Jewish community, the authority of rabbinic resolutions lies ultimately within the particular communities and their acceptance of rabbinic leadership.

Geiger's defense of local differences shapes how he perceives the role and function of the rabbinical conferences. In an essay published two days before the first conference in Brunswick (written as an apology for his absence from the first days of the meeting), he argued that rabbinic assemblies should stay clear of binding resolutions. The rabbis should "stand far away from binding norms [*von bindenden Normen*]" in order to respect the freedom and diversity of individual and autonomous communities.[49] Geiger holds a rather limited and practical conception of the conferences. The first meeting should be "preparatory rather than conclusive," practical rather than theoretical, and this because of the "diverse views and desires" represented at the conference, as well as the differing ideas about its goals and purpose. Even more, the conference must take into account the "variety of moods [*Stimmungen*] in the communities to which we as religious leaders and teachers belong," and Geiger worries of ensuing "*Geisteskämpfen*" (spiritual battles) if the conference were to issue binding norms.[50] Geiger still believes in rabbinic leadership, and writes passionately about the teaching of Jewish history to the lay community. He speaks of the "courage" and "devotion" required of the modern rabbi to serve as "*Führer*" for his community.[51]

A critical feature of Geiger's larger vision of Jewish leadership is his desire for Jewish institutes of scholarly research. A Jewish theological faculty could prepare "masters of Judaism" for their role as rabbinic and scholarly leaders. These university-trained scholars would direct their research to affect everyday life, and the Jewish presses would convey their scholarly views in a language more accessible to the layperson.[52] This top-down model of Jewish scholarship reflects Geiger's elitist views of leadership within religious communities. When he proposes future rabbinic assemblies in the late 1860s, he agrees that rabbis, communal leaders, and scholars (whom he calls "well-informed persons") should all participate. But for serious conversation, the lay Jewish public must stand aside.[53] Yet even here, rabbis, as leaders and scholars, remain so only for *their* communities. In these more open scholarly conferences, rabbis cannot impose particular beliefs and customs upon isolated groups: "there must be allowed free elbow room [*freie Spielraum*] for the peculiar convictions and special needs of the community."[54]

Yet even as Geiger calls for rabbinical conferences to be "practical, not theoretical," and to focus "on life,"[55] his defense of local differences undermines rabbinic authority. We can see this in his response to Holdheim's published article on the laws of Kashrut. The rabbinic assembly appointed Holdheim to review the dietary laws. After arguing that the laws have only a "ceremonial, symbolic nature," Holdheim declares "the religious obligation of the dietary laws [has] become extinct."[56] Geiger reacts strongly to this declaration, and writes a heated response to Holdheim's article.[57] He calls Holdheim's claim "thoroughly inappropriate" because it expresses "such a sweeping declaration."[58] The rabbinic assembly should seek practical reforms and not grand pronouncements that have little effect on life. Holdheim's declaration might apply to individual communities, but when declared for all it becomes farcical, and dismisses entirely the individual freedoms of local Jewish communities.

But the tension between rabbinic authority and particular communal customs lies even deeper. Jews do not reject the dietary laws because *Wissenschaft* authorizes it. Geiger believes there are personal issues at stake that remain outside the commanding grasp of scholarship:

> This too cannot be denied: the dietary laws have settled so deeply in the entire Jewish community that until now only a tiny part had not considered it as a central pillar of Judaism. But for the overwhelming majority of those who have ac-

> tually given up the observance wholly or at times, and under various circumstances, the authority to ignore this regulation of Judaism has not been found in another interpretation of Judaism, but instead in their individual freedom.[59]

Declaring the dietary laws "extinct" will have no effective force upon Jewish communities, even if Holdheim's scholarship proves sound (and Geiger thinks it does not). Here, as in many other areas, the authority of personal meaning carries more weight than an overreaching rabbinic resolution. The peculiar "circumstances" and individual choices, however formed, determine practice far more than theoretical claims pronounced from afar and behind the writing desk. This view mirrors Geiger's critique of Zunz's dietary practice discussed in the previous chapter: Geiger could well appreciate the social "circumstances" that would move Zunz to maintain a kosher home. But he could not understand this practice grounded in theoretical claims. Here as elsewhere, personal meaning holds sway. But only to a point. In his letter to Zunz, Geiger appeals to religious idealism to justify his attack. And Geiger spends a good deal of time discussing Holdheim's theoretical arguments, criticizing the latter's approach to symbol and rabbinic texts. Geiger simply fails to integrate his theoretical interests with his practical concern over dietary restrictions. He makes the practical point that Holdheim will not sway the broader Jewish community, but then turns to Holdheim's method and shows it to be *theoretically* inadequate. Even Geiger remains caught in the speculative game that, he claims here, has little practical value. His response to Holdheim is, unwittingly to be sure, a performative utterance that the authority of personal meaning and rabbinic authority remain worlds apart. Local "circumstances" and the freedom of individual choices undercut the authority of *Wissenschaft* and the rabbinic scholars who practice it.

The phrase *rabbinic scholars,* however, already assumes too much concerning the problem of religious authority in nineteenth-century Germany. Only liberals of one kind or another presided at these rabbinic assemblies, and most of them were quite young, with 70 percent between thirty and forty years of age.[60] But even this did not reveal the most striking peculiarity of the rabbinical conferences: scholars and lay leaders were simply not invited.[61] After all, these were *rabbinical* conferences! This closing of ranks enraged men like Zacharias Frankel, who grounded religious authority in scholarship alone.[62] Frankel withdrew in protest from the second rabbinic assembly in Frankfurt, allegedly over the question of Hebrew.

But Frankel's opposition had deeper roots. He published his article, "Concerning the projected Rabbinic Assembly," immediately before the Brunswick conference (Frankel did not attend the first meeting).[63] In that essay, Frankel reviewed the history of the rabbinic office and the image of the rabbi in Talmudic, medieval, and modern times. He works through this rather lengthy discourse to underscore two main points: 1) rabbinic authority rests not in office and title but in knowledge, for a rabbi functions as scholar (*Gelehrte*) for the community; and 2) since scholarship trumps rabbinic office, a conference of rabbis (like the one proposed in Brunswick) cannot plausibly hold binding authority and should therefore refrain from pronouncing resolutions (*Beschlüsse*).[64] Only a synod, with the participation of learned *lay* scholars, could pass such authoritative decisions as to warrant Jewish communal assent.[65] Frankel claims that "every scholar is a rabbi," which is to say that a rabbi, as the Berlin reform community had argued, serves as the learned resident of the community. Ismar Schorsch has noted that in 1835, Frankel had composed a memorandum for the Bohemian town of Teplitz on the rabbinic institutions. Frankel's piece reflects, so Schorsch argues, his "life-long commitment to revive the title and office of rabbi."[66] But now, in 1844, Frankel clearly believed the rabbinical conference had defamed, rather than revived that office and title. This assembly of rabbis, learned and unlearned alike, lacks the "democratic legitimacy"[67] for a community that demands scholarly discipline. The respected practitioner of *Wissenschaft,* Leopold Zunz, would go further than Frankel. Zunz believed the "rabbinic assembly smells of clericalism and hierarchy," and Zunz detested all forms of religious hypocrisy.[68] Honorific alone just will not do, both Zunz and Frankel argue. For Frankel, "the rabbi represents learning [*Gelehrsamkeit*], and he should recognize exactly this as the essence of Judaism."[69]

Frankel challenged the very point and goal of the Brunswick conference. To him, the convening rabbis simply did not possess, as an assembled body, the scholarly authority to pass binding resolutions, and therefore should refrain from the business of doing so. In this sense, Frankel and Geiger agree: the assembly should avoid passing overarching decisions that demand communal acceptance. But Geiger turns to the authority of personal meaning located among distinct Jewish communities to justify his censure. Frankel, instead, appeals to communities that demand legitimate scholarly leaders rather than the trappings of rabbinic office.

As one would suspect, Frankel appeared both amused and irritated by the Brunswick conference. He read the protocols as soon as they were made public, and quickly wrote a review of them.[70] He begins his essay where he left off in his previous one: condemning the whole notion of an assembly that can pass binding resolutions. The rabbis have neither the legal "right" nor the "power" to do so.[71] But in marked contrast to the earlier piece, Frankel appeals here to "the people [*Volk*]" and their sense of Jewish religious life. His is the populist stance that defends Jewish observance as it stands. For the rabbis to speak with force and authority, they must understand "the spirit of religion" as "the spirit of the people." They should discuss religion "as it is lived by a people, and not as some abstract theory or unclear speculation."[72] A rabbinical conference must focus on "existing Judaism" as lived by *das Volk,* and its religious "reflection" must derive out of this living source.[73] *Wissenschaft,* then, remains the handmaiden to authority vested in the lay community.

The rabbis at Brunswick did not leave Frankel's challenge unanswered. Holdheim and Salomon, among others, defended the conference that, in Salomon's view, represented "the better part, the kernel of the people, who *want* a reform." Frankel speaks only for the insignificant "shell" who will never demand such changes in life and law. In the end, Salomon concludes, the general populace will demand reform.[74] Frankel remained unpersuaded by these apologies, and with such contempt for the rabbinic proceedings in Brunswick, one might wonder why he chose to attend the second a year later in Frankfurt.[75]

He must have known what would be in store. And that seems to have been the case, for Frankel had prepared well his opening-day speech. He had something to say to these supposed leaders of the Jewish community, and he knew he would have a captive audience. Frankel demanded grounding principles, the very thing Geiger wished to avoid. It was "the pride of Judaism," Frankel announced, that "all decisions [*Entscheidungen*] must flow out of their principles and only through this do they acquire their validity."[76] Many of the rabbis, as it turned out, stood with Frankel in his appeal to principle. Ludwig Philippson, in his critical assessment of the third rabbinic assembly in Breslau the following year, wanted guiding principles to justify rabbinic decisions. Without such grounding tenets, the rabbis could never produce "norms for the future."[77] Holdheim as well, in a more impassioned critique of the third conference, chastised his fellow rabbis for abandoning fundamental principles for piecemeal solutions.[78]

In the second conference in Frankfurt, Frankel had labeled that grounding principle as "positive historical Judaism."[79] Yet his slogan proved sufficiently vague as to allow all rabbis present to agree to it.[80] The president of the assembly, Ludwig Stein, speaking on behalf of the conference, supported the positive and historical nature in Judaism.[81] But Frankel clearly believed otherwise. He argued that the conference acceded far too much to the "spirit of the times [*Zeitgeist*]," and should instead enrich communal observance. Reform does not mean change, but a kind of scholarly strengthening of "activities of law" that the Jewish people already perform and live by. So this conference ought to include those learned persons who, while neither rabbis nor preachers, can still encourage a scientific reform grounded in the life of the people.[82]

The ensuing discussion on Hebrew language only served to harden Frankel's view that his was a far different reform than the one presented by the majority at Frankfurt.[83] Frankel believed that the proposed question concerning the "objective" necessity for liturgical Hebrew illustrated only "a game" of intellectual obscurity. No rabbi would consider liturgical Hebrew objectively necessary, Frankel admitted. But so what? The Hebrew language "has grown together with the essence of Judaism, it is its *holy* language. For the Jews the Hebrew *name* for divinity is אדני (Adonai), far more than the German expression God [*Gott*]."[84] The language of prayer is not a theoretical issue but a practical one concerning the beliefs and rituals of a living people. The Hebrew language is objectively necessary only in the sense that it remains inextricably bound to the identity of Jews and their tradition. But the liberal rabbis at Frankfurt cite Talmud and law: they seek to reform the texts rather than conform to the authority of meaning already present in the communities they serve.

Even if Geiger could sympathize with Frankel's appeal to Jewish communal authority, he also recognized that Frankel's community reflected only one strand of European Jewry. Frankel imagined a Jew steeped in tradition and commandment, energized by communal solidarity and commitment, grounded in rabbinic text and its interpretive legacy, and rooted in the Hebrew language. For most of the rabbis at the Frankfurt conference, these communities represented legacies of their parents, and nostalgia for them signified a failure to confront modern dilemmas. In Geiger's community, among others, Hebrew resonated less with the young than with the older generation. As noted in Chapter 1, Geiger felt compelled to include German texts in the liturgy to maintain an active youth membership (alongside Hebrew, however, to satisfy the more traditional). Jewish communities exhibited noticeable diversity in Germany during the 1840s, and Frankel's argument reflects only one of many. For a good number of German Jews, God's name really was *Gott.*

Frankel, no doubt, lectured the rabbis on their understanding of Hebrew. Not just a language in which one learns or prays, Hebrew represents something far more, for "we were born and raised in it, and have been suckled in it as mother's milk and have been filled with a holy respect for it. We carry within us the scope of this inwardness."[85] Like the Jewish people, Hebrew retains a depth and richness that only distant scholarly reflection can minimize and obscure. For Geiger, by contrast, liturgical Hebrew holds value—in keeping with his religious idealism—only if it truly and clearly expresses inner feelings.[86] But for Frankel, Hebrew should neither be used nor discarded as a means to trigger deep-seated emotions. It expresses far more the whole personality and individual development. The rabbis, so Frankel believed, have discussed Hebrew as a theoretical problem without recognizing it as a living language in a practicing Jewish community. They desired a "new Judaism,"[87] and so failed in their scholarly calling to provide a learned basis for *existing* Judaism.[88]

Samuel Holdheim directly challenged Frankel's picture of communal authority. Note his critical response to the third rabbinic assembly in Breslau.[89] He was frustrated with the rabbinic failure to lead communities to more progressive and modern views of religious practice. He chastised rabbis for lacking fundamental principles for all law as they sought answers "to this and that law."[90] But the duty of every rabbi, Holdheim believes, is to instill his own convictions in the community he serves, and to motivate and lead that community according to a principled foundation. The rabbis in Breslau, however, abdicated their leadership, relying instead on communal support and assurance before enacting new resolutions. Rather than guiding, these rabbis followed the dictates of contemporary Jewish beliefs.[91]

In many ways, Holdheim's appeal to rabbinic leadership remains at odds with claims he made in Brunswick only a few years earlier about speaking "for the consciousness of our time." But Holdheim distinguishes between that consciousness and those Jewish beliefs that remain out of step with modern commitments. The rabbi must challenge uninformed beliefs so that they better reflect more progressive views. Jewish communities can stagnate in nostalgic yearning for traditional Judaism, and Holdheim's rabbi ought to replace this nostalgia with "the consciousness of our time." Holdheim argues that the Frankfurt conference won broad acceptance because Jewish communities supported rabbis who spoke with "the truth of inner conviction" and out of principle. Rabbinic authority, Holdheim argues here, lies not in the resolutions decreed, but in principles grounded in personal integrity and commitment. Although each community must decide, in the end, whether to accept and practice these new resolutions, "it is nonetheless the duty of the rabbi to seize the initiative and to procure the respect of the people through learning and conviction."[92] The rabbis at Frankfurt led by example, but in Breslau they hesitated and ultimately abandoned their duty, as Holdheim saw it, to initiate change and lead "through learning and conviction." Rabbinic authority is won through guiding convictions and principles.

The rabbis at the Frankfurt conference, Holdheim contends, maintained a principled stand on liturgical Hebrew and its place in worship.[93] Even as he opposes Frankel's conception of the rabbi as the representative scholar rather than active leader of the lay community, Holdheim nevertheless stands with him in believing that fundamental norms underlie religious reforms. Geiger was opposed to all this, and sought to limit the binding resolutions passed by the rabbinical conferences. But, of course, Holdheim and Frankel could not agree on those resolutions, much less their underlying principles. If the Frankfurt conference really stood on principle, as Holdheim believed, it was not a principle that Frankel could easily accept. He abruptly left the conference on the third day after the debate on Hebrew. But the issue of rabbinic authority would not go away with his leave.

The day after his departure, on July 18, Frankel published his reasons for leaving. Stein, the president at the second rabbinical conference, told the rabbis still at the meeting that Frankel had stormed out in protest. For all to hear, Stein read Frankel's essay to the assembly.[94] In his article, Frankel stood not only against the specific decisions (*Beschlüsse*) recommended by the rabbis at Frankfurt, but he also vehemently denounced the entire "tendency" of the conference. Appealing to a still vague "positive historical Judaism," Frankel could not but declare his protest against the rabbinic decisions by walking out.[95] Stein had written a draft response to Frankel's essay, but Geiger (the vice president in Frankfurt—he beat out Frankel by ten votes)[96] convinced the majority to confront such "arrogance" only in silence—although they would later respond to Frankel through other publications.[97]

The rabbis in Frankfurt dismissed Frankel's note and even his presence at the conference with mocked scorn. We can see this in the published printings of the conference protocols. When Stein tells Frankel on the first day that all could agree with his view of positive historical Judaism, it is written as comedy, and Stein repeats three times a version of the phrase, "Well sir, is that not our position too," and the audience voices its agreement in each case.[98] The published protocols make it unduly clear that the majority of rabbis stand with Frankel on the basic issues, and that his subsequent departure could only be interpreted as insulting and selfish. Frankel appears rather cranky and childish, arriving in Frankfurt looking for a fight.

This is so, I believe, because Frankel touched upon issues that undercut rabbinic authority. He appealed to communal meaning and not rabbinic authority, to scholars but not rabbis, all in order to ground the ideals and commitments of Jewish life in "*das Volk*." The rabbis, however, had gathered in Frankfurt to reassert their authority over lay commitment.[99] This is precisely what Holdheim believed they should do. But Frankel had come there to remind them that authority was not theirs from the start. Authority is rooted in learning and in the life of the people, Frankel had argued, but not in rabbinic office and abstract scholarship divorced from everyday concerns and activities. The rabbi must become an engaged scholar who roots his life and work in the activity of *das Volk*. Many present in Frankfurt thought they were doing just that, including Geiger. But they had done little to persuade scholars such as Frankel that authority vested in the rabbinic calling could be something other than an unwarranted usurpation of the lived authority within Jewish communities.

Lay Protest

The echoes of the debate between communal and rabbinic authority still resonated in the next and, as it turns out, last rabbinical conference in Breslau in 1846. The bulk of the discussions centered on Sabbath observance and the altered social, economic, and political landscape of modern German states.[100] Geiger presided over all of these discussions, and was a member of the Sabbath commission that presented its research to the assembly. But as Holdheim argued in his essay after the conference, the rabbis in Breslau buckled under pressure to alter sabbatical restraints to better conform to the new lived reality. Both the commission and the assembly as a whole recognized this failure.[101] Unlike the previous two conferences, the Breslau assembly pleased no one.

The "storm of opposition," as David Philipson called it, began with a letter of protest from twelve Jews from Frankfurt am Main. This infamous article, cited by many as the *Verwahrung* (protest), was reprinted in a number of German-language journals, and reached a wide audience.[102] So too the responses to the *Verwahrung*, some of which I cite below. These responses are important, for I will argue that Geiger shared much with their tenor and complaint. They uniformly deride rabbinic ordinances pronounced from above with little felt understanding of the particular and local concerns from below. Certainly Geiger could not agree with all of this, for the rabbi in his view still maintains a legitimate and guiding presence in the community. But Geiger too recoiled from abstract and universally binding resolutions, and stood with the protests in their appeal to lived religion.

Much of the *Verwahrung* centers on the Sabbath discussions, but the essay effectively restates the central problem of authority faced by the rabbinic leadership. The authors speak for "the friends of progress in Judaism," and believe that "the third rabbinic conference has lost the trust of the German Israelites." The rabbis, indeed, have "usurped" a "priestly authority" that remains entirely foreign to Judaism.[103] Here the authors echo the rabbinic candidate Dreifuß, with whom I began this chapter, and his distinction between the priests of old and the new spiritual leaders as rabbinic scholars. The rabbis in Breslau return to an older model of priestly hierarchy, and reestablish that ancient authority to undercut "the friends of progress in Judaism." The authors of the *Verwahrung* literally protest against this unwarranted assault on contemporary Judaism: "No, no, those men are not our representatives, their words are not the expression of our sensibility."[104] Leopold Stein, in his response to this essay, would quote this phrase word for word, so closely did it strike at the heart of the matter. For the authors of the *Verwahrung* could only derisively label the rabbis as "those men," not even priests or spiritual leaders but as "representatives" who had failed in their duty. Those men, indeed, usurped the priestly authority by ignoring lay concerns, and in doing so weakened Jewish progress. The authors express utter disgust with the legal discussions and logical word games that appear so divorced from their more immediate troubles.[105]

The tone and rhetorical style of the *Verwahrung* is dismissive to be sure; yet the basic challenge to rabbinic authority echoes a number of themes already circulating around and within the rabbinical conferences. If Holdheim desired a strong rabbinic presence that could lead through principled conviction, the lay authors of the *Verwahrung* would only accept leaders who reflected the "sensibility" of progressive Jewish communities. For these authors, rabbis neither acted as scholars, as Dreifuß and Frankel would have it, nor did they belong to an elite hierarchy of religious specialists. Rabbis would instead represent communal desires and needs, and reflect the everyday life of committed Jews. Rabbinic authority, for the authors of the *Verwahrung,* lies in the "sensibility" of Jewish communities immersed in historical progress.

When Ludwig Philippson reprinted the *Verwahrung* in his *Allgemeine Zeitung des Judenthums,*[106] he included an anonymous gloss to the text as a running commentary and response. Philippson may have been the author, but whoever composed it vehemently denied that the rabbis in Breslau sought "a foreign priestly authority." This commentator argued precisely the opposite: "the gentlemen from Frankfurt have hierarchical tendencies."[107] The *Verwahrung* was a base power grab from a rather small minority over the legitimate voice of the more numerous (and certainly more moderate) liberal European Jews.

This would become a common theme in many of the responses to the *Verwahrung*. Bernhard Wechsler, the rabbi of Oldenburg and himself a member of the Sabbath committee with Geiger in Breslau, directly attacked the legitimacy of such a fringe and minority group in Frankfurt. He declared that the authors of the *Verwahrung*

> wish and strive for a rash, radical alteration of Judaism in all of its present norms and institutions. They are men who, as is already publicly well known, situate their reform principles not on the historical, but on opinions and claims that at root have little to do with the development and rational progress of confessional elements. . . .[108]

By distancing the authors of the *Verwahrung* from a legitimate position within progressive Judaism, Wechsler could then claim that only the rabbinic assembly spoke for the majority of German Jews. As a conference with a wider vision, the Breslau assembly represented "the majority, the general public in their religious consciousness."[109] The *Verwahrung* witnessed to a fringe movement out of step with mainstream Judaism. Its protest referred only to a backward and historically insignificant party that, according to Wechsler, could barely find a home within "confessional elements." The rabbis in Breslau rightly distanced themselves from this and other extreme groups, and instead focused their resolutions "for the center of the various communities." Rather than assume a "priestly authority" with "hierarchical intentions,"[110] the rabbis reflected the mainstream voices and concerns of liberal Jews.

One senses Wechsler's frustration with a marginal group that provoked so many apologetic responses in the Jewish press, including his own. But clearly even such a "radical" group could uncover the anxiety of rabbinic authority that plagued the proceedings. Both in Wechsler's article and in a letter from the congregation of Alzey (published on the previous page to Wechsler's essay in the *Allgemeine Zeitung des Judenthums*), the texts quoted from the *Verwahrung* include the terms "priestly authority" (*priesterliche Autorität*) and "hierarchical intentions" (*hierarchischen Absichten*). These phrases in particular struck a nerve for those who defended the rabbinical conferences and their resolutions.[111]

The appeal to communal needs and authority surfaces in yet another letter responding to the rabbinical conference, this one from Breslau published in *Der Orient*.[112] The anonymous author, disappointed with the results of the conference, suggests that now "all eyes" look to Frankel's planned conference for "Jewish theologians." Soon after Frankel left the Frankfurt conference in protest, he proposed a very different kind of gathering for scholars and practicing rabbis.[113] Although Frankel eventually abandoned the idea after many delays, the Breslau author anticipates that Frankel's meeting will treat the laity as equals among rabbis, preachers, and learned scholars. Such a conference will respond to "the true religious needs of the community" because there will be "an active and immediate partnership with the laity." Frankel's proposed conference tapped into a popular sense, witnessed here in the anonymous letter from Breslau, that the rabbinical conferences remained entirely divorced from practicing Jewish communities. Where the rabbinic assembly claimed to speak for lay concerns, they in fact defended only "the need of hierarchy."[114]

The conference rabbis were well aware of these critiques from the beginning. Salomon opened his pamphlet on the first conference in Brunswick with a lengthy apology for a rabbinic gathering that speaks to "religious interests" and not merely to scholarly ones.[115] But in this regard, Salomon had missed the point. The Breslau letter reveals a much deeper resentment against religious authority that lies not with local communities but with a group of convening rabbis. Surely these rabbis ought to represent those communities and offer religious support for how Jews actually live their lives. The transfer of religious authority from the site of communal life to rabbinic calling appears to many Jews as an unwarranted and "foreign" return to "priestly authority" and hierarchy. Many of the rabbis in Breslau were sympathetic to the various needs of particular communities, and understood, as Geiger explained in his defense of the Breslau conference, that their resolutions were "of little authority" unless they could speak to the lived conditions of Jewish existence.[116] Even Ludwig Philippson chastised his colleagues at the Breslau conference for sinking into "casuistry" and a kind of intellectual elitism rather than engaging in practical reform.[117] Authority lies within communal standards, not logical arguments, within lived religion, not historical directives.[118]

Of course, one senses that appeals to community hide far more individual disenchantment with progressive Judaism. As Geiger and colleagues such as Wechsler well knew, Jewish communities reflected diverse bodies, both among and within them. The Breslau conference did little to encourage liberal Jews who, for example, desired a Sunday Sabbath—a resolution discussed but eventually abandoned at the rabbinic assembly.[119] To speak in the name of community often buffered direct attacks on more radical Jews within it. The "community" became a means to further individual "needs" and desires.

In many ways, the rabbinical conferences never intended to represent local Jewish communities. This view appears in a passionate response to the *Verwahrung*[120] from Leopold Stein, the president of the Frankfurt rabbinical conference. As the recently appointed rabbi of Frankfurt, Stein might have considered the local protest from his hometown (the Frankfurt *Verwahrung*) a challenge to his authority in ways not quite felt by other conference rabbis. Stein responds at once to the complaint that the rabbinic resolutions "are not the expression of our sensibility." Like many of his colleagues, Stein quotes directly from the *Verwahrung,* and focuses on the now well-known phrases "hierarchical tendencies" and "priestly authority." But with pride he appeals to "our calling" and the rabbinic office. He also disputes the claim that rabbinic resolutions are binding laws. The rabbis never intended to form law but to merely "advise," and the tally of votes allowed a minority to remain independent of majority decisions.[121] Stein disowns any sense of "spiritual power" or "any other authority" attributed to the conference. If communities wish to disregard the resolutions, then they remain absolutely free to do so.[122] To Stein, rabbinic authority was never there for the taking in the first place. Communities really do control the authority to adopt or ignore rabbinic "advice." When the *Verwahrung* and other letters complain of usurped authority by a rabbinic leadership, they simply misunderstand the nature of the rabbinic calling.

But if the rabbinical conferences can only advise without commanding presence or authority, if Stein can answer the problem of rabbinic authority by entirely dismissing it, then the conferences in Brunswick, Frankfurt, and Breslau turn into an intellectual exercise of rabbinic study. They simply fail to offer, as many of the responses to Breslau attest, practical reforms that affect real, local Jewish communities. The problem of rabbinic authority lies not in a usurped power, but in the very lack of it.

Geiger's Communal Rabbi

The liberal rabbis at the 1844–1846 conferences often complained that Frankel's rabbi only followed communal desires, but did nothing to reshape or guide them. Holdheim had forcefully presented this view, for he yearned for a more assertive and courageous rabbinate that engages conflict when there are worlds to win. But like the more radical Berlin reformers, Frankel envisioned a rabbi firmly entrenched in communal needs, for he sought to authorize in scholarly texts only what the community practiced in its living Judaism. In this sense, Frankel's *positive* Judaism refers to the real daily practices of observant Jews, and his *historical* Judaism implies the kind of *Wissenschaft* scholarship that would support and encourage "activities of law" in material Jewish practice.[123] Whatever the phrase *positive historical Judaism* may have come to mean for later Jewish thinkers, at the conferences it implied a sympathetic and scholarly apology for the ways in which Jews actually live their Judaism.

If Frankel suggested a more dialectical relation between rabbi and community,[124] this nuance was all but lost on the liberal rabbis at the conferences, Geiger chief among them. Although Geiger defended the autonomy and diversity of particular Jewish communities before legislative binding norms, he still encouraged local rabbis to open their communities to new forms of worship, to develop liberal visions of communal obligations, and to present *wissenschaftliche* approaches to the past that broadened a limited and insular communal consensus. Sympathetic to local communal meaning and authority, Geiger sought to retain a commanding authority for the modern rabbinate. He negotiated among the various commitments to scholarly training expressed by Frankel, a strengthened rabbinic leadership championed by Holdheim, and the authority of communal meaning represented by the many responses to the rabbinical conferences.

To do this, Geiger reinvented the rabbi as a progressive scholar fully immersed in the daily lives of local Jewish communities. Geiger remained, without doubt, far more critical of Jewish communities than Frankel, and once quipped that "the Jewish communities do not know what they want, and do not want what they know."[125] But a rabbinic assembly, comprised of rabbis with various sensibilities, passions, and ideals, should resist instructing from afar, as Holdheim had done, and leave communal tasks to those with more intimate knowledge. Local rabbis understand how best to guide and challenge their practicing communities. But they also remain passionately committed to communal vitality, and this in ways obscured by a rabbinical conference insulated from those passions. Geiger's rabbi moves congregants from an insular conformity to a broadened liberal practice of renewed possibilities: but not from afar, and not from within the insular program of a rabbinical conference.

For Geiger, the rabbi acts as the engaged scholar who enlivens and broadens local communal practices and ideals. Authority is local and contextual, and so rabbis engage the communities they serve and direct. Their authority rests not merely in scholarship, as Frankel argued, but also, as Holdheim would have it, in a progressive and motivated scholarship that disrupts the easy conformity and familiarity of local Jewish observance. Geiger's *positive historical* Judaism is certainly not Frankel's: *historical* Judaism recovers forgotten pasts that ground an ideal Judaism rooted in ethical principles, and *positive* Judaism embodies those principles in the material practices of the present. Rabbinic authority is rooted in an informed but directed scholarship (*Wissenschaft*) that forces local Jewish communities to fully engage and confront the moral life embodied in religious Judaism.

Geiger presents this vision of the modern rabbinate in an impassioned article written at the end of his rabbinic tenure in Wiesbaden. His "Two Different Approaches: The Writer and the Rabbi," composed in June 1838 but not published until the following year, reads as an extended apology for his rabbinic duties in Wiesbaden, and justifies his desire to leave his post.[126] Indeed, Geiger left Wiesbaden on July 2, 1838, only a few weeks after writing his article. His son, Ludwig, notes how the personal tone of "The Writer and the Rabbi" expresses Geiger's impatience with the seeming indifference and pedestrian concerns of the Wiesbaden Jewish community.[127] We know from Geiger's letters that he was unhappy there, and considered much of his work in vain. Although he worked tirelessly for reform, his congregants had little energy or desire for it. Instead, Geiger channeled much of his excitement toward the founding of his new journal, *Wissenschaftliche Zeitschrift für jüdische Theologie.* His community, so Geiger believed, was both "indifferent" and "hostile" to his liberal ideas printed in that journal.[128]

But even if written as apology and critique, Geiger's article (published, ironically, in his new journal) offers a forceful and articulate defense of the rabbinic calling. Concise and passionate, "The Writer and the Rabbi" conflates Frankel's dichotomy between scholar and rabbi to propose a new sense of authority rooted in engaged historical reflection—one that bridges past sensibilities and future possibilities in local Jewish communities. It is this sense of rabbinic calling and duty that Geiger defends at the rabbinical conferences some six years later.

As in his later work on *Judaism and Its History* (1864/65), Geiger distinguishes in this essay between two approaches to the past. The one views all historical change and development in the terms of cause and effect. Various movements and multifaceted events in history interconnect because they all extend from an original and unchanging source. History reflects a constant "spiritual direction" despite its ever-changing shape.[129] The "calm historian," says Geiger, so removed from engaging contemporary affairs, reinscribes this disinterest in his view of the past. He recovers religious ideas, forms, and laws in all areas of life, and desires only to explain the historical causes of gradual change.

The second approach, however, views every "historical element" as a revelatory expression of "the religious consciousness of a believing community." Where the first reclaims history as a general unfolding of events, and uncovers how these events develop in time, the second reveals how historical circumstances reflect the social, political, and religious concerns of particular communities. The historian of this approach fully engages the present and discovers in history "the answers to his questions." He recognizes how a past imbued with "the religious consciousness of a believing community" informs the present.[130] The "dead past" remains alive and calls forth a future that draws an "inner" relation to forgotten sensibilities. This is what historian Pierre Nora calls "the history-memory of old," in which "the present itself became a sort of recycled, up-dated past, realized as the present through such welding and anchoring." History, in this sense, is "filiation to be restored."[131] For Geiger's engaged historian, appeals to historical causes do not honor or restore the past for contemporary concerns. Instead, Geiger's historian reads the past through a modern lens in order to gaze into a possible future. But it remains a future that implicates contemporary Jewish practice as well. Geiger deliberately blurs the distinction between a past horizon of experience and contemporary interests. Histories as motivated reports uncover a past that challenges present sensibilities. The historian inscribes local and contemporary concerns into a past in order to read out of it a possible future.

Yet even as Geiger distinguishes between two kinds of histories and historians, he has in fact undermined that distinction. For the calm and detached historian remains "a son of the times" and "passionately represents the interests of the present."[132] The distant historian who claims only to reveal historical causes really is and always has been enmeshed in contemporary events, as Geiger surely was during the 1848 European revolutions, when many of his sermons touched on those chaotic times.[133] Reading the past takes stock of the present: historical writing reflects the consciousness of an embodied local community. Indeed, historians mirror the very movement of history: they interpret history as students of their own times, and so project the sensibilities of their age onto a past that, in turn, reflects motivated passions and concerns.

If Geiger seems untroubled by this subjective history, he unflinchingly confronts the longing for historical meaning and religious authority. Access to the past travels through present needs and concerns. The bifurcation between dispassionate scholar and committed rabbi really obfuscates the ways in which scholars approach history. In Geiger's deconstructive vision, the scholar becomes the communal rabbi who appropriates the consciousness of the past in order to reinvigorate and realign local religious practices. Religious authority arises from the model of past lives, even as ideas and events offer progressive moral resources for the present. This produces not an utterly subjective history, but a usable past in the service of contemporary communal desires.[134]

To be sure, Frankel understood his historical work in much the same way, and believed *Wissenschaft* should support and embrace communal material practices. But he sought to conserve contemporary practice in the face of competing obligations and opportunities. Geiger, however, challenges those practices in order to liberate modern Jews from what appear to him, and to many in his community, as confining and insular ritual customs. If Geiger responds to more progressive needs in his community, then Frankel witnesses to a prevalent anxiety that too much has been conceded to modernity. Geiger should not read into the past, Frankel might argue, but read more out of it. Yet Geiger's larger point remains: historians configure a past *as past* so that it meaningfully relates to the present. This remains as true for scholars as it does for rabbis who move their communities toward a future now read as an already past.

This configuring of the past often takes the form of a linear narrative. Events and persons (what Geiger calls "human life") develop according to their peculiar and independent trajectories, as if each event and actor form a linear story with beginning, middle, and end. But Geiger suggests that a schism (*Zwiespalt*) can disrupt this development (*Bildung*), and so undermine its "seclusion" and "inner harmony." These fractures in narrative progression reveal the messiness of historical events, and suggest a history that "makes another development necessary."[135] Constructing the past *as past,* then, should not only take the form of narrative emplotment with defined beginnings, middles, and ends. These narratives, Geiger argues here, are shot through with disruptive events that undercut a linear progressive model. The "consciousness of a believing community" is less uniform than diverse, more uneven than linear, embattled rather than secure.

The "higher historical view," as Geiger labels it here, moves beyond "the individual cultural life [*Lebensbildung*] and the small circle within which these events occur, but must recognize the prevailing contradictions in general and, in this recognition, prepare for its overcoming [*Aufhebung*]."[136] The conflicts of the past can be outmaneuvered by a thoroughgoing, "higher" historical critique. But this higher view still resists a straightforward narrative construal of the past, and instead resuscitates discarded fragments from forgotten histories. There is depth, broadness, and misdirection in historical acts and life, and configuring the past should reclaim these moments.

These differences between a linear account of the past and a rich, complex, and dynamic one prefigure Geiger's claims about the writer and the rabbi. The writer recognizes the various historical interconnections and disruptions, but cannot do so dispassionately. She relates these events to the present in order to hasten a future that skillfully evades past conflicts. The rabbi, however, can no longer remain within "the small circle" of communal Jewish life, and must broaden its borders to include opposing tendencies and political conflict. If history is messy and disruptive, then rabbis must engage those conflicts rather than withdraw from them. The rabbi moves local communal concerns beyond their insular borders, and the writer devotes her energies to a rich past that reveals new communal possibilities.

By projecting historical approaches onto the writer and rabbi, Geiger builds into history the very criteria for assessing rabbinic and scholarly authority: passionate reconfiguring of Jewish history as a usable religious (moral) past, reflective understanding of disruptive moments in history, and a sympathetic grasping of local communal needs in order to challenge and extend them. Geiger undermines the distinction between rabbi and the writer-scholar to reveal how visions of the future shape images of the past. Religious authority rests in the efficacy of that shaping. Geiger's philosophy of history is at the same time a philosophy of rabbinic and scholarly authority.

The paradox of the essay lies, of course, in how Geiger continually weakens the distinctions between writer and rabbi. This emerges even in the very naming of the professions. Geiger calls the writer "the priest of true Science" (*der Priester der wahren Wissenschaft*) and a "Jewish theological writer" (*der jüdisch-theologische Schriftsteller*). The modern priest understands "the present and its ideas in their complete unity and examines the position of Judaism in relation to it."[137] He acts much like the passionate historian who rediscovers the religious consciousness of past Jewish communities. Yet Geiger easily conflates communal activity with "Judaism," and as his later *Judaism and Its History* attests, his historian works more with ideas than actual Jews. This, too, remained central to the protests against the rabbinical conferences. These rabbis claimed to speak about Jewish life when in fact they debated Judaism.

Yet Geiger's writer draws Jewish theology into line with "true" *Wissenschaft*, and symbolizes a unified vision of scholarly work and devotional study. As scientific scholar, he recognizes modern ideas "in their complete unity," but as a Jewish-theological writer he elevates Judaism into modern scientific discourse. He bridges both Jewish and European communal space and Jewish and historical studies. The writer thus forces Judaism to abandon its "one-sidedness" and, without shedding its distinctiveness, become "an organic member of the human organism."[138] In "vivid, expressive" language, the writer motivates Jewish communities to engage broader humanistic trends, even as they maintain strong commitments to their local and particular identities. It is altogether striking that Geiger has described the rabbinic calling in much the same way, for the rabbi, too, leads the community from insular self-certainty into more expansive realms of human activity. In this, Geiger responds to those protests against the modern rabbi who wrongfully usurps the authority of the ancient priests. Geiger's "priest of true Science" unifies Jewish life and thought not from afar, but in serving local Jewish communities and their needs.

The writer is a tormented figure who valiantly and humbly serves a larger purpose. But much of this heroism goes unnoticed by the community to which she remains loyal and devoted. So the writer looks beyond the insular "house" of Judaism toward "relations of the world" and "the needs of the time."[139] Unaccepted at home, the writer reaches out for a broader community of progressive minds.

This is all no doubt autobiographical, for it fits well Geiger's own despondent position as rabbi in Wiesbaden. He clearly views himself as the modern writer and *Wissenschaft* priest as he attempts to relate his scholarly work to his rabbinic calling. He struggles for reform in both practice and history, labors to expand the communal horizons, but too often encounters contempt and scorn from his Wiesbaden congregants. So much of this article reflects Geiger's own experience in Wiesbaden and his disenchantment with the community there. Even Geiger recognizes this, for he turns directly to the reader of his essay and hopes that he "does not believe him capable of the vanity" of such a writer.[140] His readers may too easily recognize Geiger's own rabbinic experience in the essay, and thereby simply dismiss it as a vindictive rebuke of the Wiesbaden Jewish community. Geiger certainly points to what he seeks to avoid. But in doing so, he also reinforces the dual character of the writer who unifies both scholar and rabbi in his professional calling. Geiger aspires to bridge his philological and rabbinic training in the figure of the professional writer who sacrifices local fame and esteem for majestic ideals.

Geiger seems utterly nostalgic for the rabbi who remains "safe and peaceful" in comparison to the tormented writer. Geiger grew far more critical of modern rabbis in his later years. Exasperated by their silence before the challenges of the day, Geiger believed a "high conservatism" had taken hold of the rabbinic office.[141] But the nostalgic views of his youth still prove costly, Geiger admits. While the writer always looks to Jewry as a whole in its relation to other communities, the rabbi focuses instead on a "closer sphere of activities, his community, its level of education [*Bildungstufe*], and its communal relations." Many of the "disharmonies that exist in a more sweeping or open view vanish in this more immediate circle."[142] Closed in their "original innocence," Jewish communities remain insulated from modern *Zeitbildung* (contemporary culture). The rabbi who presides over a "closer sphere of activities" sweeps under the rug, as it were, the inevitable tensions that arise when Jewish communal practice engages broader historical trends. This rabbi reinforces the "original innocence" by never disturbing it. The "disharmonies" fail to surface as such, and these communities live as if outside the flow of historical time.

The naïve rabbi "hinders the negative consequences which custom could have, and so custom is allowed to stand as something innocent."[143] Yet this innocence too has a cost: "it belongs to the peculiarity of human nature that it tolerates custom [*Gewohnheit*], and even more, preserves it without protecting its roots and so drives them even further away."[144] A rabbi who hides the challenges to custom from public view undermines the very "roots" of these communal practices. These communities cannot "protect" the foundations of their customs, and so they will inevitably uproot and destroy them. The customs lack the grounded strength to keep destructive forces at bay. The writer, who has already engaged his community in the larger human enterprise, can still hope to bridge the currents of habitual custom and change. Engagement and immersion in local communities need not breed insularity, for the writer continually broadens local concerns to embrace larger trends. The rabbi and his community, isolated from historical progress, will be lost at sea. Geiger mocks this rabbi who, as a "man of peace" and a "true administrator," mingles only with the "lesser lights" in his community, and avoids its "leaders" and "prominent personalities."[145]

One senses that the Wiesbaden community desired a rabbi of this type, and Geiger refused to play that role. But even more, Geiger ridicules this innocent rabbi because he has replaced him already with the writer. The true communal rabbi, as Geiger's essay argues, is really "*der jüdisch-theologische Schriftsteller.*" Geiger utterly dismisses the more naïve sense of rabbinic authority in favor of a different kind of rabbi. This new "Jewish-theological writer" infuses the rabbinic office with scholarly passion and commitment. The writer fosters local debate and allows the power of ideas to forge new relationships and communal interests. Expecting communal resistance, the writer prepares for "the struggle that the enemies wage against him."[146]

Geiger effectively usurps the authority that Frankel vested in the scholar, and inscribes it within the professional duties of the priest of modern *Wissenschaft*. The writer unites the progressive leader with the passionate scholar—the representative of local Jewish communities with the reformer of modern Jewish practice. As the liberal rabbi, the writer engages his communities with modern "disharmonies," and thereby protects the "roots" of custom through reinvigorated and, for Geiger, honest commitment. The emergence of the modern rabbinate, as a contemporary scholar once described this movement,[147] goes through Geiger's writer as the new communal rabbi. If Geiger envisions himself as such a modern rabbi, it is only because he cannot imagine any other who could respond to the present crisis in rabbinic authority.

Fortunate indeed would a rabbi be if he could maintain an insular life of innocence. But for Geiger, the innocent and protective rabbi "is no longer the ideal" and "can no longer be carried forward."[148] The modern communal rabbi who fully engages contemporary movements must battle against all that had once been cherished: he must destroy the old way of thinking before building something new again. Geiger holds out hope that this university-trained, passionate, and engaged rabbi can unify the writer with the rabbi of old. He even claims, as he closes his essay, that he has sought to do just this in Wiesbaden. But in bridging these two roles, Geiger also recognizes their "unnatural union."[149] He honors the rabbi's naïveté, even as he knows that an innocence lost is an authority regained. The rabbi must become more worldly, more like the writer, and more fully immersed in the messiness of history. The critics of the rabbinical conferences were surely right: distant from communal concerns, these rabbis acted more like Geiger's dispassionate scholar than his committed writer. Religious authority now resides in the modern Jewish-theological writer as the engaged communal rabbi.

Though Geiger wrote his essay on "The Writer and the Rabbi" some years before the three rabbinical conferences, he clearly engages much that would go on there concerning rabbinic authority. If Holdheim desired a firmer leadership willing to challenge a complacent Jewish public, if Frankel and Philippson yearned for grounding principles to warrant future reforms, and if Stein just sought advice that communities could take or leave, then Geiger dismissed all of these factors to better position the committed and religious writer as the new communal rabbi. Leadership would be lonely, he admitted, and would at times create great personal anguish and despondency. But in moving local communities to a wider grasp of their own particular practices, the writer as communal rabbi would lead by example, and not by principle. Grounding principles were far too sweeping—as Holdheim's essay on Kashrut had been—and those who appealed to science and logic too easily attacked firmly embedded material practices. Religion attaches to deeper sources than reason, Geiger had argued, and many of those roots hold emotional power and force. The writer, with a firm grasp of local conditions and the religious members of his community, could motivate and lead according to cultural limitations and possibilities.

Better to unite a liberal practice with an impassioned retrieval of a forgotten past, so argued Geiger, than ground new practices in rational and abstract truths. In this, Geiger shares much with the many writers who protested against the rabbinical conferences and the religious hierarchy and elitism reflected there. The lay protests responded to a rabbinic deafness to local differences and cultural traditions. But the rabbinical conferences were not all bluster and show, so Geiger believed. The proof would come in embedding the conference aims and ideals in material changes. The conferences would energize new reforms, and liberal rabbis like Geiger could creatively adapt Jewish thought to lived practice. The rabbinic resolutions (*Beschlüsse*) promised more than good advice; they marked out guidelines for the young and liberal rabbis to control the future of European Jewish communities.

But the conference proceedings suggest that rabbinic control had already diminished. This Geiger surely understood as well. Indeed, as his "The Writer and the Rabbi" attests, an insular model of rabbinic leadership could never recapture such control and authority. Rabbis (liberal or otherwise) could no longer afford to cushion the blow of modernity, nor mask the instability already churning within more traditional communities. Learned in secular culture and, what is more, educated by and within it, the modern writer as engaged communal rabbi could recoup an authority lost only by recovering a moral religious past. For Geiger's writer unearths forgotten history in order to reinvigorate contemporary Jewish moral practice. The nostalgic past would become a usable ethics for contemporary reformers. Rabbinic authority would again command lay assent if the recovered past could reveal a better future.

For Geiger, too, how to control that future preoccupies his essays on rabbinic office and his arguments at the conferences. As was the case with many of his colleagues, Geiger refused to cede that future to the more radical elements in Berlin, and to the more conservative forces that surrounded him in his hometown of Breslau. But rabbinic authority was under siege by both camps, and the conferences in Brunswick, Frankfurt, and Breslau witnessed more to the demise than the resurgence of rabbinic command. But as the waning rabbinic hegemony came increasingly in conflict with the "sensibilities" of particular Jewish communities, Geiger positioned the modern rabbi within communal practices, rather than from the distant reaches of the rabbinical conferences.

But the rabbi would still lead. Geiger could not appeal to *das Volk* and the power of communal authority, as Frankel often did in his early writings. With Holdheim and others, Geiger shared a fear of a nostalgic and uneducated public. If for nothing else, the rabbinical conferences would house a professional society of learned scholars and educators who could talk shop without the disheartening dismissal that Geiger routinely absorbed in Wiesbaden. The conferences would provide a bulwark against an increasingly frustrated public that cared less for rabbinic subtlety and more for economic health amid the many Sabbath restrictions. If the rabbinic elite could not solve these problems, many of the protesters had claimed, then appeals to rabbinic leadership carried little weight, and the rabbis appeared all too close to the ancient priests who belatedly defended their fading power.

Liberal rabbis like Geiger helped to create the very problem they now confronted. When Geiger, Holdheim, and so many others dismissed the rabbis of old as closed, elitist, and stubborn, their liberal communities adopted that very rhetoric to denounce the rabbinic office. It is as if rabbinic authority could never quite catch up to itself, as if it would always trail behind the demands of communal meaning and assent. It is this very sense of "catching up" that runs throughout the protocols of the rabbinical conferences and the reactions to them. It is also this sense of belatedness that links Geiger's time to contemporary Jewish practice. Liberal rabbis today, as they did then, carve out their authority in response to the daily material practices of committed Jews. If rabbis seek to reassert a guiding authority now, then they reflect the anxiety of leadership that prevailed among the liberal rabbis of the 1840s in Germany, and the public insistence that religious authority lies in communal acts of lived religion. Geiger's essay on rabbinic authority recovers much of this tension. Yet he also believed that the new religious writer could energize communal practice only from within. This is, to be sure, how Geiger understood his own calling and the challenge of rabbinic leadership. It is a rabbinic authority in the making, then and now.

Jewish Education and the Authority of Personal Meaning

5

Geiger's education as a youth, like that of so many of his liberal colleagues, reflected a traditional upbringing that slowly, but ever gradually, blossomed into more critical studies of Jewish history that included humanistic disciplines. Raised in a strict observant household, Geiger learned Hebrew texts at an early age, and soon added German as well as mathematics to his Talmudic studies. At eleven, he absorbed Latin and Greek from private tutors, and after the death of his father in 1823, Geiger increasingly turned to his older brother Salomon (1792–1878) for instruction in classical Jewish texts.[1] In his diaries, Geiger complained about this constricted educational focus, and how he felt unprepared for broader studies in history, literature, and philosophy. Ludwig Geiger recalls that "the spirit of Enlightenment and German intellectual development remained thoroughly untouched" in Geiger's household.[2] What Geiger could get of it would be "left to chance."[3] But the youngest child of a family rooted in Frankfurt for over 200 years would soon enter that progressive, enlightened universe when, in April 1829 and at the age of nineteen, Geiger abandoned his home for a university education in Heidelberg. There a world opened for him: lectures in philosophy, archaeology, history of literature, and philology. Forgoing his early desire to study theology, Geiger left Heidelberg after less than a year to pursue oriental languages at the University of Bonn, where he entered the faculty of law and philosophy, and remained there until 1833.[4] Geiger's educational development mapped the terrain of a good many traditional Jews who yearned for the liberal, humanistic studies at German universities. Grounded in classical Jewish texts, he then redirected the study of them through his own education in philology, history, linguistics, and philosophy.

As a rabbi and scholar, Geiger sought to bridge his academic training with local Jewish communal desires. He returned to the Jewish community and remained there, writing essays and books for an imagined enlightened audience, even as he carefully integrated his scholarship to better advance communal reforms. This is, indeed, how Geiger came to understand the role of the new theological-writer: the modern rabbi who could unite *Wissenschaft* with the rabbinic calling. But Geiger was pulled by two competing worlds: the scholarly life of academic study, and the obligations and commitments demanded of a community leader. To be sure, Geiger's educational philosophy reflects these two worlds and the strains invoked within them. He seeks to train young adults who could enter gracefully into European culture and university training, even as they, like him, would employ that education to further local Jewish needs and communal projects. Geiger wanted for the younger generation what he had so passionately struggled for in his own life:

an education that united academic and local traditions, and one that utilized scholarship to deepen, rather than abandon, the roots of Jewish identity in communal religious goods and obligations.

Geiger appropriated the lessons from his own educational upbringing to transform Jewish pedagogy in his communities. He opened his first educational school in Breslau on May 7, 1843. There were six classes altogether, three for girls and three for boys. The girls studied translations of Hebrew prayers, analyzed biblical history and texts, and were instructed in basic teachings about God, religion, and ethics. The boys also learned translations of Hebrew prayers, and studied the Pentateuch and its history (together with more general Jewish history). But the young men also moved beyond this curriculum to absorb Hebrew with religious education (including examples from the *Ursprache*).[5] In the main, only boys and not "the female race" would learn Hebrew.[6]

This focus on biblical studies, history, ethics (for the girls), and language (at least for the boys) marked Geiger's school as a modern Reform institution.[7] The Bible replaced the Orthodox emphasis on the Talmud, compilations and catalogues yielded to history, law ceded to ethics, and Hebrew (not, for example, Aramaic) became the most significant religious language of study. This new curriculum, Geiger argued, offered an appropriate and necessary response to the times. It was moderate, contemporary, and grounded in the sources, yet was also practical and worldly. Earlier generations could simply educate their young men in Hebrew Bible and Talmud, and then quickly launch them into a world with "a decisive line of thought." Jewish women, in turn, could easily learn the practical features of homemaking most suited to their "profession." But if these earlier generations appeared less practiced in the "clear concepts of religious truths," they nonetheless followed the impulses of their time.[8] Such impulses would no longer prove compelling now, when women advanced beyond the home and enjoyed new freedoms,[9] and men entered professional trades where their Talmudic studies offered little help and, it appeared to many, even stunted their professional advancement. Emancipation for both sexes, Geiger believed, required a revolution in Jewish education.

Yet Geiger recognized that social emancipation brought with it another kind of revolution: a profound "indifference" to Jewish educational studies. He had to fight for his school, in part because of the apathy to all things Jewish among his laity. Enlightened parents insisted that learning respond to "the demands of life." So the parents of young Jewish children proved both indifferent and dissatisfied, for with new access to the professional goods of European society, these parents wanted more for their children than they had won for themselves. Geiger admits that "the parents themselves demanded that religion give way to instruction in music, dance, French, and the like." These parents desired "virtuosos and salon men,"[10] educated in European culture, philosophy, the arts, and high society. Geiger's new, liberal Jewish education sought to appease these parental concerns and student desires.

Jewish studies, once the only educational game in town, now competed with other cultural sport. Geiger knew this, and so he forcefully defended (if not apologized for) his Breslau Jewish educational program. One should not teach a few religious truths and send Jewish children into a world of new professional and social demands. Teachers must impress these truths in memory. But even more, these truths "must develop out of the spirit and disposition of the pupil":[11]

> Religion is not merely a branch of knowledge, and so the instruction of it must arouse the deepest feelings, and stimulate the most inner part of our being. Religious instruction is, at the same time, the sermon for the younger generation.[12]

The modern rabbi both instructs and edifies.[13] Such education, left to the professional, well-trained rabbi (*wissenschaftlich gebildete Rabbiner*), stimulates "the most inner part of our being."

These new rabbinical functions transformed Jewish educational philosophy. Jewish education no longer imparts information through texts, dogmas, and laws. It must be personal and "arouse" heartfelt longings that stimulate and motivate inner dispositions. It must stir passionate convictions that confer upon religious studies the necessary authority to command allegiance. Mordechai Eliav calls this period in Jewish education "the century of pedagogy" and "pedagogical innovations."[14] Geiger's liberal Jewish education edifies by invoking personal meanings, and only in this way will it command allegiance within the marketplace of values.

Those personal meanings invoked by Jewish education integrally relate to social life. Geiger claims that his educational program moves beyond "the foundational principles of Judaism" to train young children as full "members of the community."[15] For Geiger and others within the German Enlightenment tradition represented by Humboldt,[16] "the essential business of education is the *formation of character* [*Charakterbildung*]." Liberal Jewish education prepares Jewish children for universal ends, and instills the virtues and dispositions necessary to succeed in the larger community.[17] Access to this broader, cosmopolitan society requires, however, a firm footing in one's own, more limited community:

> One must be grounded upon a fixed point . . . and work out of this solid standpoint. The concept of "world citizenship" must necessarily be restricted. One belongs to humanity through belonging to a particular circle, in which and for which and *by means* of which one acts for the whole.[18]

The road to European salons and professional advancement goes through the Jewish community, and not at the expense of it. This is no less true today for Jews in America and elsewhere. A worldly Jew, or the Jew with *Charakterbildung,* becomes so by acting for and in the Jewish circle. Geiger's Jewish education appeals to the authority of personal meaning to ground modern Jews in local communities, and through this "particular circle" to absorb and participate in the larger cultural world.

The University and Local Jewish Communities

Geiger's view of communal education, while drawing upon the German Enlightenment tradition, nonetheless remains at odds with it. Humboldt and Fichte described the German university as the guardian of German culture and national character (*Bildung*). The university, especially for Fichte, inscribed a national ethnic identity upon its students. Even for Humboldt, the university served the ends of the state in cultivating a unified citizenry.[19] But Geiger understood that this social world, despite the enlightened rhetoric, marked a distant one still closed to Jewish elites.[20] Aware that "world citizenship" enthralls more as propaganda than real possibility, Geiger argued for a socially contingent and local space of Jewish learning. He could not endorse pedagogical reforms to cultivate a world citizenry, as some liberal educators do today.[21]

But parents in Breslau did see in their children new world citizens, cultured in middle-class manners and dance, all the while moving beyond national and religious borders. Jewish education should enable this kind of social advancement, they believed, and teach less religious home-truths and more practical and worldly ones. For Geiger, this notion of "world citizen" only separates Jewish children from their historical and local environment. Jews cannot simply leap out of their skin and form bourgeois characters disentangled from their personal history and memory. Persons approach universal ends "through belonging to a particular circle," and within that social nexus Jews work for larger ends. Geiger senses that Jewish education can just as easily weaken as strengthen local ties. In stressing music, dance, and foreign languages, the parents in Breslau wanted more for their children but less for the Jewish community. Geiger seeks a middle ground that educates Jewish youth in culture and virtue (*Charakterbildung*), but grounds that character in Jewish communities, "in which and for which and *by means* of which one acts for the whole." Liberal Jewish education gains communal allegiance by developing cultured persons who empower and enliven local communities.

Geiger appealed to notions of character and the virtues of community to argue that Jewish education is neither backward nor damaging. Above all, Jewish education must be *meaningful,* and not merely necessary for Jewish practice. Yet by appealing to inner convictions and a practical Jewish curriculum, Geiger recognized that Jewish education no longer binds and commands. For now parents could choose how to educate their children, and some, at least in Breslau, opted to educate their boys and girls at home.[22] Geiger challenged these parents to reconsider the value of Jewish character formation, the strong ties to particular Jewish communities, and the ethical values nurtured within them. He entered the secular world in which religious education now competed in the marketplace for the minds and hearts of young adults. The authority of Jewish education would rest in how well it prepared Jewish boys and girls for a future in Europe. Geiger educated *in* and *by means of* the Jewish community, but also *for* a polity firmly entrenched in broader historical trends.

Geiger's pedagogical developments respond to two competing tendencies: his desire to strengthen and cultivate local Jewish communities, and the certain need to fully integrate those communities within the broader German society. He appeals to education from within, as it were, even as his schools in Breslau encourage "practical" knowledge that prepares for "the demands of life." If liberal education only advances the broader cultural landscape (the ideal of German *Bildung*), then Geiger would surely lose the progressive and affluent Jewish children to more integrated Christian schools or to private tutors.[23] For with music, geography, natural science, and above all, French and German as the centerpieces of enlightened education, Jewish parents would find a better market for those services in the Christian schools (and, to be sure, many of them did).[24] Unable to compete, Geiger alters the terms of pedagogical discourse. His Jewish schools, so he claims, can produce both identity and character, a committed Jew and a cultured personality, without sacrificing the one for the other. Geiger offers a unified vision of learning in which young Jewish adults seamlessly integrate within German society *as* committed Jews. Under Geiger's tutelage, young liberal Jews would be well prepared for the "demands of life" and the responsibilities of Jewish citizenship.

The pull of German society moves even Geiger beyond the confines of the Jewish community. For Geiger, that pull carries the power and prestige of the German university. For many of his educated Jewish colleagues who desired university positions that would never materialize, the German university signified the cultured and social center of liberal society. This is no less true for Geiger.[25] Imagining the university with full romantic sentiment, Geiger calls it the "beautiful flower of the spiritual German life" that maintains "the universal scientific approach to cultured education [*die universelle wissenschaftliche Bildung*]."[26] So it seems clear to Geiger that a prestigious German university should house a Jewish theological institute. The theological task requires careful scientific scholarship coupled with practical knowledge and sensitivity to communal needs. Whereas the *Wissenschaft* scholar can ascend the heights of rational inquiry, the theologian must draw practical conclusions from such distant research.[27] In this sense, Jewish theology can unite *Wissenschaft* with "questions concerning life." Traditional concern with the Talmud as the book "sufficient for all of life" still dominates Jewish learning, and this because Jewish scholarship remains too parochial and confined. But scholars like Geiger, nurtured in secular studies, have opened new areas of research concerning biblical authority, textual meaning and language, historical proof, and authorial intent.

New questions, Geiger argues, call for a new kind of theology and a revised pedagogical system.[28] Jewish theology must become a science (*Wissenschaft*) to regain the communal authority that it clearly once owned but has since lost. A science, open to secular inquiry but grounded in the practical life of local Jewish communities, yields a "Jewish theology in the spirit of current trends in education [*Bildung*], in which training is necessary for its effective application in practical life." Theologians must unite, in a practical way, scientific scholarship with the demands, questions, and needs of particular communities.[29] Geiger dedicates his Jewish theological institute to this very ideal.[30] It is a task to be carried out only within the halls of the German university (Geiger suggests Breslau and Tübingen as two possible centers for Jewish *Wissenschaft*).[31] A Jewish faculty, as a branch of the university, would "work and strive according to the German sense." The theologian enters the halls of secular power and knowledge only to return to local

Jewish communities with practical solutions rooted in scientific learning, much in the way that Geiger himself did after his university training. A theological authority lost will be dramatically regained through association with the German university.

Such a faculty would never materialize in a German university in Geiger's lifetime. The university, as Fichte imagined it, would foster citizens of the state as an ethnic unity. A Jew might enter as a Jew, but as a cultured person, he would leave as a German citizen. To work "according to the German sense" could only mean the sacrifice of local and particular commitments in the name of German *Bildung*. Geiger's Jewish theological institute did not fit this model, for it required a university that encouraged local ties, and so cultivated particular commitments. Returning to the Jewish community from the university, however, proved far more problematic than Geiger would admit openly. In many ways, Geiger felt more at home in academic life than he did as a Jewish leader and rabbi. But Geiger never abandoned his rabbinic duties, and passionately engaged his communities with progressive theological currents and ideas.

A university faculty dedicated to Jewish studies, and one staffed by and for Jews, would do more than move scholarship forward; it would also advance the educational institutions already in place. Or so Geiger believed. For scholarship and life, as this dualism came to be known, rarely integrated well within the rhythms of the Jewish religious community. Geiger imagined that *Bildung* and the German university could help unify strong religious commitment (life) with rational and critical inquiry (scholarship). They would ground inner sensibilities and personal meanings upon the bedrock of Jewish *Wissenschaft*. Those individual meanings would not produce inflamed passions but reasonable commitments embedded in communal life. The university would inspire and justify a cultured Judaism that nurtured and strengthened local Jewish attachments. But German *Bildung* did not bend to Geiger's Jewish sensibilities, and Fichte's university ensured that it would not. The authority for liberal Jewish education would travel through other venues closer to home.

Hebrew Education

Both German high culture and the vitality of local Jewish communities attracted Geiger, and much of his work attempted to unify these distant spaces. He fervently believed that the German university could profitably serve the needs of Jewish life. Yet even Geiger was troubled by this convergence, and his many essays reflected the tension between his academic commitments and his rabbinic calling. His "The Writer and the Rabbi," discussed in the previous chapter, focused on these competing pressures and Geiger's effort to overcome them.

These tensions also come to the fore in Geiger's position on the proper role and function of Hebrew in the Jewish prayer service. In previous chapters, I have discussed the place of Hebrew in liturgical reform (Chapter 1) and its centrality to discussions of rabbinic leadership (Chapter 4). The role and power of Hebrew language certainly occupied the minds of the early reformers. A mere glance at the minutes from the rabbinical conferences of the mid-1840s reveals how central, and thus how divisive, the use of Hebrew language in the synagogue had become.[32] In this chapter, I turn to the role of Hebrew in Jewish education, and in particular Geiger's view of it. Hebrew studies absorbs many of the issues raised earlier, but in tones and colors quite distinct and important. The present chapter, as the concluding study in this book, echoes themes discussed earlier, but helps to bridge the many accounts of religious authority running throughout Geiger's works.

Geiger defends the careful use of the German language in religious services, despite his commitment to Hebrew as a language of historical richness:

> There now remains the irrefutable truth that prayer can only arouse a complete solemnity and devotion if it is held in the mother tongue, and this not merely because the understanding of it should above all be required, but rather because with the mother tongue all our feelings are connected in the most innermost way. But with a foreign language the word must first go through the medium of understanding, the function of translation, before it penetrates the heart.[33]

Authority lies in the heart rather than in understanding—and this no less for Hebrew than for German. Geiger believes that German prayers, particularly those that immediately precede and follow the sermon, have "a penetrating effect in a way that no other Hebrew prayer is felt."[34] Certainly Geiger retained many of the Hebrew prayers in his edited prayer books. He did so, in part, because he presided over a diverse Jewish community, and for many of his congregants, German (and not Hebrew) remained a foreign language. But Geiger also understood the value of strong communal memories associated with the Hebrew prayers. The language matters less than the way in which prayers move Jews "in the most innermost way." To be effective, prayers must arouse the deepest emotions, and edify and strengthen devotion to God; prayer is "the language of sensibility,"[35] instructing less and reflecting more our innermost concerns and desires. Hebrew as a "foreign language" blocks the immediacy of emotions by first encountering the logical mind. The act of translation filters out, and so disturbs, personal resonances and memories. This foreign "medium" all but ruins the required solemnity and piety necessary for devotional prayer. Liturgical prayers require a language that speaks from and to the heart.

Geiger admits that a German prayer arouses more intense feelings in him than a Hebrew one, however much one might call Hebrew his true first language (for Geiger first learned Hebrew before German).[36] But he recognizes the role that Hebrew plays in connecting Jewish learning to historical memories, and he supports such education in his schools for boys. In Breslau, young Jewish men must learn the *Ursprache* to become familiar with and translate Hebrew prayers. Though no longer a language of feeling, Hebrew still educates and, Geiger admits, roots Jewish children in the language and culture of the Bible.[37] Young Jewish women, with fewer prospects to learn Hebrew to the same degree, cultivate their deepest emotions through the German prayers. The German language enables women to enter public ritual and liturgy as common speakers of the German mother tongue. Though Geiger includes the study of Hebrew in his educational program, he emphasizes its philological and grammatical richness. One senses that Geiger holds a more scholarly appreciation of Hebrew as a complex, ancient language, but recognizes less its liturgical value. Hebrew cannot do what Geiger says the language of prayer must do: arouse strong emotional attachments and commitments to Jewish communal needs. Even for the older generation, Hebrew appeals more to nostalgia for Geiger than to a language of sensibility. If Hebrew no longer awakens the holy within, then Jews should turn to other, more expressive languages to guide liturgical worship.

Geiger's scholarly delight in Hebrew struck Ludwig Philippson and other liberal colleagues as far too minimalist and shallow. Philippson responded to Geiger's critique of liturgical Hebrew in his *Allgemeine Zeitung des Judenthums,* and countered that Hebrew establishes deeper roots than mere utilitarian ones. He mockingly recalled that children learn Hebrew even in Geiger's hometown of Breslau, and for reasons that went beyond its cultural import. For Philippson, Jewish education and liturgical practice enriched each other: "the Israelite prayer service must ground itself in the Bible, and this must be the essential component of the prayer service."[38] Liturgy not only edifies; it also teaches. The "medium of understanding" proved no less effective for Philippson than the opening of the heart. In Philippson's view, Geiger too easily distanced the academic study of Hebrew from the liturgical power to educate Jews in their history and tradition.

For Philippson, the synagogue stands as an educational institution, yet it reaches for something more as well. Within the synagogue, Hebrew and German fuse "organically" in the Jewish liturgy.[39] Prayer reflects, for Philippson too, the language of the heart "that is not a thing of understanding, but much more of sensibility."[40] But Hebrew also marks a "minority" from the stifling conformity of the "majority."[41] The Hebrew language serves a pedagogical role in fashioning Jewish identity. It is more than an emotional trigger: "The Israelite *prayer service* does not merely consist in *prayer* as an expression of feeling. Surely, an essential part of its expression remains the recognition of the content of Israelite religion in its dogmatic and historical connection."[42]

Hebrew represents the language of both heart and mind, and can thereby unite strong emotions with dogma and history. Every people has a mission, Philippson insists, and so too the Jews as "the people of religion." Their mission requires a special language, and Hebrew is "the most complete religious language" because it both edifies and instructs.[43] In the synagogue, Jews engage their history and sacred texts. But they also learn about their different, chosen heritage. The Hebrew prayers and texts help to fashion a Jewish identity apart.[44]

An identity rooted in the organic unity of liturgical Hebrew and German would shape a distinctive religious sensibility within broader cultural trends—an identity apart, to be sure, but one firmly entrenched in European society. Philippson's view of Hebrew as an edifying language that instructs a "people of religion" dovetails well with "the content of Israelite religion in its dogmatic and historical connection." For Philippson, Judaism is all of a piece, and a unified one at that. In a lengthy essay published in 1879 entitled "The Unity of the Ideas in the Holy Bible," Philippson argued that the entire Hebrew text could be subsumed under "a unity of ideas, teachings, and views as they really appear in the books of our holy Bible." He called his study a "work of critique" in the service of religious faith and conviction, one grounded in a "serious, scientific standpoint."[45]

Where Geiger highlighted in his *Urschrift* political and social tension in historical context, Philippson believes "the teaching of God the creator in its simplicity, clarity, and decisiveness stands in complete opposition to all cosmogonies of the ancient world—the Egyptian, Indian, Persian and Greek."[46] Singular and unique, the Hebrew God creates humanity "in the image of God, harmoniously composed of body and spirit."[47] Philippson repeats these tropes throughout his work, attending to moments of clarity, harmony, and organic unity within the sacred text. The laws of Kashrut, for example, teach us "the most inner connection" and "harmony" of body and spirit, so that our bodily functions regulate and nourish the soul.[48] Not only the Pentateuch, but the entire Hebrew Bible describes the covenant (ברית) as "a unified organic whole."[49] Biblical unity grounds and fashions a unified Jewish identity. Philippson need not agonize, as Geiger sometimes does, about the distance between Israelite religion and modern sensibilities. The "organic unity" discovered in the Hebrew Bible imposes itself even now upon modern European Jews. The Hebrew language reinforces this biblical unity, and returns modern Jews to "the content of Israelite religion in its dogmatic and historical connection."

Yet for Geiger, Hebrew has lost its power to awaken religious desires. It can, he admits, offer compelling connections to the biblical heritage and historical Judaism. But a "dogmatic and historical connection," as Philippson would have it, will not support Jewish commitment: for Geiger, "the direction of the young to religion can be truly realized only when it moves hand in hand with powerful and arousing religious conviction."[50] The Hebrew language cannot stimulate such emotions for Geiger, and neither should it instruct young Jews in religious dogmatism. Geiger associates dogmatic principles with a kind of religious catechism that seeks to prove rather than arouse faith. Catechisms alone cannot instill religious emotions and sensibilities for a lasting belief. Philippson's appeal to dogma and history suits better Jewish *Wissenschaft* than pedagogical reform, although he introduced his unified, dogmatic approach to Jewish children studying for confirmation and bar mitzvah.[51]

Geiger preferred to study Hebrew, but not to pray in it. German resonated with personal meanings because it spoke directly to the heart, and opened the Jewish community to social and political goods. Philippson rooted Jewish identity in dogmatic and organic biblical unity. But Geiger grounded that identity within the self, and in so doing found no dogma or unity there.

Dogma, Catechism, and Personal Meaning

One maintains an insular Jewish identity, so Geiger believes, only through appeals to religious dogma. Such is the case for Philippson, but not only him. Geiger's more contextually sensitive, local, and communal approach to Jewish identity differed significantly from Philippson's grounded, objective view. Religious dogmatism reflected more than a theoretical concern, however, for Geiger's thinking on identity and Jewish education. It opened deeply personal wounds as well. Manuel Joël, Geiger's successor in Breslau, published in 1869 his "Toward an Orientation on the Question of the Cultus."[52] Geiger read the piece as a personal slight that undermined his own, more pragmatic approach to Jewish liturgy. He was clearly affronted by Joël's attack, and Geiger's tone in his written response is nasty and sardonic.[53] The main thrust of Geiger's reply concerns Joël's commitment to religious dogmatism. He quotes Joël directly—"Judaism has concepts of faith that can never be placed in question"[54]—and returns to this quotation often, as if the very claim warrants the overthrow of Joël's entire theoretical edifice. Joël's "Cultus" is religious dogmatism, so Geiger argues in the next fifty pages of his article, and it reflects a very dangerous kind of pedagogical reform in Jewish education.

In Geiger's view, Jewish faith and dogma transform over time, and one cannot "once and for all" establish or fix Jewish principles of faith.[55] Unlike moral truths, dogmas "have a moving history and have never been fixed."[56] Judaism demonstrates great diversity in this regard. Geiger notes the "dialectical fierceness of Talmudic discourse, and the fantastic depths of Jewish mysticism that retained the freshness of spirit."[57] Joël's dogmatic thinking, Geiger claims, draws heavily from Christianity and represents a foreign religious movement, one far less tolerant and open to theological diversity; Joël "offers up his 'either', but he gives us no 'or'."[58] Geiger worries that grounding norms of faith only creates illegitimate borders of identity. Dogmatic principles serve only to disenfranchise Jews who remain outside the established margins. But Joël's theology appears to claim, "here is a Jew, there a non-Jew."[59] His theology, on Geiger's reading, is both groundless and dangerous: it could lead to schism and the most serious religious persecutions.

Rather than Joël's hard and "subjective" limits, Geiger seeks "*approximate* borders that are not so tightly determined. What are we to make of such indeterminate borders? That each and every person must do for themselves, and no other can put something in their conscience."[60] But Joël *has* put something in their conscience, and has thereby falsely limited the various ways Jews imagine themselves and their tradition. Geiger places much of the blame on Mendelssohn's understanding of Judaism as a religion "of mere laws and statutes." Mendelssohn yielded "a death judgment on Judaism," for as "a skeleton without a living soul," Judaism could not become what Geiger believes it surely is: a moral tradition both personal and communal that continually progresses and inspires.[61] Joël has adopted Mendelssohn's "dryness" and developed a limited system of dogmatic truths that undermine Jewish creativity and development.

But a Jew should appeal less to dogmas, Geiger stresses, and more to "*the way in which he considers himself closely connected to Jewry.*"[62] Not theology, but personal experience outlines the vague borders that define Jewish tradition and one's commitment to it. Authority resides in the relation between personal conviction and Jewish community, between inner "sensibility" and Judaism. This kind of authority proves neither subjective nor chaotic, Geiger insists. *Wissenschaft* "alone" decides the true and false paths. Geiger imagines a science that offers greater clarity in the choices Jews make, and provides reasonable grounds for more worthy projects. Only *Wissenschaft,* and not Joël's dogmatic theology, can determine, ultimately and in some broad sense, the contours of Jewish identity. The difference lies, according to Geiger, in how Joël places inflexible limits on theological investigation. The ideal of *Wissenschaft* requires free and open research, but Joël has placed some "facts beyond question."[63] Although Geiger has elsewhere undermined *Wissenschaft* as an agenda-free, "positive" science, here he recognizes its claim to open and free exploration.

The real force of Geiger's critique lies in the autonomy of personal choices and the limits of Jewish allegiance. Dogmatic theology usurps the authority that resides in individual commitment. To argue for certain fundamental issues to remain "beyond question" wrongly limits the power of religious sensibilities. Appealing to "facts beyond question" is bad theology and bad science.

Geiger makes these same points in his review of Samson Raphael Hirsch's *Nineteen Letters on Judaism.* The *Letters* consist of a series of questions by the student Benjamin, with answers (apparently Hirsch's own) by Benjamin's teacher Naphtali. In his lengthy critique, Geiger focuses his attention at one point on the meaning of Hirsch's phrase, "the Torah is fact like heaven and earth."[64] Just as we investigate nature through impartial reason, we can now, so argues Hirsch, understand religious laws, principles, and goals without preconceived notions or assumptions. But such objectivity denies the role of spirit in history, Geiger replies, and approaches the text as a closed fact.[65] This reflects yet another form of dogmatic theology that resists creative interpretive techniques to reveal local meanings. Geiger even presses Hirsch with questions that Benjamin himself refused to consider. In short, Geiger takes up the character of Benjamin, and then forces Naphtali to reply to more critical questioning. If, as some scholars have noted, Hirsch modeled Benjamin on his friend Geiger, then Geiger, taking on the role himself, tells us what Benjamin *should* have asked.[66] This literary technique performs Geiger's philosophical point: certain issues remain beyond question for dogmatic thinkers such as Hirsch and Joël. We require "another kind of reform," Geiger concludes, one far more progressive and critical than such "groundless faith."[67] This new reform defends the free choices of individual Jews to determine the limits of their faith. The authority of theological inquiry must bend to the authority of personal meaning.

This is no less true for Jewish education, for especially here the authority of personal meaning grounds the authenticity of religious practice. Jewish education, in Geiger's view, accesses the inner life that motivates and sustains Jewish communities. Schooled in doctrine, grammar, and texts through memorization and other heuristic practices, Jews will inevitably leave such knowledge and skills behind—or more likely, employ them for secular gain. But even more, such pedagogical techniques never approach the authority of science. *Wissenschaft*, as the proper and critical study of history and religion, opens deeper sources of inner spirituality to empower religious practices.

But Jewish learning through doctrine became a leading pedagogical tool in early nineteenth-century liberal Judaism. The local, flexible, and creative approaches that Geiger favored in education were often abandoned for general, stringent, and dogmatic views. Jewish catechisms in the first half of the nineteenth century dominated the educational scene in many liberal Jewish circles (but not only here), especially as these works prepared young students for confirmation.[68] As many conservative Jewish educators employed catechisms in their teaching (and many liberals chose other methods), scholars of nineteenth-century Judaism such as Jacob Petuchowski and Mordechai Eliav highlight the Christian foundations for Jewish catechisms, and their focus on dogma and universal principles of faith.[69] Even Geiger employed a catechism in his confirmation classes. His son and biographer, Ludwig Geiger, ruefully defends its limited use. Even so, the catechism's pedagogical utility also highlights that other distinctive feature of Geiger's educational program: the authority of personal meaning to counter the deadening effects of dogma.

An illustrative example of the liberal catechism is Samuel Hirsch's *Systematischer Katechismus der Israelitischen Religion*, published in Luxembourg in 1856.[70] The liberal Samuel Hirsch, though unrelated to the Orthodox Samson Raphael Hirsch, still shares with him a dogmatic view of Jewish theology and practice that, for Geiger, only suffocates Jewish creativity. Hirsch's catechism results from some twenty years of communal reflection upon the "essence of the Jewish religion" and the "foundations, concepts and views" that sustain the spiritual life.[71] The catechism solidifies and distills the two central tenets of Hirsch's liberal Judaism: 1) religion lies within inner sensibilities and responds to a "need of the human heart," such that one must only "learn to read the language of one's own heart in order to discover all the teachings of religion"; and 2) Judaism represents "this religion of the heart, indeed, it is only this, and this entirely."[72] Like many other religious works of this period, Hirsch's text begins with a discourse on religion, and only then moves to a particular form of it (in this case, Judaism) as the most fitting exemplar of the religious life. The meaning and value of Jewish practice would now rely upon the new and universal arena of religious experience. For Hirsch, and indeed for Geiger as well, Judaism represented the most vibrant and expressive religion in the modern period.

Though Hirsch warns that his catechism should not displace the spiritual yearnings of the heart, the very nature and form of the work effectively do so.

Hirsch divides his catechism into five books: *History, Revelation, Teaching, Worship,* and *Life*. Each book contains numerous chapters with subtitles. The book *History*, for example, includes chapters on The Human Being, The Garden of Bliss, and The Laws of Kashrut, among others. The formulaic style established in the very first chapter of *History* runs throughout the catechism. Hirsch opens with the question, "Why do we need religious instruction?" The answer immediately follows, but in a much larger type size: "In order to discover how we should live so that we live up to the goal that we have to fulfill here on earth." Hirsch then cites two biblical sources (Deut. 30:20 and Deut. 32:46–47) as proof texts. He then moves on to a second question that builds upon the first: "How does the Bible describe the goal that human beings must fulfill on earth?" Hirsch's response again follows in larger script, but here he interweaves biblical texts in his reply.[73] The pattern continues right through: first a question printed in reduced font, then Hirsch's answer in larger type that may include biblical texts. Often, but certainly not in every case, Hirsch cites biblical sources only after he responds thoroughly to the question. In this way, the reader approaches the biblical text through Hirsch's reading of it. One senses that Hirsch cites these sources only to boast, "see, the Bible really does claim what I am arguing here." He invites neither critical scrutiny nor interpretive probing, but only basic knowledge of the biblical texts that best support the principles of his liberal Judaism. The effect is cumulative: each question builds upon the previous answer, and the student assembles a base of knowledge in order to cite relevant biblical texts to support the foundations of Jewish faith. Memorizing the sources, then, rather than learning "to read the language of one's own heart," becomes the key pedagogical tool for Jewish education.

But even the biblical sources cannot sustain Hirsch's theological agenda. In the third book (*Teaching*) under the chapter "I am the Lord," Hirsch asks this question: "Where should we search for God?" He supports his answer ("We will not find God anywhere if we do not search in our own hearts and in the experience of our own lives") with four proof texts—Job 28:12–14 and 28, Psalms 111:10, Proverbs 1:7, and a Mishnaic text known as the Sayings of the Fathers (*Pirkei Avot*) 3:11. But none refer to the God within, in heart or in personal experience. They each speak to wisdom and fear of the Lord. Hirsch understands the problem, and so adds a rare footnote to the last citation (only a handful of footnotes appear in this catechism). The footnote clarifies the true meaning of the cited works: "the true God is spirit [*Geist*], and can therefore only be found when we proceed out from our spirit, that is, from our spiritual-ethical life [*von unserem geistig-sittlichen Leben*]."[74] The weight of Hirsch's theological commitments bears down upon the biblical texts to impose a reading of wisdom and fear that better aligns with a spiritual God. If the texts cannot stand alone and perform as proof texts, then Hirsch must add some interpretive gloss to prod them along. In still other places, Hirsch explicitly challenges a more literal reading of the Bible. Responding to a question concerning God's creation of the world in six days, Hirsch asserts: "for God there is no earthly day and no earthly night," and so Genesis cannot reasonably be a historical record of God's acts.[75]

As a pedagogical tool, the catechism instills Hirsch's own doctrinaire theology through repetitious patterns of question, answer, and (sometimes) proof text. For the student who fails to memorize all the answers to Jewish faith, Hirsch gratefully appends a "confession."[76] Rather than listening to the "language of the heart" to find both God and Judaism, Jewish students learn to read Hirsch's catechism and speak the language of spiritual religion. This is dogmatic imperialism by other means.

Geiger never wrote a catechism for young Jewish adults, though he did institute a confirmation class for his religious schools in Breslau, and the final exam consisted of an oral question-and-answer session for the young men and (more often) young women.[77] When Ludwig Geiger describes these exams in the synagogue, he recalls the "flood of words" and the "immediate, personal" tone of the event that always left an "unforgettable impression" on those present.[78] Though written as apologetic, Ludwig's account still regards this more expressive confirmation as working "against conventions," and as one that offers something "new and more powerful" for child and parent alike. Despite protocol and precedent, Geiger "as a born teacher" infused his confirmation classes with a "living freshness."[79] This account fits nicely with Geiger's approach to Jewish education. For neither claims to universal dogmas, nor learning through catechism reaches "the language of the heart" that Hirsch sought but would never find. The authority of personal meaning determines the nature and scope of Geiger's educational philosophy and practice.

The *Hochschule* Lectures: The Authority of Language and History Reconsidered

Geiger's lectures at the *Hochschule für Wissenschaft des Judenthums* in Berlin in the years 1872–1874 counter the repressive pedagogical direction of Hirsch's catechism. The *Hochschule* grew out of discussions during the Leipzig synod of "moderately progressive" rabbis, scholars, and lay leaders in 1869, but it also represented the fruits of Geiger's first call for a Jewish theological faculty in 1836.[80] Coalesced under the title "A General Introduction to the Critical Study [*Wissenschaft*] of Judaism,"[81] Geiger's lectures cover a broad area of scholarship and analysis of Jewish history. He weaves together themes that I have previously discussed in various chapters of this book, and so provides a kind of summary of his theological and educational concerns. In the lectures we discover Geiger as Jewish educator at the very end of his life, still hopeful for progress in Jewish *Wissenschaft,* still master of Hebrew grammar and textual nuance, still critical of dogmatic prejudices and unwarranted assumptions. His introduction suits young Jewish leaders and rabbis who seek both instruction and inspiration, as well as Jewish learning with spiritual vigor. In many ways, the lectures defend his own training as philologist, historian, and linguist. The new leadership should be trained as Geiger once had been, and they too must appreciate how the authority of personal meaning generates and expands the Jewish spirit.

Geiger distinguishes three critical spheres of study, but he lectures on only two—linguistics and history (Geiger never discusses the third, philosophy and ethics). The relation between language and history had earlier dominated Geiger's critique in his *Urschrift*. Now, however, both language and history offer a balanced view of the Jewish past—one that, while elusive, is too often surrendered for clearer but far less imaginative critical studies. Yet that balanced view should not be conceded too readily, for a common hermeneutical enterprise unites linguistic and historical studies. The truly critical historian and linguist "observe the peculiar direction of the spiritual life," much as they did in Geiger's early popular lectures, *Judaism and Its History*. The only Judaism worth studying remains one that develops and maintains its "vitality" in the life of *Geist*.[82] Resonating with Hegel's sense of historical movement and progression, and capturing the inner motive force of historical practice, Geiger's notion of *Geist* is still far less than Hegel's dialectical movements and growing self-awareness. But it nonetheless captures a view of spirit that animates all "vital" human acts. Geiger understands *Geist* as the spiritual force that motivates, enlivens, and makes possible all human activities, practices, and ideals. Judaism participates in the life of *Geist* insofar as it mirrors and develops this vitality. There are moments of Jewish history, for example, that fall too far afield from their spiritual sources. For *Geistesleben* really does have a "peculiar direction," so Geiger thinks, and the historian and linguist must learn how to trace it. *Wissenschaft des Judenthums* is a critical study of how *Geist* directs, motivates, and sustains human practices.

Linguistic studies reveal the Jewish spiritual life. Jews recognize themselves in their language as the very "corollary of its spirit":[83]

> The *Hebrew language* is not merely the pleasing robe in which original thoughts are contained, in which it comes before us as a visible appearance. The Hebrew language lies much closer and is a more representative expression. The knowledge of Hebrew is therefore not merely an aid to knowledge of Judaism, but rather it is itself an indispensable part of it.[84]

Here again Geiger distances Hebrew from Jewish prayer only to recapture it for Jewish *Wissenschaft*. The value of Hebrew lies in its revelatory power to uncover the Jewish historical spirit. Hebrew is more than mere garment, more than an outer form to be replaced by other languages. Geiger compares Hebrew to similar Near Eastern languages, including Aramaic, and finds them all "so much flatter" and "lifeless" in comparison to Hebrew "vitality."[85] Only such a vibrant and *geistige* language offers "a picture of the whole inner life," and without such a "healthy sense of language," the "living spirit" cannot progress and mature.[86] Hebrew becomes not only a language of study, but also a language of spiritual meaning. Students of Jewish history must thoroughly understand Hebrew grammar, philology, and history to better appreciate and account for that spirit. Geiger's students learn Hebrew to gain access to the movement of *Geist* in Judaism.

But *how* should one educate students in the study of Hebrew? If languages really do provide "a complete picture of the times," as Geiger believes, then the method of linguistic study must conform to how languages reflect spiritual movements. The appropriate method would draw from "the most inner strivings of the Jewish spirit" and offer "a complete mirror image" to it. Linguistics thus provides "the critical methodological approach to the Bible."[87] But with the final redaction of the biblical text, together with a new concern for textual purity, scholars focused on the "externals" of vocalization, grammatical rules, and the like. Geiger blames Saadia Gaon and the Masoretic tradition for adopting "an objective consciousness," modeled on Islamic reading practices, in their treatment of Hebrew literature. Yet such objectivity obscures the "inner strivings of the Jewish spirit," and neglects how language reflects moral ideals and passions.

A proper, critical study of Hebrew, Geiger contends, must be subjective in the sense that it recognizes how language expresses inner desires. Language is alive and attuned to the movements of spirit, and so too must be the modern *Wissenschaft* scholar. If one merely explains how language functions without exposing the meaning it has for those who speak and write it, then one offers a dry, cold, and "external" account of a dead language. But for Geiger, language reveals personal meanings, and so the critical linguist must uncover its richness and power. All *Wissenschaft,* Geiger concludes, "produces wonder."[88] By making Hebrew alive again, Geiger evokes in his readers the scientist's own sense of awe and amazement. To be attuned to the personal resonance and richness in language is to study it in a critical, *Wissenschaft* mode.

Geiger's *Wissenschaft* scholar uncovers the spiritual resonance of language through a linguistic translation that remains pure, "immediate," and "fresh."[89] One can, apparently, access the immediacy of language only in study, but not in prayer. In the synagogue, Hebrew often obscures the inner sensibilities that properly trained linguists magically recover. Where Geiger elsewhere privileges the work of theologians, rabbis, and historians, here Geiger attributes to the linguist all that Hegel before him had ascribed to the philosopher. Language reflects not only "the word of a people's ideas"; it suggests even more "the history of that people's activity."[90] Jewish education requires both knowledge of and passion for linguistic history.

What remains, then, for other kinds of history? If the study of language covers the thought and activity of a people, what does history do? Geiger seems well aware of the question, and gently works around it. History encounters a problem unknown to the study of language: not all history is pregnant with meaning, and so not all history reveals the contours and movements of *Geist.* Geiger had previously alerted his readers to such a distinction in his *Judaism and Its History* (1864/65). There Geiger understood history in two senses: the first as a "great world-historical phenomenon," and the second as "merely a historical consideration." The first sense corresponds to what Geiger calls in these later lectures "a history of spiritual activity." But the second approach he labels as "external history that has value only as a substrate, only as the conditions under and according to which spiritual activity becomes a historical phenomenon." There is history, and then there is "spiritual and therefore world-shaping history."[91] Jewish history stands with the world-shaping kind, and the historian uncovers those features that witness to Jewish "spiritual activity." Only in this sense can it be a science of *Judaism,* emphasized in italics by Geiger to stress the relation between *Geist* and *Judenthum.* A *science* of Judaism, on the other hand, with the emphasis on *Wissenschaft,* focuses attention on the critical method for approaching spirit. Sources must be authentic, the data reliable and accountable, such that "history is recognized as science."[92]

But all this does not yet turn history, even spiritual history, into a recognizable discipline of critique. For linguists, too, employ the same critical skills to flesh out the "spiritual activity" of a historical people. Even if historians extract that activity from the more mundane "substratum," history still appears as a sub-discipline to the more commanding study of language. But the historian, unlike the linguist, recognizes "the whole later development of spirit already prefigured in the growth and development of its original seeding."[93] The organic metaphor evokes the continuity and progressive movements of spirit, such that spiritual fruits still reflect the seeds of more humble beginnings. Spiritual activity matures from "more modest" roots, and the historian reveals how later flourishings of spirit develop out of "more chaste" foundations.

If linguists uncover spiritual activity at particular historical moments, then historians piece those moments together to reveal organic continuity and development. Geiger's historian reads the present into the past. Historians interpret the past in their own terms because the present exhibits in a sharper, clearer way what remained inchoate and murky long ago. Indeed, the past speaks meaningfully only through contemporary idioms. We recognize the past as *our* past through historical narratives of continuity. These narratives, however, do not assume a linear model of development. Geiger asks his students to recover spiritual moments from within the debates he described in his *Urschrift.* Geiger's liberal rabbis weave together a continuous narrative of spirit out of the social and political struggles of the Jewish past. In this, they create a usable past as a meaningful and progressive tradition. Geiger's notion of *Geist* guarantees such continuity and progress, and justifies how the historian understands the past better than the past could do so itself. History is, for Geiger, the hegemonic power to observe the past as a mirror to the present.

History awakens commitment to a liberal Jewish practice modeled on a usable past. Geiger believes that good history rejuvenates and enlivens contemporary Judaism. But to do so, history must speak to the lived circumstances and hopes of modern persons. It must become, Geiger claims, the very opposite of myth as "pure poetic imagination."[94] Myth begins from "inner dark representations" and forms only "personalities that all reality surpasses." In short, myth "stands in absolutely no relation to real times." It could never "rejuvenate a people or a religion, and reveals only the decline of the old spirit."[95] History, by contrast, evolves out of the lives of real persons. It remains of this world; myth searches for another.

Geiger favors history to myth in order to position Judaism as the religion of personal meaning. The life of Jesus in Christian theology succumbs to pure mythological play. It therefore retains only a vitality for "the old spirit." Judaism supersedes Christianity with its practical, meaningful, and this-worldly spiritual history, and triumphs as well over Islam. In his very early work, *Judaism and Islam* (1833),[96] Geiger employs this mythological approach to describe "the striving and aims of Muhammad, with the mind of his time and the constitution of his surroundings."[97] Grounded in history, the biblical narratives contrast sharply with Muhammad's stories "draped in the most marvelous garb of fiction" that "appealed to the poetic fancy of Muhammad, and suited the childish level of his contemporaries."[98] In his *Judaism and Its History,* written some thirty years after his book on Islam, Geiger attributes all creativity in Islam to Jewish influence, and concludes that "Islam enters without new creative impulse, rude and poor in ideas, wild, and with stormy rattling of arms."[99] Judaism, distinct from both Islam and Christianity, is progressive and contemporary. It produces a history that can "rejuvenate" modern religious practice. Christianity, like Islam, remains a mythological abstraction—a fanciful flight from lived reality. A vibrant history within lived social life resides in Judaism alone.

Geiger's lectures at the *Hochschule* affirm the vibrant progressive sources of Jewish life and thought, and ridicule the more sterile, otherworldly, and debased forms of Christianity and Islam. Susannah Heschel has noted how Geiger, in the last years of his life, became increasingly spiteful toward Christianity and its scholars, and these lectures only confirm that view.[100] But they also reveal a Geiger taking stock of his educational past, imparting his own pedagogical concerns to the younger generation of liberal rabbis and scholars. He weaves together themes discussed in his earlier works, both popular and more academic. Geiger provides a summary of his theological and educational concerns.

His lectures at the *Hochschule* endorse the linguistic development first pioneered in Geiger's *Urschrift,* and they recast the "spiritual" moments of Jewish tradition that echo *Judaism and Its History.* But where the *Urschrift* targeted an elite scholarly audience, and *Judaism and Its History* focused instead on lay readers, Geiger's lectures at the *Hochschule* define the future of Jewish studies for young students and future rabbis. The lectures neither inculcate dogma nor justify sweeping and objective claims, but instead demand a passionate commitment to the vibrancy and spiritual power of Jewish history. Geiger believes that only this kind of history can trigger the emotional powers of personal commitment. An enlivened and spiritual history—a history of *Geist*—awakens individual attachments that command beyond the self to embrace the wider concerns of local and particular communities. Geiger's lectures attempt to fashion committed, engaged, and progressive young educators who will soon translate the knowledge of the *Hochschule* into local idioms. If future scholars become attuned to the political, religious, and social ideas in language and history, they also further Geiger's lifelong scholarly projects. With his first lectures at the *Hochschule* in 1872, Geiger constructed future rabbis and scholars in his own image. The future would indeed arise from the progressive seeds of the past.

Geiger's educational model awakens personal commitments to a progressive Judaism shaped by the linguistic and historical resources of the tradition. It seeks to motivate individual Jews to strengthen edifying ties to local communities, and through them build a broader, integrative commitment to the wider social public. Jewish education begins with embodied persons, so Geiger believes, and moves them to embrace communal concerns and practices.

In his *Commandments and Concerns*, contemporary scholar Michael Rosenak distinguishes between two "orientations" toward Jewish education. The "explicit" paradigm focuses upon the text as "constituting the spiritual reality being encountered," and understands Judaism as a peculiar language game that teachers master and students learn. The "implicit" view, however, concentrates upon student concerns and the environment of educational learning. This model emphasizes "environments and significance-perceived-by-pupils," whereas the explicit paradigm stresses "subject matter and teacher competence."[101] One might assume that Geiger falls somewhere in the implicit camp of Jewish theologians and educators, for he recognizes the "significance-perceived-by-students" as the crucial starting point for engaged learning. While the Jewish catechism reflects the "explicit" model by providing the language and structure of Jewish discourse, Geiger's pedagogical concerns focus on individuals and their local environments. Geiger simply will not prescribe the "spiritual reality being encountered," but instead will move his students to generate that reality through reflective and passionate study of classical Jewish sources. Religious authority cannot be found ready-made, but is created through emotional struggle with the tradition and one's commitment to it. Jewish education, in other words, commands through evocative appeals to the "environment" of personal significance.

But Geiger also harbors "explicit" claims that ground Jewish education in classical Jewish texts. He channels students into the spiritual waters of historical Hebrew, and shows how language uncovers religious value and conflict. History too opens new political and social concerns that map out important religious positions on law, theology, and belief. The textual world still remains the central site of Jewish pedagogical concern, and Geiger seeks to enliven that world by redescribing it. Students engage texts to discover the resources for progressive Judaism. The classical texts seduce readers in locating modern commitments within it—as if the seeds of liberal Judaism were planted long ago, anticipating readers such as Geiger's students to cultivate and employ them.

To be sure, the "implicit" model still holds in Geiger's pedagogical practice. The text neither controls the "language game" nor the methodological commitments of the reader. But Jewish learning and identity remain nonetheless rooted in textual language and grammar. Only the texts and their interpretations—to rephrase Geiger's title for his *Urschrift*—reveal the contours and vibrancy of Jewish tradition. These texts represent classics for Geiger because they expose the ever-present possibility for spiritual and religious progress.[102] They open up a world that challenges readers to reconstruct the present in light of the radical possibilities of the past. Geiger's Jewish education cultivates "implicit" claims to personal significance in order to revive the "explicit" appeals of classical Jewish texts. He initiates a dialogical encounter in which students translate the progressive tendencies in ancient sources to better inform the local and particular needs of the present.

Geiger educates Jewish students to become committed citizens to local Jewish communities before they become "citizens of the world."[103] Or more precisely, students become world citizens only in and through their local communities. Liberal educators, such as Martha Nussbaum, argue that "world citizenship requires transcending the inclination of both students and educators to define themselves primarily in terms of local group loyalties and identities."[104] But Geiger admires students for their individual talents and concerns *because* of their rootedness in particular communities. Young Jewish adults attain world citizenship "through belonging to a particular circle, in which and for which and *by means* of which one acts for the whole."[105] Geiger certainly fails to explain how one moves from local to more diverse spaces of human culture. He confines his pedagogical model to those particular circles within which Jewish education is both effective and necessary. Yet one does not give up "the world" by attending to local concerns—indeed, only in this way can one engage the world at all. But giving up would be to abandon local ties in favor of broader cultural trends. So Geiger situates Jewish education within the needs and desires of particular Jewish communities. Only there can a practical, effective, and commanding educational practice inspire Jewish commitment. Parents in Breslau surely yearn for children schooled in French, European literature, and philosophy. They desire "virtuosos and salon men" who thrive among "the demands of life." But Jewish communities generate their own demands, Geiger warns. One of those demands is the capacity to view "acts for the whole" through "a particular circle." Jews become world citizens, as it were, by strengthening and enlivening their local Jewish communities. Geiger inspires his students in his *Hochschule* to mediate the world through more immediate concerns and spaces.

Once within those local areas of concern, however, Geiger distances his educational program from dominant cultural trends to instill knowledge and commitment. Samuel Hirsch's catechism is but one of many that mold young Jewish adults in the ideological and dogmatic image of liberal Judaism. Programmatic Judaism, if we can call it this, educates through responsible knowledge of religious history and ideas. Hirsch promotes a core education that responds not to indifference but ignorance, not to passion but argument, not to emotional triggers but to logic. His catechism builds the edifice for Jewish commitment, and provides the proof texts for liberal Judaism. Geiger's more pragmatic and contextual view resists this move to foundations and security. He rejects Joël's "dogmatic" approach to "concepts of faith" because it too easily minimizes religious conflict within Jewish history. Attending to the grammatical and linguistic development of Hebrew reveals that political, religious, and social debates had always been in play. As Ludwig Geiger notes, Geiger did employ a catechism in his educational program. But only to a degree, and one senses the anxiety (at least for Ludwig) in relying upon it. Perhaps here Geiger bent to the dominant educational practices of his times. Yet the whole tenor of his pedagogy opposes the dogmatic thrust of learning through catechism. If Geiger's education seeks personal commitment, Hirsch's catechism instills core knowledge; if Geiger's student critically engages the sources to reveal the developments and tensions within Jewish history, students of Hirsch's catechism turn to those sources as proof texts; if Geiger situates Jewish education within local communal needs and resources, Hirsch's catechism responds to "the demands of life" and the desire for world citizenry. For Hirsch, knowledge confers power to engage the world at large. For Geiger, knowledge engenders responsibility to rebuild and energize particular Jewish communities.

The authority of personal meaning dominates Geiger's educational program and his turn to the particular and local needs of Jewish life and practice. Rather than Hirsch's proof texts in catechism, or Joël's dogmatic claims, deep-seated commitments empower the authority of liberal Jewish education. Geiger seeks to unearth those commitments through appeals to "implicit" meanings, charting the movement of Jewish education from personal significance to communal goals. Grounding Jewish studies in the meaning things have for us, Geiger opens the self to political and religious concerns that bind individuals to social goods. Educational authority moves from "implicit" to "explicit" dimensions, from the inner world of spiritual vitality to the social world of religious practice.

In this, Geiger's pedagogical practice mirrors his philosophical idealism. Here too, the "implicit" claims of personal significance materialize in the public practices of local Jewish communities. For Geiger, education begins with the self, enlivens it with appeals to personal meanings, and then channels those meanings to inform and reform Jewish social space. Without that binding inner significance, Jewish education surrenders its authority to command allegiance from its young students. For in the end, Geiger's educational programs in Breslau and Berlin offer less substance than personal engagement, less history than usable memories, less ancient texts than interpretive meanings. Geiger's Jewish education opens up a world of significance, and in doing so produces knowledge intimately related to the authority of personal experience.

Conclusion: The Practice of Authority

Abraham Geiger's many appeals to the authority of personal meaning resonate with contemporary Jewish lives. This is true because he rejected philosophy as "completely pre-suppositionless" and solely derived from "pure rational teaching." Rational philosophy, in Geiger's view, seeks universal ends that undermine personal commitment and character. But Jewish philosophy, so Geiger argues, works within systems of value and concern, and cultivates embodied persons attached to particular communities and traditions.[1] Geiger empowers a kind of Jewish philosophy that grounds authority in historical practice, local communities, and personal meaning. It is philosophy that attends to particular communal ends, and employs deliberative techniques that appeal to personal commitments and religious reform. Geiger's Jewish philosophy regains modern Jewish authority through provocative readings of texts and history that engage, even as they challenge, local Jewish communities and their practices.

There is a good deal of evidence to suggest that modern Jewish communities, particularly in America, respond to this call for local attachments that inspire and command. Steven Cohen and Arnold Eisen document that as moderately affiliated American Jews abandon organizational life within the public sphere, they turn instead to more intimate concerns of family, synagogue, and the "sovereign self."[2] The authority of personal meaning overrides commitments to Israel, social organizations, and political action committees. Communal obligations run through the self, as it were, and persons seek meaning and authority grounded in self-expression and fulfillment. Loyalty to religious denominations gives way to fidelity to particular rabbis and their synagogues; public acts of religious ritual cede to family and the home; and the "second language" of community obligation recedes into the "first language" of the autonomous individual.[3]

A philosophy attuned to these local attachments and meanings, as Geiger's is, can both inform and challenge modern Jewish identity. The issues discussed in this book—historical memory, sacred texts, gendered ritual practices, the rabbinic calling, and educational philosophy—all have decidedly influenced contemporary Jewish observance. Indeed, modern Jewry creates and discovers the authority of personal meaning within those religious practices that Geiger cared so much about. The practice of authority becomes authentic through the very making of it—through memories that command, texts that inspire, rituals that inform, rabbis who lead, and schools that energize. In these sites of religious practice, Geiger's Jewish philosophy can help shape the contemporary search for religious authority and identity.

For Geiger the *Wissenschaft* scholar, religious authority and identity cannot be found in objective or linear histories of the past. Though he protected the methodological strictures of scientific *Wissenschaft,* Geiger nonetheless expanded them to reclaim forgotten moral sources. He reawakened Judaism as a "great world-historical phenomenon" that could command modern allegiance through renewed moral strength. To be sure, history could justify modern religious reforms; but even more, that history would be a remembered one that shaped, even as it was shaped by, contemporary political and ethical debates. Geiger constructed historical memory to strengthen modern commitments to it. This was no positivist history in Assmann's sense, but a meaningful shaping to create a usable moral past.

Geiger's moral idealism, for all its metaphysical claims, remains far more pragmatic in its recovery of moral sources that command allegiance. For Geiger's historical writing recovers less the Jewish experience (as Graetz would have it), and far more a reflective sense of religious meaning. This is no less true for Geiger's edited prayer books. The point of liturgical worship is not to recall an experience, much less to relive it, but rather to harness its moral truth to reinvigorate modern commitments. History commands because it furnishes the sources for Jewish ethical reflection. Geiger positions history and historical memory as the ethical context within which Jews reimagine the meaning of their lives.

History becomes a source for religious meaning rather than a bearer of truth, and historical memories recapture and enliven those meanings as personal, ethical, and commanding. In his powerful meditation on the ethics of memory, Avishai Margalit distinguishes between the "literary" and the "scientific" picture of a life.[4] The scientific view judges life by measuring the quality of our experiences; the literary recovers a life as we remember it. Only the literary picture seeks out historical meaning through reflective memory.[5] Persons texture their remembered past with ethical concern, for memories contribute to self-understanding in a narrative mode. We recall past events, and as Margalit argues, even relive them, to better situate our ethical lives in the present. Objects, persons, and events from the past reappear in our memories as sources for emotional reflection. We reawaken their capacity to inform and shape our moral landscape, and situate our lives within this narrative of continuity. But it is a narrative ever reworked by present concerns and struggles, and so historical continuity is always challenged, reworked, negotiated.

Geiger claims that in this struggle for *historical* meaning, the authority of *personal* meaning commands ever more. Situating the self within this community of memory underscores the weighty influence of the dead upon the living, and their ancient power to command allegiance even in our very struggle to move beyond them. Historical memory roots authority in the evocative cadence of events and persons recalled, and in the ethical challenges that such memories expose. In locating identity within this extended community, Geiger grounds religious authority in the web of interlocking threads that bind individuals to communal practices. Historical memory is less personal than shared—it is a kind of historical fabric that, while torn and frayed, still manages to weave broader cultural trends within self-reflection and remembering. Memories are surely personal, and convey meaning in and through private moments and places. But reflective memories in a narrative mode require more than a private language of meaning; they engage broader sites of value that texture and inform personal identity. The authority of personal meaning binds the self to communal frameworks that enable and support it.

Yet we often recall the past in ways that conceal the social context of our reflections, and these narratives in turn appear far more nostalgic and clean. Loyalty to a moral ideal often betrays a blindness to cultural tensions and historical contingency. Geiger himself appeals to a "natural sense" of Scripture that evokes the moral purity of the ancient prophets. Even as he criticizes the rabbis of the Mishnah and Talmud for replacing this inner spirituality with the "outer" life of law and ritual, Geiger transforms the "natural sense" into the more immediate experiential relation of the self and God. But this immediate experience also evokes the individual, expressive, and spiritual commitments noted by those sovereign selves in Cohen and Eisen's study. Those Jews describe their relations to God in ways divorced from their cultural and social moorings, as Geiger did himself in his account of the "natural sense" of Scripture.

So it is all the more important that Geiger rejected this solitary religious experience in his *Urschrift* to better account for the political struggles embedded in sacred texts. Rather than assume a natural sense that later readers corrupted, Geiger now claimed that revisionary readings go all the way down, as it were, to the biblical core. Biblical meaning appears natural only because particular readings won out. Geiger recovers those lost interpretations in order to reconstitute the cultural and political debates that form the textual background. Traces of those debates lie within the biblical text and in its many translations. Sacred texts become so, Geiger argues in his *Urschrift,* because they mask the social strains that produce textual readings and revisions. The Hebrew Bible apparently harbors natural and sacred meanings; but underneath lurks an *Urschrift* shot through with cultural debate and social struggle. So too, then, are individual religious experiences embedded in this social fabric.

How can the archaeology of textual history challenge and shape Jewish historical memory? For Geiger, the Bible is a public document always already shaped and reworked by a community of readers. He situates the text within a public discourse rooted in political and social claims. When modern readers re-enact this public struggle over textual meaning, they revivify (to employ Margalit's language)[6] biblical religious politics. They bring to life the cultural struggles that animated ancient Israelite society, and color them with modern concerns and desires. Historical memory shapes this textual dialectic in revisiting the lost meanings suppressed by the canonical text. For by reconstituting that memory to include forgotten cultural and political struggles, Geiger enchants a world deadened by the written word. The biblical text comes alive in its political depth and cultural richness. It can once again serve as an authority for personal meaning as readers situate their religious lives within the broader landscape of Geiger's *Urschrift.*

But if Geiger reconnected with one political party—as he did in his "Sadducees and Pharisees" article—then he also pointed to how communities of memory inform personal meaning. To read means to locate the self within a communal discourse of cultural struggle; it is to place one's self within a historical community of readers. If Geiger imagines his liberal readers as devoted followers of the Pharisees of old, he also reawakens a sense of historical continuity and struggle. Personal meanings are never entirely individual; they are embedded within a tradition of reading practices. When Geiger exposes those practices in his *Urschrift,* he invites a practice of religious wrestling that confronts, even as it continues, the biblical legacy.

In Geiger's world of bourgeois sensibility and refinement, only middle-class Jewish males could perform this sense of religious wrestling. His reading of female and male biblical characters reveals the powerful hold of nostalgia and private innocence. If public life proved demanding and lonely, as it was for Geiger in Wiesbaden and, at times, in Breslau and Frankfurt, then males could imaginatively recoup that lost stature in the private world of home and family. Women could wrestle with their biblical heritage only as enablers of male ritual performance. They harnessed their natural feminine spirituality to strengthen the public moral life of their husbands and sons. Yet I argued in Chapter 3 that even as Geiger's idealism underwrites this view of feminine interiority and male public practice, his gendered politics effectively denies it. For ritual performance determines and shapes feminine spirituality—the precise inverse of what Geiger's religious idealism demands. Public males delimit the scope and power of the inner private life.

This deconstructive gendered reading suggests a performative model of ritual practice. We should reject Geiger's religious idealism, and the politics it establishes and supports, and instead reconsider how public ritual informs the meaning of religious ideals. Geiger believes we begin with some original moral idea, and then seek to embody it in ritual. But he also exposes how ritual practices shape the meaning things have for us. Modern readers need not accept Geiger's gendered preferences to recognize how material performances elicit strong emotional attachments. The act itself confers meaning and religious authority. But for rituals to deliver a sense of *personal* meaning, they must be as textured and open as the persons performing them. Religious practice is surely optional, in the sense of being noncompulsory and diverse. But even the moderately affiliated Jews that Cohen and Eisen track in their study discover meaning in ritual acts, such that "practice is seen as a potent source of meaning in its own right, one which may stimulate the quest for reasons which make sense of it."[7]

I am none too sure that such a quest will take place; nor am I convinced that it should. For the personal meaning within the practice "in its own right" may be enough to center and captivate modern religious lives. It can do so precisely because Jews enact this practice in communities—even if those communities reflect more familial attachments. Rituals open the self to other public actors, and move persons to seek recognition from a community (or a family) of practitioners. Even the most private of rituals are shared in the sense that they adopt, revise, or challenge communal norms and cultural practices. A performative model of ritual would help the post-modern self to recognize the social location of ritual acts. Embedding the self in local communities of practice, religious ritual dramatizes the social movements of personal identity. The authority of personal meaning need not appeal to reasons, moral or otherwise. Instead, persons can respond to the reflective emotional triggers of memory and community elicited in ritual practice.

It is precisely this personal but shared sense of memory and meaning that the liberal rabbis of the 1840s rejected in favor of an overarching institutional framework. The failure of the three rabbinical conferences had less to do with their stature than with their lack of rootedness. Holdheim's dismissal of dietary eating requirements, and Geiger's heated response to it, illustrate well the diverging opinions between the liberal rabbinic establishment and Geiger's contextual approach to rabbinic authority. In his search for authentic rabbinic leadership, Holdheim appealed to general moral and religious principles that would obligate by pure rational force. If the dietary laws were both historically outmoded and irrational, then Jews would do well to abandon them altogether. Geiger rebuffed Holdheim's conclusions because the sources of religious authority go further down than logical analysis. Recall Geiger's message:

> This too cannot be denied: the dietary laws have settled so deeply in the entire Jewish community that until now only a tiny part had not considered it as a central pillar of Judaism. But for the overwhelming majority of those who have actually given up the observance wholly or at times, and under various circumstances, the authority to ignore this regulation of Judaism has not been found in another interpretation of Judaism, but instead in their individual freedom.[8]

Jewish dietary laws, embedded "so deeply" in communal practices, shape Jewish identity. But even for the very few who have abandoned these restrictions, the authority for doing so lies less in "another interpretation of Judaism," and far more in the "various circumstances" that inform individual conscience. Rabbis cannot instruct or lead from afar, much less command through scholarly argument and committee. They must engage modern Jews in their "individual freedom," and in their appeal to that "sovereign self" who authorizes through personal decree.

Geiger defended the "Jewish-theological writer" as the embedded and engaged local rabbi who situated individual freedom within the broader frameworks of local and communal interests. Even in Geiger's criticism of Zunz's kosher practices, he appealed to the social context of the dietary laws. For Geiger could well understand how Zunz, as the leader of a local Jewish community, could observe Kashrut as a communal standard—one that enacted a communal consensus of valued observance. He could not comprehend, however, how Zunz could ground his practice in what were, to Geiger, outmoded rational principles. If those dietary laws are indeed rational, then so too the practices, according to Geiger's religious idealism. But the meaning of those laws is best reflected in the performance of them. So too, rabbinic leadership flows from within communal practices, and not from standards adjudicated and agreed upon by abstract thinkers and institutions. In this, Geiger echoed the concerns and challenges of the lay responses to the rabbinical conferences. For they too defended communal consensus in the face of rabbinic usurped authority, and sought to recoup that authority within local attachments and deliberation. For these protesters, and for Geiger as well, rabbinic authority lies within local practicing communities.

Geiger envisioned a far more decentered model of Jewish leadership than someone like Holdheim could stomach. For Geiger's model suggests that local communal autonomy outstrips the demands from organizational centers. This is already the case today for many moderately affiliated Jews in America. Synagogue affiliation relies more on local and dedicated communities, and much less on institutional relations and commitments.[9] Geiger, I imagine, would neither be surprised nor worried. Indeed, as local religious communities creatively determine the shape and breadth of their practices, they broaden their appeal to the various ways in which modern Jews express their identities. Rabbinic leadership can help create spaces of authority, such that the modern Jewish self locates authenticity in shared communal practices and concerns. The authority of Jewish leadership lies in these openings of the self to a world beyond it.

In moving beyond more insular concerns, Jews of the nineteenth century, and certainly their descendants in the twentieth, desired an education that opened doors to secular pursuits and goods. The parents of Geiger's students in Breslau sought "salon men" who, learned in music, dance, and philosophy, could easily move within the cultured circles of European high society. Geiger would have to fight for his Jewish schools in the language of personal fulfillment. But he also channeled that discourse toward a more communal understanding of human flourishing. For Geiger claimed that "[o]ne belongs to humanity through belonging to a particular circle, in which and for which and *by means* of which one acts for the whole."[10] Cultured Jews become so through local attachments, and do not gain some imagined "world citizenship" by abandoning these commitments. To better convince the Breslau parents, and even more the children educated in his schools, Geiger appealed to personal meanings that would inspire commitment to local Jewish communities. He revealed just how situated and rooted those meanings are within communal practices of learning.

If contemporary Jews recognize only the "sovereign self," then Geiger inextricably grounds those selves in local communities of meaning and memory. They become the cultured selves that they are in the local communities that support and shape them. This communal practice of human flourishing provides the context within which the authority of personal meaning acquires strength. For if catechisms instruct through moral and religious ideas, then Geiger's "implicit" model appeals to personal memories and narratives. But it also relates those meanings to the "explicit" context of textual traditions and communities. Geiger's Jewish education exposes how personal meaning correlates with social life and practice. In a very different sense of moving beyond, Geiger's education dislodges the sovereign self and reconnects it to the goods and values of communal life.

Individualism may be the first language of much contemporary Jewry, but modernity belies a second language that situates the self within broader circles of commitment.[11] Geiger's liberal Judaism appeals to the authority of personal meaning in order to recenter those meanings within communal practices. Historical Judaism connects the individual to a moral tradition that inspires and supports communities of memory. Sacred texts absorb political and cultural debates that inform, even as they are dialectically shaped by, contemporary reading practices. Rituals expose the material cultural expressions of the self, and situate it within a performance of public meaning. Rabbis harness this public energy to better elicit the shared import of personal meaning. And Jewish education centers the self within a map of cultural expectations, and builds the avenues for human flourishing. This is how religious authority should be lived—in historical memories and reading practices, in the embodied rituals and local communities that provoke and obligate in their own right, and in the education of social actors who flourish within strong communal attachments. These are the "thick relations"[12] that inspire Geiger's liberal Judaism. Jewish authority is in the making of those relations, in the everyday practices that yield personal meanings that command, inspire, and ground modern Jewish identity.

Notes

Introduction

1. See Michael Meyer, "Rabbi Gedaliah Tiktin and the Orthodox Segment of the Breslau Community, 1845–1854," *Michael: The Diaspora Research Institute of Tel Aviv University* 2 (1973), 92–107; Meyer, "Universalism and Jewish Unity in the Thought of Abraham Geiger," in *The Role of Religion in Modern Jewish History,* edited by Jacob Katz (Cambridge: Association for Jewish Studies, 1975), 91–104; Meyer, "Abraham Geiger's Historical Judaism," in *New Perspectives on Abraham Geiger,* edited by Jakob Petuchowski (Cincinnati: Hebrew Union College Press, 1975), 3–16; Meyer, "Reform Thinkers and Their German Intellectual Context," in *The Jewish Response to German Culture,* edited by Jehuda Reinharz and Walter Schatzberg (Hanover-London: University Press of New England, 1985), 64–84; Meyer, *Response to Modernity: A History of the Reform Movement in Judaism* (Oxford: Oxford University Press, 1988), 89–99; and the collection of essays in Meyer, *Judaism within Modernity: Essays on Jewish History and Religion* (Detroit: Wayne State University Press, 2001); Jay Harris, *How Do We Know This? Midrash and the Fragmentation of Modern Judaism* (Albany: State University of New York Press, 1995), 157–65, 184–90; Jakob Petuchowski, *Prayerbook Reform in Europe: The Liturgy of European Liberal and Reform Judaism* (New York: The World Union for Progressive Judaism, Ltd., 1968); Petuchowski, ed., *New Perspectives on Abraham Geiger* (Cincinnati: Hebrew Union College Press, 1975); Petuchowski, "Abraham Geiger and Samuel Holdheim: Their Differences in Germany and Repercussions in America," *Leo Baeck Institute Year Book* 22 (1977), 139–59; Ismar Schorsch, "Emancipation and the Crisis of Religious Authority: The Emergence of the Modern Rabbinate," in *Revolution and Evolution: 1848 in German-Jewish History,* edited by Werner Mosse, Arnold Paucker, and Reinhard Rurup (Tübingen: J. C. B. Mohr, 1981), 205–47; Schorsch, "The Emergence of Historical Consciousness in Modern Judaism," *Leo Baeck Institute Year Book* 28 (1983), 413–37; Schorsch, "Scholarship in the Service of Reform," *Leo Baeck Institute Year Book* 35 (1990), 73–101; Andreas Gotzmann, *Jüdisches Recht im kulturellen Prozeß* (Jerusalem/Tübingen: J. C. B. Mohr/Leo Baeck Institut, 1997); and Gotzmann, *Eigenheit und Einheit* (Leiden: Brill, 2002).

2. Ludwig Geiger, *Abraham Geiger: Leben und Lebenswerk* (Berlin: Georg Reimer, 1910). See also Max Wiener, *Abraham Geiger and Liberal Judaism: The Challenge of the Nineteenth Century* (Philadelphia: The Jewish Publication Society of America, 1962).

3. Susannah Heschel, *Abraham Geiger and the Jewish Jesus* (Chicago: University of Chicago Press, 1998), 2–3. For the notion of "counterhistory," see Amos Funkenstein, *Perceptions of Jewish History* (Berkeley: University of California Press, 1993), 36–40; and David

Biale, *Gershom Scholem: Kabbalah and Counter-History* (Cambridge, Mass.: Harvard University Press, 1979).

4. Heschel, *Abraham Geiger and the Jewish Jesus,* 23.

5. Susannah Heschel, "Revolt of the Colonized: Abraham Geiger's *Wissenschaft des Judentums* as a Challenge to Christian Hegemony in the Academy," *New German Critique* 77 (1999), 64.

6. Meyer, *Response to Modernity,* 89.

7. Ismar Schorsch, "Ideology and History in the Age of Emancipation," in *Heinrich Graetz: The Structure of Jewish History and Other Essays,* edited by Ismar Schorsch (New York: Jewish Theological Seminary of America, 1975), 1–62; see also Heschel, *Abraham Geiger and the Jewish Jesus,* 220.

8. See Geiger's letter to M. A. Stern (August 1843) in Abraham Geiger, *Nachgelassene Schriften* V, edited by Ludwig Geiger (Berlin: Louis Gerschel, 1878), 168.

9. Abraham Geiger, *Das Judenthum und seine Geschichte* (Breslau: Schletter, 1865), 9–10. All translations are mine and follow closely upon, though at times deviate from, Abraham Geiger, *Judaism and Its History in Two Parts* (Lanham, Md.: University Press of America, Inc., 1985), 21. Hereafter, citations will be noted as Geiger, *Judenthum,* 9–10; *Judaism,* 21. The first six lectures were originally published in Geiger's journal, *Jüdische Zeitschrift für Wissenschaft und Leben* 2 (1863).

10. See Arnold Eisen and Steven Cohen, *The Jew Within: Self, Family, and Community in America* (Bloomington: Indiana University Press, 2000). I will offer further reflections on Cohen and Eisen's study in the conclusion to this book.

11. I traverse only summarily here the biographical history that Ludwig Geiger, in his *Abraham Geiger: Leben und Lebenswerk,* has well documented. For excellent and succinct accounts of Geiger's life, see Heschel, *Abraham Geiger and the Jewish Jesus,* 23–49; and Meyer, *Response to Modernity,* 89–99. Note as well Ludwig Geiger, "Abraham Geigers Briefe an J. Derenbourg, 1833–1848," *Allgemeine Zeitung des Judentums* 60, no. 5 (1896), 52–55.

12. Geiger, *Nachgelassene Schriften* V, 4.

13. Heschel, *Abraham Geiger and the Jewish Jesus,* 24.

14. Geiger, *Nachgelassene Schriften* V, 4–7.

15. Ibid., 6.

16. Ibid., 17–19.

17. Heschel, *Abraham Geiger and the Jewish Jesus,* 50–52.

18. Ibid., 31.

19. Geiger, *Nachgelassene Schriften* V, 67, 75, 77.

20. Ibid., 3; Heschel, *Abraham Geiger and the Jewish Jesus,* 43–44.

21. Ludwig Geiger, *Abraham Geiger: Leben und Lebenswerk,* 176; Heschel, *Abraham Geiger and the Jewish Jesus,* 43–44.

22. Heschel, *Abraham Geiger and the Jewish Jesus,* 44.

23. See, for example, Michael Berger, *Rabbinic Authority* (Oxford and New York: Oxford University Press, 1998); Bruce Chilton and Jacob Neusner, *Types of Authority in Formative Christianity and Judaism* (London & New York: Routledge, 1999); Schorsch, "Emancipation and the Crisis of Religious Authority: The Emergence of the Modern Rabbinate," 205–47; and Jeffrey Stout, *Flight from Authority* (Notre Dame, Ind.: University of Notre Dame Press, 1981).

24. Note such diverse texts as Terry Eagleton, *The Ideology of the Aesthetic* (Oxford:

Basil Blackwell, 1990); Stuart Hampshire, *Innocence and Experience* (Cambridge, Mass.: Harvard University Press, 1989); Franz Rosenzweig, *The Star of Redemption* (Notre Dame & London: University of Notre Dame Press, 1970); Ismar Schorsch, *From Text to Context: The Turn to History in Modern Judaism* (Hanover, N.H.: Brandeis University Press, 1994); and Charles Taylor, *Sources of the Self: The Making of Modern Identity* (Cambridge: Cambridge University Press, 1989).

25. The term, as well as the thorough sociological analysis, has been made famous by Peter Berger, *The Sacred Canopy* (New York: Anchor Books, 1969).

26. For conceptions of *Bildung* as the cultivated personality, and its influence upon nineteenth-century German conceptions of the self, see David Sorkin, "Wilhelm von Humboldt: The Theory and Practice of Self-Formation (*Bildung*), 1791–1810," *Journal of the History of Ideas* 44 (January 1983), 55–73; and Sorkin, *The Transformation of German Jewry, 1780–1840* (Oxford: Oxford University Press, 1987).

27. Moses Mendelssohn, *Jerusalem, or On Religious Power and Judaism* (Hanover, N.H.: University Press of New England, 1983), 89–94.

28. Arnold Eisen, "Divine Legislation as 'Ceremonial Script': Mendelssohn on the Commandments," *AJS Review* 15, no. 2 (Fall 1990), 239–67.

29. Mendelssohn, *Jerusalem,* 127, 133.

30. Max Weber, *Economy and Society* I (Berkeley, Los Angeles, London: University of California Press, 1978), 241–44, 266–67; Max Weber, *Wirtschaft und Gesellschaft* I (Tübingen: J. C. B. Mohr, 1956), 140–41, 155–56. For a helpful article on Weber's notion of charisma, see Edward Shils, "Charisma, Order, and Status," *American Sociological Review* 30, no. 2 (1965), 199–213.

31. Weber, *Economy and Society* II, 1112–13; Weber, *Wirtschaft und Gesellschaft* II, 663.

32. See Roy Rappaport, *Ecology, Meaning, and Religion* (Richmond, Calif.: North Atlantic Books, 1979).

1. Historical Memory and the Authority of Religious Judaism

1. See Geiger's literary correspondence in Ludwig Geiger, "Abraham Geigers Briefe an J. Derenbourg, 1833–1848."

2. See Heschel, *Abraham Geiger and the Jewish Jesus,* 33.

3. Wiener, *Abraham Geiger and Liberal Judaism,* 86 (letter dated November 8, 1836); and Heschel, *Abraham Geiger and the Jewish Jesus,* 33.

4. See Arnold Eisen, "Constructing the Usable Past: The Idea of 'Tradition' in Twentieth-Century American Judaism," in *The Uses of Tradition,* edited by Jack Wertheimer (New York and Jerusalem: The Jewish Theological Seminary of America, 1992), 429–61.

5. Jan Assmann, *Moses the Egyptian: The Memory of Egypt in Western Monotheism* (Cambridge, Mass.: Harvard University Press, 1997), 22, 9. Also see his *Die Mosaische Unterscheidung oder der Preis des Monotheismus* (Munich: Carl Hanser, 2003).

6. The literature on historical memory is enormous. The works that have been most insightful and pertinent to this chapter are Assmann, *Moses the Egyptian;* Assmann, "Collective Memory and Cultural Identity," *New German Critique* 65 (1995), 125–33; Richard Bernstein, *Freud and the Legacy of Moses* (Cambridge: Cambridge University Press, 1998); Jacques Derrida, *Archive Fever: A Freudian Impression* (Chicago and London: University of Chicago Press, 1995); Amos Funkenstein, *Perceptions of Jewish History* (Berke-

ley: University of California Press, 1993); Wulf Kansteiner, "Hayden White's Critique of the Writing of History," *History and Theory* 32 (1993), 273–95; Daniel Schacter, ed., *Memory Distortion: How Minds, Brains, and Societies Reconstruct the Past* (Cambridge, Mass.: Harvard University Press, 1995); Yosef Hayim Yerushalmi, *Zakhor: Jewish History and Jewish Memory* (Seattle and London: University of Washington Press, 1982 and 1996); Yerushalmi, *Freud's Moses: Judaism Terminable and Interminable* (New Haven and London: Yale University Press, 1991); Yerushalmi, "The Moses of Freud and the Moses of Schoenberg: On Words, Idolatry, and Psychoanalysis," *The Psychoanalytic Study of the Child* 47 (1992), 1–20.

7. Assmann, *Moses the Egyptian,* 9.

8. Abraham Geiger, "Samuel Holdheim: Sein Leben und seine Werke, von Immanuel Ritter. Eine Recension," *Jüdische Zeitschrift für Wissenschaft und Leben* 3 (1864–65), 216, where Geiger compares his work to Holdheim's more "dogmatische, dialektische Natur" by stating: "meine Richtung war und ist eine überwiegend historische."

9. Heschel, *Abraham Geiger and the Jewish Jesus,* 40; Jakob Petuchowski, "Abraham Geiger, the Reform Jewish Liturgist," in *New Perspectives on Abraham Geiger,* 42. On the historical background for *Judaism and Its History* and the prayer books, as well as general discussion, see Ludwig Geiger, *Abraham Geiger: Leben und Lebenswerk,* 144–52, 184–89.

10. Abraham Geiger, "Das Judenthum unserer Zeit und die Bestrebungen in ihm," *Wissenschaft Zeitschrift für Jüdische Theologie* 1 (1835), 12.

11. Ibid., 2.

12. Ibid., 3.

13. See Meyer, *Response to Modernity,* 70–72, 201; and Jay Harris, *Nachman Krochmal: Guiding the Perplexed of the Modern Age* (New York: New York University Press, 1991); Emil Fackenheim, "Samuel Hirsch and Hegel," in *Studies in Nineteenth-Century Jewish Intellectual History,* edited by Alexander Altmann (Cambridge, Mass.: Harvard University Press, 1964), 171–201; and Fackenheim, *The Religious Dimension in Hegel's Thought* (Bloomington: Indiana University Press, 1967).

14. Schorsch, "Ideology and History in the Age of Emancipation," 9.

15. Abraham Geiger, "Jüdische Geschichte: Recension," *Wissenschaft Zeitschrift für Jüdische Theologie* 1 (1835), 175.

16. For a helpful overview of the terms and central issues of this kind of scholarship, see Schorsch, "The Emergence of Historical Consciousness in Modern Judaism," 413–37; and Ismar Schorsch, "The Ethos of Modern Jewish Scholarship," *Leo Baeck Institute Year Book* 35 (1990), 55–71.

17. Schorsch, "The Emergence of Historical Consciousness in Modern Judaism," 416–19.

18. See Abraham Geiger, "Grätz' Geschichte," *Jüdische Zeitschrift für Wissenschaft und Leben* 6 (1868), 220–22.

19. For helpful background to this essay, as well as Jewish and non-Jewish responses to it, see Nathan Rotenstreich, "The Bruno Bauer Controversy," *Leo Baeck Institute Year Book* 4 (1959), 3–36.

20. A published book under the same title appeared the following year in 1843.

21. See, for example, Abraham Geiger, "Die Aufgabe der Gegenwart," *Wissenschaftliche Zeitschrift für jüdische Theologie* 5 (1844), 1–35.

22. See Schorsch, "Ideology and History in the Age of Emancipation," 19–21; and Schorsch, "Emancipation and the Crisis of Religious Authority: The Emergence of the Modern Rabbinate," 238–42.

23. Bruno Bauer, "Die Juden-Frage," *Deutsche Jahrbücher für Wissenschaft und Kunst,* no. 274–82, Nov. 17–26 (1842), 1102.

24. Ibid., 1093–94.

25. Ibid., 1094.

26. Ibid., 1096.

27. Ibid., 1096–97.

28. Ibid., 1107.

29. Ibid., 1113.

30. Gotthold Salomon, *Bruno Bauer und seine gehaltlose Kritik über die Judenfrage* (Hamburg: Perthes-Besser und Mauke, 1843), 38–40.

31. Ibid., 47–48.

32. Ibid., 73.

33. Ibid., 48.

34. Abraham Geiger, "Bruno Bauer und die Juden," *Wissenschaftliche Zeitschrift für jüdische Theologie* 5 (1844), 199; and Rotenstreich, "The Bruno Bauer Controversy," 11.

35. For a notion of counterhistory as "a form of polemic in which the sources of the adversary are exploited and turned 'gegen den Strich,' see Heschel, *Abraham Geiger and the Jewish Jesus,* 14.

36. Geiger, "Bruno Bauer und die Juden," 204–206, 210.

37. Ibid., 211–12.

38. Ibid., 335.

39. Abraham Geiger, "Der Kampf christlicher Theologen gegen die bürgerliche Gleichstellung der Juden, namentlich mit Bezug auf Anton Theodor Hartmann," *Wissenschaftliche Zeitschrift für jüdische Theologie* 1 (1835), 349.

40. See, for example, Geiger, "Bruno Bauer und die Juden," 332. Also see Schorsch, "Ideology and History in the Age of Emancipation," 8–9, for his discussion of Hegelian influence on Jewish historical writing in nineteenth-century Germany.

41. Geiger, "Bruno Bauer und die Juden," 200.

42. Ludwig Geiger, *Leben und Lebenswerk,* 184–85.

43. Geiger, *Judenthum,* 1; *Judaism,* 13.

44. Friedrich Schleiermacher, *On Religion: Speeches to Its Cultured Despisers* (San Francisco: Harper & Row, 1958); and Heschel, *Abraham Geiger and the Jewish Jesus,* 147.

45. See also the excellent discussion by Andreas Gotzmann on Judaism as a religion in his *Eigenheit und Einheit* (Leiden: Brill, 2002), 111–13, 184–211.

46. Geiger, *Judenthum,* 2; *Judaism,* 14.

47. See Arnold Eisen, "Secularization, 'Spirit,' and the Strategies of Modern Jewish Faith," in *Jewish Spirituality II: From Sixteenth Century Revival to the Present,* edited by Arthur Green (New York: Crossroad Publishing Company, 1987), 283–316.

48. Geiger, *Judenthum,* 7; *Judaism,* 18–19.

49. Ibid., 7; 19.

50. Ibid., 9; 21.

51. See Friedrich Schleiermacher, *On Religion: Speeches to Its Cultured Despisers.*

52. See Wayne Proudfoot, *Religious Experience* (Berkeley: University of California Press, 1985), xv, 1–40.

53. Geiger, *Judenthum,* 2; *Judaism,* 14.

54. Ibid., 9; 21.

55. Ibid., 9–10; 21.

56. Ibid., 10; 22.

57. Ibid., 11; 23.

58. This is true, as well, for Schleiermacher's account of Christianity as the preeminent religion of feeling.

59. For a short review of this literature and the general terms of comparison, see Ken Koltun-Fromm, *Moses Hess and Modern Jewish Identity* (Bloomington: Indiana University Press, 2001), 76–78; Peter Gay, *The Enlightenment, an Interpretation: The Rise of Modern Paganism* (New York: Alfred Knopf, 1966), 33; and the foundational article by Matthew Arnold, "Hebraism and Hellenism," in *The Works of Matthew Arnold* (London: Macmillan and Co., 1903), 120–40.

60. Geiger, *Judenthum,* 15–17; *Judaism,* 26–29.

61. Ibid., 17; 29.

62. Ibid., 26; 38.

63. I will be employing the term *religious Judaism* in this sense throughout the chapter. *Religious Judaism* always refers to Geiger's understanding of the term as the historical embodiment of universal moral truths.

64. Geiger, *Judenthum,* 19; *Judaism,* 31.

65. Abraham Geiger, "Nothwendigkeit und Maass einer Reform des jüdischen Gottesdienstes," in *Nachgelassene Schriften* I, 205. Also see Jakob Petuchowski's translation of this passage in his "Abraham Geiger, The Reform Jewish Liturgist," in *New Perspectives on Abraham Geiger,* 49.

66. Abraham Geiger, "Unser Gottesdienst," *Jüdische Zeitschrift für Wissenschaft und Leben* 6 (1868), 2.

67. Ibid., 4.

68. Funkenstein, *Perceptions of Jewish History,* 20.

69. Yerushalmi, *Zakhor,* 94.

70. Ibid., 116. For an insightful critique of Yerushalmi's reading of Freud and the historian's craft, see Derrida, *Archive Fever,* 33–81.

71. Heinrich Graetz, *Die Geschichte der Juden* XI (Leipzig: Oskar Leiner, 1870), 449; Heinrich Graetz, *History of the Jews* V (Philadelphia: Jewish Publication Society of America, 1895), 590.

72. Schorsch, "Ideology and History in the Age of Emancipation," 31–32. See also Harris, *How Do We Know This?* 184–87.

73. Graetz, *Die Geschichte der Juden* XI, 502–503; Graetz, *History of the Jews* V, 626–27.

74. Schorsch, "Ideology and History in the Age of Emancipation," 37.

75. Ibid.; and Harris, *How Do We Know This?* 179–86.

76. I am referring to the first volume in the series (volume I) rather than the first published volume, since Graetz published volume IV in 1853 as the first of his many volumes. The fourth volume covers the important period of early Christianity and emerging rabbinic Judaism from 70–500 C.E. By publishing the fourth volume first, Graetz clearly wanted to weigh in on the most controversial period of religious history in the West. See Schorsch, "Ideology and History in the Age of Emancipation," 46–47; and Harris, *How Do We Know This?* 178.

77. See Schorsch, "Scholarship in the Service of Reform," 73–101, especially 74–78; and Schorsch, "From Wolfenbuttel to Wissenschaft: The Divergent Paths of Israel Markus Jost and Leopold Zunz," *Leo Baeck Institute Year Book* 22 (1977), 109–28.

78. I. M. Jost, *Geschichte der Israeliten seit der Zeit der Maccabäer bis auf unsre Tage, nach den Quellen bearbeitet* (Berlin: Schlesinger, 1820), 1–2.

79. Graetz, *Die Geschichte der Juden* XI, 456; Graetz, *History of the Jews* V, 595.

80. Abraham Geiger, *Nachgelassene Schriften* V, 76.

81. Also see Gotzmann, *Eigenheit und Einheit,* 189–90, for his view of Graetz and Geiger's reading of Jost.

82. See Schorsch, "Ideology and History in the Age of Emancipation," 5, especially fn. 6: "Indeed, the title [*Geschichte der Israeliten*] bespeaks the widespread embarrassment of emancipated Jews with the word *Juden,* which had become a pejorative term." Jost discussed his use of the term *Israeliten* in the opening pages of his work, arguing that for historical reasons the term fits the national group, and only as a religious community did *Israeliten* become *Juden.* See Jost, *Geschichte der Israeliten,* xii; and Heschel, *Abraham Geiger and the Jewish Jesus,* 133. Note as well that in his *Schulchan Aruch* (1833–1840), a text that explores Talmudic readings of the Bible, Michael Creizenach (1789–1842) discusses this issue on the very first page, and opts for the term *Judenthum* despite its "nasty and even suspicious sense." Creizenach will instead use the term in its "true sense." See Michael Creizenach, *Schulchan Aruch* I (Frankfurt am Main: Andreä, 1833–1840), v.

83. Graetz, *Die Geschichte der Juden* XI, 449; Graetz, *History of the Jews* V, 589–91.

84. The only interesting exception to this rule that I discovered was Graetz's labeling of "Abraham, the *Hebrew.*" Graetz does not italicize Abraham's name, but only the appending descriptive term. See Graetz, *Die Geschichte der Juden* I, 449.

85. Graetz, *Die Geschichte der Juden* XI, 448; Graetz, *History of the Jews* V, 589. I have altered the English translation somewhat to better express the original German.

86. Graetz, *Die Geschichte der Juden* III, 272–73, 281–82; Graetz, *History of the Jews* II, 141–42, 148–49. Also see Heschel, *Abraham Geiger and the Jewish Jesus,* 131–37, 151.

87. Abraham Geiger, "Umschau," *Jüdische Zeitschrift für Wissenschaft und Leben* 4 (1866), 145–50.

88. Ibid., 145–46.

89. Ibid., 146.

90. Ibid. See also Schorsch, "Ideology and History in the Age of Emancipation," 47, where he quotes the more extended passage in full.

91. Geiger, "Umschau," 146.

92. Ibid., 147–48.

93. Ibid., 146.

94. Manuel Joël, Geiger's rabbinic successor in Breslau, also recognized this tension in Geiger. See Manuel Joël, *Zur Orientirung in der Cultusfrage* (Breslau: Schletter, 1869); and Geiger's quick refutation of inconsistency in Abraham Geiger, "Etwas über Glauben und Beten: Zu Schutz und Trutz," *Jüdische Zeitschrift für Wissenschaft und Leben* 7 (1869), 1–59.

95. See Petuchowski, "Abraham Geiger, The Reform Jewish Liturgist," 44–48; and Petuchowski, *Prayerbook Reform in Europe,* 31–43. For an overview of the Hamburg Temple prayer book and the controversy surrounding it, see Meyer, *Response to Modernity,* 57–61, 114–19. Also note David Ellenson's account of Geiger's critique of the Hamburg liturgy in his fine article, "The *Israelitische Gebetbücher* of Abraham Geiger and Manuel Joël: A Study in Nineteenth-Century German-Jewish Communal Liturgy and Religion," *Leo Baeck Institute Year Book* 44 (1999), 143–64, especially 150–56.

96. Geiger, *Nothwendigkeit,* 215.

97. Abraham Geiger, "Die religiösen Thaten der Gegenwart im Judenthume," *Wissenschaftliche Zeitschrift für jüdische Theologie* 6 (1847), 2.

98. See Meyer, *Response to Modernity,* 91.

99. Petuchowski, *Prayerbook Reform in Europe,* 32.

100. See David Ellenson, *Between Tradition and Culture: The Dialectics of Modern Jew-*

ish Religion and Identity (Atlanta: Scholars Press, 1994), 60–61, 71–73; and Ellenson, "The *Israelitische Gebetbücher* of Abraham Geiger and Manuel Joël," 157–58.

101. See Gotzmann, *Eigenheit und Einheit,* 192–201, especially 194.

102. Petuchowski, *Prayerbook Reform in Europe,* 33–34. See my Chapter 4, "Rabbinic Authority," for a more lengthy discussion of some of these issues.

103. Geiger, *Unser Gottesdienst,* 7–8.

104. David Philipson, *The Reform Movement in Judaism* (New York: Ktav Publishing House, 1931), 168–69. Also see Arnold Eisen, *Rethinking Modern Judaism* (Chicago: University of Chicago Press, 1998), 124–25, for the consensus scholarly assessment that Geiger did not appreciate, as Zacharias Frankel did, how the Hebrew language was "interwoven with the very life of Judaism."

105. Geiger, *Unser Gottesdienst,* 8.

106. Petuchowski, *Prayerbook Reform in Europe,* 151; Abraham Geiger, ed., *Israelitisches Gebetbuch für den öffentlichen Gottesdienst im ganzen Jahre* (Breslau: Julius Hainauer, 1854), vii.

107. David Ellenson emphasizes the political nature of prayer-book reform, and the compromises necessary to appease all members of the Jewish community. See Ellenson, *Between Tradition and Culture,* 60–62.

108. Geiger, *Nothwendigkeit,* 208–209.

109. Geiger, *Unser Gottesdienst,* 10.

110. Quote taken from Petuchowski, *Prayerbook Reform in Europe,* 165. See Abraham Geiger, ed., *Israelitisches Gebetbuch für den öffentlichen Gottesdienst im ganzen Jahre* (Berlin: Louis Gerschel, 1870), viii. This section of the preface was taken from Geiger's *Denkschrift* written in 1869, and reprinted in full in Abraham Geiger, "Plan zu einem neuen Gebetbuche," *Jüdische Zeitschrift für Wissenschaft und Leben* 7 (1869), 245–46.

111. Geiger, *Israelitisches Gebetbuch* (1870), xiv.

112. Abraham Geiger, "Der Hamburger Tempelstreit, eine Zeitfrage," in *Nachgelassene Schriften* 1, 170.

113. Geiger, *Unser Gottesdienst,* 10.

114. Ibid., 12. For a similar account of the *Akedah,* see Geiger, "Etwas über Glauben und Beten: Zu Schutz und Trutz," 41. See also Ludwig Geiger, *Abraham Geiger: Leben und Lebenswerk,* 151.

115. Heschel, *Abraham Geiger and the Jewish Jesus,* 182.

116. Geiger, *Unser Gottesdienst,* 13.

117. Ibid.

118. See Heschel, *Abraham Geiger and the Jewish Jesus,* 181–82.

119. Geiger, *Unser Gottesdienst,* 14.

120. Ibid., 16.

121. Quoted from Petuchowski, *Prayerbook Reform in Europe,* 151; also see Geiger, *Israelitisches Gebetbuch* (1854), vii.

122. Geiger, *Israelitisches Gebetbuch* (1854), vii.

123. Ellenson, "The *Israelitische Gebetbücher* of Abraham Geiger and Manuel Joël," 147. See also David Ellenson, *After Emancipation: Jewish Religious Responses to Modernity* (Cincinnati: Hebrew Union College Press, 2004), 227–31, where Ellenson discusses Geiger's liturgical innovations.

124. Ellenson, "The *Israelitische Gebetbücher* of Abraham Geiger and Manuel Joël," 161, where Ellenson claims that "Joël's imitation of Geiger is also apparent in other prayers he composed. Like Geiger in 1854, Joël left the traditional Hebrew text of the first two

blessings of the *Amidah* undisturbed. However, like Geiger, he used translation as a vehicle to obviate meanings he found disturbing."

125. Note Ellenson's argument that "the translations transform the manifest content of the prayers [their "overt meanings"], while the retention of the traditional Hebrew formulas permits their symbolic associations [their "latent content"] to remain inviolate." See Ellenson, *Between Tradition and Culture,* 75.

126. For examples of how Geiger introduced his reform principles into his prayer books, see Ellenson, *Between Tradition and Culture,* 73–76.

127. Geiger, *Israelitisches Gebetbuch* (1854), 100–101. Geiger's 1870 prayer book follows the 1854 rendition.

128. See Ellenson, *Between Tradition and Culture,* 69, for the views of Mannheimer, Stein, and Samson Raphael Hirsch on resurrection of the dead in Jewish liturgy. Also see Meyer, *Response to Modernity,* 186.

129. Geiger, *Israelitisches Gebetbuch* (1854), 121. Geiger's 1870 prayer book follows the 1854 rendition.

130. The English translation is taken from *The Complete Artscroll Siddur* (New York: Mesorah Publications, 1984), 445.

131. *Gebetbuch für die öffentliche und häusliche Andacht der Israeliten, nach dem Gebrauch des Neuen Israelitischen Tempels in Hamburg* (Hamburg: B. S. Berendsohn, 1845), 75. In addition, Geiger's prayer books opened from right to left in the traditional manner, while the Hamburg prayerbooks opened from left to right.

132. Geiger, *Israelitisches Gebetbuch* (1854), 115–16. Geiger's 1870 prayer book follows the 1854 rendition.

133. Michael Sachs, ed., *Festgebete der Israeliten* (Breslau: Jacobsohn & Co., 1896), 150–51.

134. Geiger, "Etwas über Glauben und Beten."

135. See Meyer, *Response to Modernity,* 186–87.

136. I will deal more on this issue, and with Joël's essay, in Chapter 5, "Jewish Education and the Authority of Personal Meaning."

137. Geiger, "Etwas über Glauben und Beten," 19.

138. Ibid., 19–22.

139. Ibid., 31.

140. See Cohen and Eisen, *The Jew Within,* 7.

141. Ibid., 185.

142. Samuel Hirsch, *Die Humanität als Religion* (Trier: C. Troschel, 1854), 213–14; also see Ken Koltun-Fromm, "Public Religion in Samson Raphael Hirsch and Samuel Hirsch's Interpretation of Religious Symbolism," *The Journal of Jewish Thought and Philosophy* 9 (1999), 100.

143. Assmann, *Moses the Egyptian,* 9.

2. The Practice of Hermeneutical Authority

1. See Geiger's journal entry in Ludwig Geiger, *Nachgelassene Schriften* V, 13.
2. Ibid.
3. See Heschel, *Abraham Geiger and the Jewish Jesus,* 25–26.
4. Ludwig Geiger, *Nachgelassene Schriften* V, 13.
5. Heschel, *Abraham Geiger and the Jewish Jesus,* 26.
6. Bauer, "Die Juden-Frage," 1103–1104.

7. Geiger, "Bruno Bauer und die Juden," 199–234, 325–71.

8. See Harris, *How Do We Know This?* 161–62, 172.

9. Abraham Geiger, "Das Verhältniss des naturlichen Schriftsinnes zur thalmudischen Schriftdeutung," *Wissenschaftliche Zeitschrift für jüdische Theologie* 5 (1844), 53–81, 234–59. Geiger's essay, however, had already been in circulation by 1842. See Harris, *How Do We Know This?* 312 n. 84; and Schorsch, "Emancipation and the Crisis of Religious Authority: The Emergence of the Modern Rabbinate," 224 n. 60. Harris also believes that two essays (with the same title) appear in this journal, with the latter (pages 234–59) "written in response to criticism." He admits, however, that both essays maintain "the basic thesis without reservation" (312 n. 84).

10. Abraham Geiger, *Urschrift und Übersetzungen der Bibel* (Breslau: Julius Hainauer, 1857).

11. See Harris, *How Do We Know This?* 189, where despite his remark that the *Urschrift* represents "a near total transformation of his earlier thinking," Geiger still reinscribes that earlier thinking into the *Urschrift* because he recognizes "an inextricable link between the natural sense of Scripture and the stultifying conservatism of a portion of the rabbinic elite of the second century." Harris recognizes the ingenuity of the *Urschrift,* but he reads it in the terms set by his earlier essay, "Das Verhältniss des naturlichen Schriftsinnes zur thalmudischen Schriftdeutung."

12. See Schorsch, "Scholarship in the Service of Reform," 89: "The *Urschrift und Übersetzungen der Bibel,* which appeared in 1857, for all its sparkling novelty, is best treated as a continuation of Geiger's central research agenda of the thirties and forties. What ultimately distinguishes it is not so much substance but tone."

13. See Abraham Geiger, "Sadducäer und Pharisäer," *Jüdische Zeitschrift für Wissenschaft und Leben* 2 (1863), 11–54. Susannah Heschel discusses how Geiger's *Urschrift* attends to Pharisaic and Sadducean religious and political tendencies, and Christian reactions to it. This, despite admitting that "it is striking that there is little direct mention in the *Urschrift* of Christianity," a lack made up for in Geiger's 1863 essay. Yet she also claims that "Geiger's assertion of a parallel between Reform Judaism and Protestantism is common to his work, particularly in the later *Urschrift,* where he compares the Pharisees to Protestants and the Sadducees to Catholics" (36). But Geiger makes this claim in his later 1863 essay on "Sadducees and Pharisees," and not in his *Urschrift.* I will have more to say about the relationship between the *Urschrift* and the later essay, "Sadducäer und Pharisäer," later in this chapter. See Heschel, *Abraham Geiger and the Jewish Jesus,* 36, 83–98, especially 98.

14. Leopold Löw, "Review of Urschrift und Übersetzungen der Bibel," *Ben Chananja* 1 (1858), 94–95.

15. Feliz Perles, "Bibel," in *Abraham Geiger: Leben und Lebenswerk,* 318. In an article published five years after his *Urschrift,* Geiger claimed that *Symmachus* (a Greek biblical translation) clearly reflected the needs of the times, and the translator "expresses quite firmly his dogmatic convictions in his translation." See Abraham Geiger, "Symmachus, der Uebersetzer der Bibel," *Jüdische Zeitschrift für Wissenschaft und Leben* 1 (1862), 40.

16. Heschel, *Abraham Geiger and the Jewish Jesus,* 122. Note, however, that Heschel buries this astute comment in a chapter on the Tübingen school, rather than highlighting it where it should be—in an account of Geiger's *Urschrift.*

17. Abraham Geiger, "Einiges über Plan und Anordnung der Mischnah," *Wissenschaftliche Zeitschrift für jüdische Theologie* 2 (1836), 489–90.

18. Abraham Geiger, "Karaische Litteratur," *Wissenschaftliche Zeitschrift für jüdische Theologie* 2 (1836), 96–97.

19. See Harris, *How Do We Know This?* 184, 200–202, 312 fn. 84.

20. Geiger, "Das Verhältniss des naturlichen Schriftsinnes zur thalmudischen Schriftdeutung," 81. The more conservative Berlin rabbi Michael Sachs quickly understood the radical nature of Geiger's critique, and attempted to undermine it in a book published a year after Geiger's essay. See Michael Sachs, *Die religiöse Poesie der Juden in Spanien* (1845) (Berlin: M. Poppelauer, 1901), 146–62. Also see Schorsch, "Ideology and History in the Age of Emancipation," 25–26; and Harris, *How Do We Know This?* 176–77.

21. See Harris, *How Do We Know This?* 161–62, and Schorsch, "Scholarship in the Service of Reform," 86–87, for their rendering of "natural sense" as *peshat.* Schorsch even translates the German title "naturlichen Schriftsinnes" into "the Literal Meaning of Scripture."

22. Geiger, "Das Verhältniss des naturlichen Schriftsinnes zur thalmudischen Schriftdeutung," 56.

23. For a helpful summary of Geiger's position, see Harris, *How Do We Know This?* 162–63.

24. Geiger, "Das Verhältniss des naturlichen Schriftsinnes zur thalmudischen Schriftdeutung," 56–57.

25. Ibid., 58.

26. See as well Abraham Geiger, "Die nordfranzösische Exegeten-Schule im 12. Jahrhundert," in *Beiträge zur jüdischen Literatur-Geschichte* II, edited by S. L. Heilberg (Breslau: H. Sulzbach, 1847), 1–44. Throughout this article, Geiger speaks of the "natürlichen Sinn" or "natürlichen Verständnisse" as the "peshat" reading (3).

27. Geiger, "Das Verhältniss des naturlichen Schriftsinnes zur thalmudischen Schriftdeutung," 244, 248.

28. Abraham Geiger, "Ist der Streit in der Synagoge ein Zeichen von ihrem Zerfalle oder von ihrem neuerwachten Leben?" *Wissenschaftliche Zeitschrift für jüdische Theologie* 5 (1844), 147–48.

29. See, for example, Abraham Geiger, "Commentary on the *Urschrift* (Hebrew)," in *Ozar Nechmad,* edited by Ignaz Blumenfeld (Vienna: Knöpflmacher & Söhne, 1860), 1–15, especially 12–15.

30. Schorsch speaks of Geiger being "propelled by the exhilaration of fresh insight" and quotes a letter from Geiger to Steinschneider in March 1855, in which Geiger apologizes for his recent silence: "How can you grumble with someone in love . . . No, my dear friend, I am really quite serious; I am in love . . . I'm in love with my work. I am so completely immersed in it, it absorbs me so fully that I neither hear nor see anything else." Quote taken from Schorsch, "Scholarship in the Service of Reform," 90. See as well Heschel, *Abraham Geiger and the Jewish Jesus,* 80.

31. Schorsch, "Scholarship in the Service of Reform," 89.

32. Susannah Heschel agrees with Schorsch that Geiger's *Urschrift* emerged from his interest in Karaite history. See Heschel, *Abraham Geiger and the Jewish Jesus,* 41, 80.

33. Schorsch, "Scholarship in the Service of Reform," 89–90. See Geiger, *Nachgelassene Schriften* V, 296; and Wiener, *Abraham Geiger and Liberal Judaism,* 127–28.

34. Geiger, *Urschrift,* 11. Geiger also notes the finding by Elijah Levita (1468/69–1549), that a very different vocalization from the Masoretic one existed in early biblical texts (see Levita's *Masoret ha-Masoret,* 1538).

35. Geiger, *Urschrift,* 13–16.

36. See Zacharias Frankel, *Vorstudien zu der Septuaginta* (Leipzig: Vogel, 1841), 32–38, and Frankel's claim that "ihre Fehler [of the Septuagint] entspringen häufig aus dem

missverstandenen hebräischen Texte" (37). See also Zacharias Frankel, *Über den Einfluss der palästinischen Exegese auf die alexandrinische Hermeneutik* (Leipzig: Barth, 1851). This later work continues and deepens the argument from Frankel's *Vorstudien.*

37. Geiger, *Urschrift,* 16–17.

38. Ibid., 18.

39. See Zacharias Frankel, *Darkhe ha-Mishnah* (Leipzig: H. Hunger, 1859), 1–21; and Ismar Schorsch, "Zacharias Frankel and the European Origins of Conservative Judaism," *Judaism* 30, no. 119 (1981), 344–54, especially 352–53; and Schorsch, "The Emergence of Historical Consciousness in Modern Judaism," 413–37, especially 429.

40. Geiger, *Urschrift,* 19.

41. Ibid., 40–41. See also Abraham Geiger, "Die neusten Fortschritte in der Erkenntniß der Entwickelungsgeschichte der Judenthums und der Entstehung des Christenthums," *Jüdische Zeitschrift für Wissenschaft und Leben* 5 (1867), 256.

42. Geiger, *Urschrift,* 47.

43. Heinrich Graetz, "Der jerusalemische Talmud im Lichte Geigerscher Hypothesen," *Monatsschrift für Geschichte und Wissenschaft des Judenthums* 20 (1871), 127.

44. Geiger, *Urschrift,* 90.

45. Ibid., 65.

46. Ibid., 72.

47. Ibid.

48. Ibid., 94–95.

49. On this point see Schorsch, "Scholarship in the Service of Reform," 90. Schorsch's summary is both helpful and right: "Geiger's *Urschrift,* then, is above all a study of how Jews during the period of the Second Temple and the *Mishnah* preserved the relevance of their sacred literature. During the early centuries, while the text still possessed a degree of fluidity, Geiger contended, Jews did not hesitate even to rewrite passages that no longer accorded with their political needs or ethical sensibilities. Such frequent incursions help to explain the many divergences between our text of the canon and the first translations of it into Greek and Aramaic. It was the original that had been tampered with."

50. Geiger, *Urschrift,* 75–76, 81–82.

51. Ibid., 75–77. See also Abraham Geiger, "Zur Theologie und Schrifterklarung der Samaritaner," *Zeitschrift der Deutschen morgenländischen Gesellschaft* 12 (1858), 133–34.

52. See Geiger's 1872–1874 lectures, "Einleitung in die biblischen Schriften," in *Nachgelassene Schriften* IV, 55–58, for a similar reading of Genesis 33:18; also note Samuel Posnański's essay on Geiger's reading of the biblical text, "Geschichte der Sekten und der Halacha," in *Abraham Geiger: Leben und Lebenswerk,* 355.

53. See also Geiger, "Symmachus, der Uebersetzer der Bibel," 60–64, for Geiger's discussion of the ways in which later Hebrew affects biblical translation.

54. Geiger, *Urschrift,* 235, 239–43.

55. See Geiger, "Symmachus, der Uebersetzer der Bibel," 60.

56. See Abraham Geiger, "Allgemeine Einleitung in die Wissenschaft des Judenthums," in *Nachgelassene Schriften* II, 35–245.

57. Geiger, *Urschrift,* 97.

58. Ibid., 251, 254.

59. Ibid., 21, 24.

60. See Heinrich Ewald, "Übersicht der 1857–1858 erschienenen Schriften zur Biblischen Wissenschaft," *Jahrbücher der Biblischen Wissenschaft* 9 (1858), 104.

61. See Louis Finkelstein, "The Pharisees: Their Origin and their Philosophy," *Har-*

vard Theological Review 22, no. 3 (July 1929), 185–261; Ralph Marcus, "The Pharisees in the Light of Modern Scholarship," *Journal of Religion* 32, no. 3 (July 1952), 153–64; and Julius Wellhausen, *Die Pharisäer und die Sadducäer* (Greifswald: L. Bamberg, 1874).

62. Geiger, *Urschrift,* 103.

63. On this point see Posnański, "Geschichte der Sekten und der Halacha," in *Abraham Geiger: Leben und Lebenswerk,* 360, where Posnański insists that "Sadducees and Pharisees are in actuality not sects in the common sense of the word, but much more two parties, two directions [*Richtungen*] with more political and ecclesiastical than religious tendencies [*Tendenzen*]." Even this is not quite right, for Geiger does not describe these two parties as "*Tendenzen,*" as my discussion on the Tübingen school below makes clear.

64. See too Geiger, "Symmachus, der Uebersetzer der Bibel," 40.

65. Geiger, *Urschrift,* 452.

66. Abraham Geiger, "Der Ursprung der Schlachtregeln nach der älteren und der jüngeren Halacha," *Jüdische Zeitschrift für Wissenschaft und Leben* 9 (1871), 38–43; see too Heschel, *Abraham Geiger and the Jewish Jesus,* 43.

67. Geiger, "Der Ursprung der Schlachtregeln nach der älteren und der jüngeren Halacha," 43.

68. Ibid., 40.

69. Geiger, *Urschrift,* 158. This turn away from the Babylonian Talmud in favor of renewed interest in the Palestinian is characteristic of *Wissenschaft* scholarship in nineteenth-century Germany. It also represents a partial rejection of the rabbinic heritage that many Reformers found so burdensome. See Ismar Schorsch, "The Myth of Sephardic Supremacy," *Leo Baeck Institute Year Book* 34 (1989), 47–66. Also see Harris, *How Do We Know This?* 157–210.

70. Harris, *How Do We Know This?* 189.

71. Geiger does indeed favor Akiba over Ishmael in more ideological tones in later texts. See Abraham Geiger, "Dispensation von der Schwagerehe und Weigerung der Unmündigen (Chalizah und Mëun)," *Jüdische Zeitschrift für Wissenschaft und Leben* 2 (1863), 88–108.

72. Geiger, *Urschrift,* 434–35. See Perles, "Bibel," in *Abraham Geiger: Leben und Lebenswerk,* 319. Perles also believes that Geiger appeals to the *Mechilta* and *Sifre* for their "Überreste der alten Halacha gegenüber der später." Also see Posnański, "Geschichte der Sekten und der Halacha," in *Abraham Geiger: Leben und Lebenswerk,* 372–73, for the same point.

73. Geiger, *Urschrift,* 436. See also Abraham Geiger, "Mechiltha und Sifre," *Jüdische Zeitschrift für Wissenschaft und Leben* 4 (1866), 96–126, especially 99.

74. See Schorsch, "The Myth of Sephardic Supremacy," 47–66.

75. See too Geiger, "Mechiltha und Sifre," 99.

76. Geiger, *Urschrift,* 452.

77. See Harris, *How Do We Know This?* 189.

78. Geiger, *Urschrift,* 437.

79. Ibid., 480. See too Posnański, "Geschichte der Sekten und der Halacha," in *Abraham Geiger: Leben und Lebenswerk,* 382–84: "The views of the Karaites agree in most cases with those of the Samaritans and the Sadducees, and so too with the old *halakhah*" (384).

80. For the connection between the Karaites and Sadducees, see Abraham Geiger, "Die Levirats-Ehe, ihre Entstehung und Entwickelung," *Jüdische Zeitschrift für Wissenschaft und Leben* 1 (1862), 28–34.

81. Geiger, *Nachgelassene Schriften* V, 296; see also Wiener, *Abraham Geiger and Liberal Judaism,* 127–28.

82. Geiger, *Urschrift,* 128–31.

83. Ibid., 132.

84. Ibid., 133–34.

85. Ibid., 139–40.

86. Ibid., 150.

87. Ibid., 170.

88. Ewald, "Übersicht der 1857–1858 erschienenen Schriften zur Biblischen Wissenschaft," 104. See also, Heschel, *Abraham Geiger and the Jewish Jesus,* 192–93.

89. See Horton Harris, *The Tübingen School* (Oxford: Oxford University Press, 1975).

90. On Heinrich Ewald's conservative historical theology, see Heschel, *Abraham Geiger and the Jewish Jesus,* 191–94; and John Rogerson, *Old Testament Criticism in the Nineteenth Century: England and Germany* (London: SPCK, 1984), 91–93.

91. See, for example, Heschel, *Abraham Geiger and the Jewish Jesus,* 118, where she states that despite "serious criticisms" of Baur's Christian prejudices and assumptions, "the methods Geiger used for interpreting Second Temple Judaism and rabbinic literature were taken over from Baur and the Tübingen school, as Heinrich Ewald originally pointed out in his review of the *Urschrift.*" See too Hans Liebeschütz, *Das Judentum in deutschen Geschichtsbild von Hegel bis Max Weber* (Tübingen: J. C. B. Mohr, 1967), 117–25.

92. Schorsch, "Scholarship in the Service of Reform," 91.

93. See Ferdinand Christian Baur, *Das Christenthum und die Christliche Kirche* (Tübingen: L. Fr. Fues, 1853), 49–53.

94. Heschel, *Abraham Geiger and the Jewish Jesus,* 205; and Geiger, *Judaism and Its History,* 181.

95. Heschel, *Abraham Geiger and the Jewish Jesus,* 118.

96. Peter Hodgson, *The Formation of Historical Theology: A Study of Ferdinand Christian Baur* (New York: Harper and Row, 1966), 209.

97. See Hans Rollmann, "From Baur to Wrede: The Quest for a Historical Method," *Studies in Religion* 17, no. 4 (1988), 445–47.

98. See Posnański, "Geschichte der Sekten und der Halacha," in *Abraham Geiger: Leben und Lebenswerk,* 364.

99. Abraham Geiger, "Die wissenschaftliche Ausbildung des Judenthums in den zwei ersten Jahrhunderten des zweiten Jahrtausends bis zum Auftreten des Maimonides," *Wissenschaftliche Zeitschrift für jüdische Theologie* 1 (1835), 36; and Abraham Geiger, "Die gesetzlichen Differenzen zwischen Samaritanern und Juden," *Zeitschrift der Deutschen morgenländischen Gesellschaft* 20 (1866), 527–73. Also see Gottlieb Klein, "Praktische Theologie," in *Abraham Geiger: Leben und Lebenswerk,* 285, for a similar point; and Posnański, "Geschichte der Sekten und der Halacha," in *Abraham Geiger: Leben und Lebenswerk,* 352–53.

100. Geiger, "Sadducäer und Pharisäer," 11.

101. Ibid., 11, 34.

102. Ibid., 42–54.

103. Ibid., 38.

104. Ibid., 33–35, 41.

105. Ibid., 41.

106. Geiger, *Urschrift,* 106.

107. Geiger, *Nachgelassene Schriften* I, 289.

108. Geiger, *Nachgelassene Schriften* II, 279.

109. See, for example, Abraham Geiger, "Die gesetzlichen Differenzen zwischen Samaritanern und Juden," 527–73; and Abraham Geiger, "Die Levirats-Ehe, ihre Entstehung und Entwickelung," 19–39.

110. Geiger, *Nachgelassene Schriften* V, 297.

111. Ibid., Letter to M. A. Stern (June 1864), 289–90.

112. Ibid., Letter to L. R. Bischoffsheim (October 1872), 350.

113. Ibid., 134, in Ludwig Geiger's introduction to Abraham Geiger's letters in Breslau (1838–1863).

114. Geiger, *Urschrift,* 426–27, 431–32.

115. Ibid., 426–27.

116. Ibid., 423.

117. Gotzmann, *Jüdisches Recht im kulturellen Prozeß,* 207.

118. For a helpful discussion of Holdheim's view of the state see Gotzmann, *Eigenheit und Einheit,* 225–28, 237–39.

119. Meyer, *Response to Modernity,* 82.

120. Harris, *How Do We Know This?* 166.

121. I take the term from Proudfoot's *Religious Experience.*

122. Samuel Holdheim, *Über die Autonomie der Rabbinen und das Princip der jüdischen Ehe* (Schwerin: C. Kürschner, 1843).

123. Ibid., viii.

124. Ibid., vii.

125. Samuel Holdheim, *Vorträge über die Mosaische Religion für denkende Israeliten* (Schwerin: Kürschner, 1844).

126. Ibid., 38–39.

127. Holdheim, *Über die Autonomie der Rabbinen und das Princip der jüdischen Ehe,* 26–27. Gotzmann concludes from this paragraph that obligations to the body are, for Holdheim, "religious obligations." But this cannot be so if we take into account Holdheim's distinction between religion and politics. See Gotzmann, *Jüdisches Recht im kulturellen Prozeß,* 208–209.

128. Holdheim, *Vorträge über die Mosaische Religion für denkende Israeliten,* 41.

129. In his review of *Rabbinic Autonomy,* Zacharias Frankel complained that Holdheim turned religion into an empty shell, wholly subsuming and subordinating it to the state. Holdheim's reply to Frankel, published in 1845 as a separate book titled *The Religious and the Political in Judaism,* illustrates well the restrictive purity of the religious sphere. Religion, Holdheim argues, will never conflict with the common civic good because that common good itself reflects religious ideals. Yet the civic sphere in no way tampers with or impairs the eternal and pure nature of religion. Even as the religious idea underwrites all true political goals, those ideas remain free of political developments. See Gotzmann, *Jüdisches Recht im kulturellen Prozeß,* 205; and Samuel Holdheim, *Das Religiöse und Politische im Judenthum* (Schwerin: Kürschner, 1845), 13.

130. Samuel Holdheim, *Der religiöse Fortschritt im deutschen Judenthume* (Leipzig: Fritsche, 1840), 9.

131. Holdheim, *Vorträge über die Mosaische Religion für denkende Israeliten,* xiv; see also Meyer, *Response to Modernity,* 84.

132. Gotzmann, *Jüdisches Recht im kulturellen Prozeß,* 200–48, especially 206 on Holdheim.

133. Abraham Geiger, "Eine Erinnerung an frühere Zeiten: Glückwunschschreiben

an Herrn Dr. L. Zunz in Berlin zur Vollendung des siebzigsten Jahres am 10. August 1864," in *Nachgelassene Schriften* I, 301.

134. Geiger, *Urschrift,* 75. For the notion of textual shock (*anstössig*), see examples on pages 244 and 347.

135. Ludwig Geiger, *Abraham Geiger: Leben und Lebenswerk,* 180.

3. The Gendered Politics of Authority

1. See Heschel, *Abraham Geiger and the Jewish Jesus,* 42.

2. Wiener, *Abraham Geiger and Liberal Judaism,* 94–96. See too Ludwig Geiger, *Abraham Geiger: Leben und Lebenswerk,* 166.

3. Ludwig Geiger, *Abraham Geiger: Leben und Lebenswerk,* 72.

4. Wiener, *Abraham Geiger and Liberal Judaism,* 95.

5. Funkenstein, *Perceptions of Jewish History,* 20.

6. See Isabel Hull, *Sexuality, State, and Civil Society in Germany, 1700–1815* (Ithaca and London: Cornell University Press, 1996), 207: "The 'intimate sphere' tailored to the presumed needs of the new male citizen was one of the most successful ideological creations of late Enlightened discourse. It was a product, not a cause, of the larger project to redraft the 'public' according to the requirements of civil society."

7. See Benjamin Maria Baader's forthcoming book, *Gender, Judaism, and Bourgeois Culture in Germany, 1800–1870,* to be published by Indiana University Press in 2006.

8. See Judith Butler, *Gender Trouble: Feminism and the Subversion of Identity* (New York and London: Routledge, 10th Anniversary edition, 1999), especially 56, where Butler adopts Lacan's approach in asking, "how is 'being' instituted and allocated through the signifying practices of the paternal economy?" Butler wants to understand how discourses of power produce and construct sex and gender for political ends. In this sense, I want to ask what work do Geiger's gendered constructions perform in the political economy of ritual reform?

9. Geiger, *Judenthum,* 44; *Judaism,* 56.

10. Geiger, *Judenthum,* 44; *Judaism,* 56.

11. Paula E. Hyman, *Gender and Assimilation in Modern Jewish History* (Seattle & London: University of Washington Press, 1995), 25.

12. Ibid., 17–18; also see Shulamit Magnus, "Pauline Wengeroff and the Voice of Jewish Modernity," in *Gender and Judaism: The Transformation of Tradition,* edited by T. M. Rudavsky (New York & London: New York University Press, 1995), 186.

13. Marion A. Kaplan, *The Making of the Jewish Middle Class: Women, Family, and Identity in Imperial Germany* (New York and Oxford: Oxford University Press, 1991), 16.

14. Paula Hyman, "Gender and the Jewish Family in Modern Europe," in *Women in the Holocaust,* edited by Dalia Ofer and Lenore Weitzman (New Haven & London: Yale University Press, 1998), 27.

15. Kaplan, *The Making of the Jewish Middle Class,* 16.

16. See Carroll Smith-Rosenberg, *Disorderly Conduct: Visions of Gender in Victorian America* (New York: Alfred A. Knopf, 1985) for her discussion of the "Cult of True Womanhood" during the American Great Awakening. Nineteenth-century American women founded reform movements that fractured domestic private space by opening new channels for public female expression (109–28). These women also "dominated the Second Great Awakening's revivals and spiraling church membership" (129). Religious women "created a public and powerful role for themselves as a female conscience and moral voice crying in a

wilderness of male corruption" (130), even if these new powers and access to the public sphere were restricted within a Christian theology of submission (154). See also Karla Goldman, *Beyond the Synagogue Gallery: Finding a Place for Women in American Judaism* (Cambridge, Mass., and London: Harvard University Press, 2000), especially 38–68. I thank Laura Levitt for bringing these issues and relevant sources to my attention. For an analysis of "True Womanhood" in nineteenth-century America that attributes "piety, purity, submissiveness and domesticity" to "mother, daughter, sister, wife," see Barbara Welter, "The Cult of True Womanhood: 1820–1860," *American Quarterly* 18, no. 2 (1966), 151–74.

17. Hull, *Sexuality, State, and Civil Society in Germany,* 188.

18. Ibid., 184.

19. Geiger, *Judenthum,* 44; *Judaism,* 56. The sexual undercurrent in Geiger's description of Rebecca is somewhat lost in the English translation. Geiger describes Rebecca in her "*unbefangener Jungfräulichkeit,*" which refers to her natural virginity, but is translated into English as "maiden of innocence."

20. Quote taken from Hull, *Sexuality, State, and Civil Society in Germany,* 322. A translation of the original text can be found in Johann Gottlieb Fichte, *The Science of Rights,* trans. A. E. Kroeger (London: Trübner & Co., 1889), 417–18, 441.

21. Geiger, *Judenthum,* 45; *Judaism,* 57.

22. Hull, *Sexuality, State, and Civil Society in Germany,* 298.

23. Geiger, *Judenthum,* 45–46; *Judaism,* 58.

24. Ibid., 46; 58.

25. Ibid.

26. Ibid.

27. Ibid.

28. Hull, *Sexuality, State, and Civil Society in Germany,* 411.

29. Ibid., 207.

30. Geiger, *Judenthum* 46; *Judaism,* 58–59.

31. Kaplan, *The Making of the Jewish Middle Class,* 34.

32. Geiger, *Judenthum,* 47; *Judaism,* 59–60.

33. Ibid., 48; 60.

34. Graetz, *Geschichte der Juden* I, 111–13.

35. Heinrich Graetz, *The Structure of Jewish History and Other Essays,* edited by Ismar Schorsch, 75–76; Heinrich Graetz, *Die Konstruktion der jüdishen Geschichte* (Berlin: Schocken, 1936), 24. For the original German essay, see Heinrich Graetz, "Die Construction der jüdischen Geschichte," *Zeitschrift für die religiösen Interessen des Judenthums* 3 (1846), 81–97, 121–32, 361–81, 413–21.

36. For a thorough review of Hirsch's life and works, and especially his relationship with Geiger, see Robert Liberles, *Religious Conflict in Social Context: The Resurgence of Orthodox Judaism in Frankfurt am Main, 1838–1877* (Westport, Conn: Greenwood Press, 1985); also helpful on Hirsch's biography is Noah Rosenbloom, *Tradition in an Age of Reform: The Religious Philosophy of Samson Raphael Hirsch* (Philadelphia: The Jewish Publication Society of America, 1976), 37–65.

37. Samson Raphael Hirsch, *Hirsch Commentary on the Torah* VII, translated by Isaac Levy (London: The Judaica Press, 1966), 150. See too Samson Raphael Hirsch, *Judaism Eternal* II, translated by I. Grunfeld (London: Soncino Press, 1956), 81. Hirsch originally published *The Jewish Woman* as "Das Jüdische Weib" in his journal, *Jeschurun* 10/1, 3–4, 11–12 and 11/1–3 (1863–1864). His discussion of Deborah occurs in *Jeschurun* 11/1 (1864), 3.

38. Hirsch, *Judaism Eternal* II, 54; *Jeschurun* 10/1 (1863), 7.

39. Hirsch, *Judaism Eternal* II, 81; *Jeschurun* 11/1 (1864), 3.

40. Hirsch, *Hirsch Commentary on the Torah* VII, 626–30.

41. Hirsch, *Judaism Eternal* II, 81; *Jeschurun* 11/1 (1864), 3.

42. See A. M. Silbermann, *Chumash with Targum Onkelos, Haphtaroth and Rashi's Commentary* (Jerusalem: Feldheim Publishers, 1934), 79.

43. Hirsch, *Hirsch Commentary on the Torah* II, 202.

44. Ibid., I, 392, 398. See too Hirsch, *Judaism Eternal* II, 66–75; and *Jeschurun* 10/11 (1864), 359–68.

45. Hirsch, *Judaism Eternal* II, 89; *Jeschurun* 11/2 (1864), 42.

46. Geiger, "Bruno Bauer und die Juden," 335.

47. Ibid., 336.

48. See Samuel Hirsch, *Die Religionsphilosophie der Juden* (Leipzig: Heinrich Hunger, 1842), 9–11. For a general account of Hirsch's philosophy and its relation to Hegel, see Emil Fackenheim, "Samuel Hirsch and Hegel," in *Studies in Nineteenth-Century Jewish Intellectual History,* edited by Alexander Altmann (Cambridge, Mass: Harvard University Press, 1964), 171–201; and Gershon Greenberg, "Samuel Hirsch: Jewish Hegelian," *Revue des études juives* 129 (1970), 205–15.

49. See, for example, Hirsch's distinction between prophetic content and form in *Die Religionsphilosophie der Juden,* 599–610 (especially 607).

50. Hirsch, *Die Religionsphilosophie der Juden,* 35.

51. See Ismar Schorsch, "From Wolfenbuttel to Wissenschaft: The Divergent Paths of Israel Markus Jost and Leopold Zunz," *Leo Baeck Institute Year Book* 22 (1977), 122; and Leopold Zunz, *Die gottesdienstlichen Vorträge der Juden* (Berlin: A. Asher, 1832).

52. Schorsch, "From Wolfenbuttel to Wissenschaft," 123.

53. See Schorsch, "Ideology and History in the Age of Emancipation," 27.

54. See Geiger, *Nachgelassene Schriften* V, 180–84; for a partial English translation, see Wiener, *Abraham Geiger and Liberal Judaism,* 113–15.

55. Geiger, *Nachgelassene Schriften* V, 181.

56. Ibid.

57. Ibid., 182.

58. Ibid., 182–83.

59. Schorsch, "Ideology and History in the Age of Emancipation," 28.

60. Geiger, *Nachgelassene Schriften* V, 184.

61. Ibid., 182.

62. See Schorsch, "Ideology and History in the Age of Emancipation," 27.

63. Abraham Geiger, "Die Stellung des weiblichen Geschlechtes in dem Judenthume unserer Zeit," *Wissenschaftliche Zeitschrift für jüdische Theologie* 3 (1837), 1–14.

64. D. Caro, "Ueber die Würde der Frauen in Israel," *Allgemeine Zeitung des Judenthums* 1, no. 87, 90, 93 (1837), 345–47, 58–59, 70–72.

65. Geiger, *Nachgelassene Schriften* V, 102.

66. Geiger, "Die Stellung des weiblichen Geschlechtes in dem Judenthume unserer Zeit," 2–3.

67. Ibid., 4.

68. Ibid., 5.

69. Ibid., 7–9.

70. Ibid., 13.

71. Ibid., 14.

72. Abraham Geiger, "Die Versammlung zu Leipzig und die zu Philadelphia," *Jüdische Zeitschrift für Wissenschaft und Leben* 8 (1870), 11–12. See too Michael Meyer, "German-Jewish Identity in Nineteenth-Century America," in *Toward Modernity: The European Jewish Model,* edited by Jacob Katz (New Brunswick, N.J.: Transaction Books, 1987), 247–67. I thank Michael Meyer for pointing out the sources for this material.

73. Geiger, *Judenthum,* 60–61; *Judaism,* 72–73.

74. Geiger, "Unser Gottesdienst," 10–13.

75. Geiger, *Judenthum,* 98; *Judaism,* 112.

76. Ibid., 101–102; 115–16.

77. Ibid., 102; 117.

78. Ibid., 100; 115.

79. Magnus, "Pauline Wengeroff and the Voice of Jewish Modernity," 185–87.

80. Ibid, 187.

81. Geiger, *Judenthum* 104, 107; *Judaism,* 118, 121.

82. Ibid., 107; 121.

83. Hull, *Sexuality, State, and Civil Society in Germany,* 322.

84. In the 1846 rabbinical conference in Breslau, the Reform rabbi Samuel Adler presented a rather lengthy report on the religious status of women, yet Geiger, as president of the conference, delayed its discussion for the next rabbinic meeting. But that next conference, in part due to the 1848 European upheavals, was never held. The fact that these liberal rabbis never openly debated the status of women in Judaism suggests more than a failure of time or historical contingency. It reveals a deep-seated fear and uncertainty about female ritual performance. See *Protokolle der dritten Versammlung deutscher Rabbiner, abgehalten zu Breslau* (Breslau: F. E. C. Leuckart, 1847), 253–66. Also note, however, Karla Goldman's discussion of the Hamburg Temple, in which the open gallery for women contrasted sharply with features of traditional observance. See Goldman, *Beyond the Synagogue Gallery,* 47.

85. Riv-Ellen Prell, "The Vision of Woman in Classical Reform Judaism," *Journal of the American Academy of Religion* 50, no. 4 (1982), 575–89, especially 584–86.

86. Kaplan, *The Making of the Jewish Middle Class,* 18.

4. Rabbinic Authority

1. Geiger, *Nachgelassene Schriften* V, 7; see too Heschel, *Abraham Geiger and the Jewish Jesus,* 25, for her discussion and translation of this passage.

2. Heschel, *Abraham Geiger and the Jewish Jesus,* 25.

3. M. Dreifuß, "Kennt das Judenthum einen Unterschied zwischen Geistlichen und Laien?" *Allgemeine Zeitung des Judenthums* 9, no. 29 (1845), 434–36.

4. Ibid., 436.

5. Ibid.

6. See Schorsch, "Emancipation and the Crisis of Religious Authority: The Emergence of the Modern Rabbinate," 205–47; Heschel, *Abraham Geiger and the Jewish Jesus,* 34; Meyer, "Rabbi Gedaliah Tiktin and the Orthodox Segment of the Breslau Community, 1845–1854," 92–107; Meyer, *Response to Modernity,* 100–42, especially 110–12. Note Meyer's summary: "The prolonged clash which followed assumed symbolic proportions. Tiktin came to be seen as the champion of stable traditionalism, the venerable representative of the old ways, committed to stemming the tide of modernization at all costs. Geiger came to symbolize both contemporary historical criticism at its most radical and the persistent impulse for practical reforms in Jewish liturgy and law" (Meyer, *Response to Modernity,* 110).

7. Solomon Tiktin, *Darstellung des Sachverhältnisses in Seiner Hiesigen Rabbinats-Angelegenheit* (Breslau: Heinrich Richter, 1842), 29.

8. Ibid., 28, 30.

9. Schorsch, "Emancipation and the Crisis of Religious Authority: The Emergence of the Modern Rabbinate," 235–36.

10. Ibid., 236–37.

11. Ibid., 228, 234.

12. Ibid., 210–11.

13. Ibid., 233.

14. Steven Lowenstein, "The 1840s and the Creation of the German Jewish Religious Reform Movement," in *Revolution and Evolution: 1848 in German-Jewish History,* edited by Werner Mosse, Arnold Paucker, and Reinhard Rurup (Tübingen: J. C. B. Mohr, 1981), 255–97.

15. Ibid., 267–68.

16. See Meyer, *Response to Modernity,* 131–42, for a general overview of the rabbinical conferences; also see Philipson, *The Reform Movement in Judaism,* 140–224; and *Protocolle der ersten Rabbiner-Versammlung abgehalten zu Braunschweig* (Braunschweig: Friedrich Vieweg und Sohn, 1844), 73.

17. *Protocolle der ersten Rabbiner-Versammlung abgehalten zu Braunschweig,* 19, 94–98. Also note the short but helpful account by Andreas Brämer in his excellent book, *Rabbiner Zacharias Frankel: Wissenschaft des Judentums und konservative Reform im 19. Jahrhundert* (Hildesheim, Zürich, and New York: Georg Olms, 2000), 230.

18. Gotthold Salomon, *Die Rabbiner-Versammlung und ihre Tendenzen: Eine Beleuchtung für ihre Freunde und Feinde* (Hamburg: B. S. Berendsohn, 1845), 1–8.

19. Philipson, *The Reform Movement in Judaism,* 149; and Meyer, *Response to Modernity,* 28.

20. *Protocolle der ersten Rabbiner-Versammlung abgehalten zu Braunschweig,* 55. See also Meyer, *Response to Modernity,* 83.

21. *Protocolle der ersten Rabbiner-Versammlung abgehalten zu Braunschweig,* 64.

22. Ibid., 65–66.

23. Ibid., 67.

24. Meyer, *Response to Modernity,* 134.

25. *Protocolle der ersten Rabbiner-Versammlung abgehalten zu Braunschweig,* xvi.

26. Ibid., 13.

27. Ibid., 14.

28. Ibid., 15. See also Philipson, *The Reform Movement in Judaism,* 145.

29. *Protocolle der ersten Rabbiner-Versammlung abgehalten zu Braunschweig,* 16; Philipson, *The Reform Movement in Judaism,* 145.

30. *Protocolle der ersten Rabbiner-Versammlung abgehalten zu Braunschweig,* 17.

31. Ibid.

32. A group of seventy-seven Orthodox rabbis also protested against the proceedings in Brunswick. Their "Manifesto" wholly condemned the assembly and its "perverted religious thoughts and actions." They considered all the resolutions published by these "Karaites" as "contrary to the statutes of our holy law, conceived in a perverted spirit, and based on a rotten foundation." See "Manifesto of German Rabbis," *The Voice of Jacob* IV, no. 100, 101 (1845), 136–37, 142–43.

33. "Aufruf an unsere deutsche Glaubensbrüder," *Allgemeine Zeitung des Judenthums* 9,

no. 16 (1845), 234–36; the full English translation can be found in Philipson, *The Reform Movement in Judaism,* 231–34.

34. Philipson, *The Reform Movement in Judaism,* 231; see Meyer, *Response to Modernity,* 123–31, for background on the Berlin Reform group.

35. Philipson, *The Reform Movement in Judaism,* 231–32; "Aufruf an unsere deutsche Glaubensbrüder," 234–35.

36. Philipson, *The Reform Movement in Judaism,* 232; "Aufruf an unsere deutsche Glaubensbrüder," 235.

37. *Protokolle und Aktenstücke der zweiten Rabbiner-Versammlung abgehalten zu Frankfurt am Main* (Frankfurt am Main: Ullmann, 1845), 240–46.

38. Ibid., 242.

39. Ibid., 243.

40. "The Rabbinical Assembly at Frankfort, for Effecting Innovations in Judaism," *The Voice of Jacob* IV, no. 109 (1845), 219.

41. *Protokolle und Aktenstücke der zweiten Rabbiner-Versammlung abgehalten zu Frankfurt am Main,* 243–44.

42. Ibid., 246.

43. *Protokolle der dritten Versammlung deutscher Rabbiner, abgehalten zu Breslau,* 14.

44. Meyer, *Response to Modernity,* 131.

45. *Protokolle und Aktenstücke der zweiten Rabbiner-Versammlung abgehalten zu Frankfurt am Main,* 70.

46. Geiger, "Die Versammlung zu Leipzig und die zu Philadelphia," 1–27.

47. Ibid., 3–4.

48. Ibid., 3.

49. Abraham Geiger, "Die erste Rabbinerversammlung," *Allgemeine Zeitung des Judenthums* 8, no. 25 (1844), 339. This article was reprinted as Abraham Geiger, "Amtsbrüderliches Sendschreiben an die in Braunschweig versammelten Rabbiner," in *Nachgelassene Schriften* I, 197–202. See also Brämer's comparison of Geiger and Frankel's understanding of the conference in *Rabbiner Zacharias Frankel,* 227. Brämer reads their differences as a function of Geiger's more radical reform view and Frankel's more conservative or "middle position." But I think it has less to do with the burgeoning religious movements, and more with conceptions of rabbinic authority.

50. Geiger, "Die erste Rabbinerversammlung," 337–39.

51. See Abraham Geiger, "Was thut Noth?" *Jüdische Zeitschrift für Wissenschaft und Leben* 3 (1864/65), 252.

52. Ibid., 254.

53. See Abraham Geiger, "Die Versammlung von Rabbinern in Cassel," *Jüdische Zeitschrift für Wissenschaft und Leben* 6 (1868), 241 and 245; and Abraham Geiger, "Die gegenwärtige Lage. Die wiedererstehende Rabbiner-Versammlung," *Jüdische Zeitschrift für Wissenschaft und Leben* 6 (1868), 170.

54. Geiger, "Die erste Rabbinerversammlung," 339.

55. Ibid., 338.

56. Samuel Holdheim, "Die Speisegesetze," *Wissenschaftliche Zeitschrift für jüdische Theologie* 6 (1847), 62–63.

57. Abraham Geiger, "Nachschrift: Die Speisegesetze," *Wissenschaftliche Zeitschrift für jüdische Theologie* 6 (1847), 63–75.

58. Ibid., 64.

59. Ibid., 65.

60. Lowenstein, "The 1840s and the Creation of the German Jewish Religious Reform Movement," 265.

61. See Meyer, *Response to Modernity,* 133.

62. For a different reading of Frankel's image of rabbinic authority, one that stresses "the universal category of religion," see Schorsch, "Emancipation and the Crisis of Religious Authority: The Emergence of the Modern Rabbinate," 212.

63. Zacharias Frankel, "Ueber die projectirte Rabbinerversammlung," *Zeitschrift für die religiösen Interessen des Judenthums* 1 (1844), 89–106.

64. Ibid., 92–93.

65. See Brämer, *Rabbiner Zacharias Frankel,* 226–27.

66. Schorsch, "Emancipation and the Crisis of Religious Authority: The Emergence of the Modern Rabbinate," 211.

67. Brämer, *Rabbiner Zacharias Frankel,* 227.

68. See Nahum Glatzer, ed., *Leopold and Adelheid Zunz: An Account in Letters, 1815–1885* (London: East and West Library, 1958), 124; and Zunz's letter to Geiger dated May 1845 in Abraham Geiger, *Nachgelassene Schriften* V, 184—reprinted in English in Wiener, *Abraham Geiger and Liberal Judaism,* 115; also see Schorsch, "Emancipation and the Crisis of Religious Authority: The Emergence of the Modern Rabbinate," 239–40.

69. Frankel, "Ueber die projectirte Rabbinerversammlung," 104.

70. Zacharias Frankel, "Die Rabbinerversammlung zu Braunschweig," *Zeitschrift für die religiösen Interessen des Judenthums* 1 (1844), 289–308; and see Brämer, *Rabbiner Zacharias Frankel,* 230–34.

71. Frankel, "Die Rabbinerversammlung zu Braunschweig," 290.

72. Ibid., 290.

73. Ibid., 291.

74. See Salomon, *Die Rabbiner-Versammlung und ihre Tendenzen,* 69–70; and Samuel Holdheim, *Die erste Rabbinerversammlung und Herr Dr. Frankel* (Schwerin: Kürschner, 1845).

75. Brämer finds Frankel's attendance puzzling as well. See Brämer, *Rabbiner Zacharias Frankel,* 235.

76. *Protokolle und Aktenstücke der zweiten Rabbiner-Versammlung abgehalten zu Frankfurt am Main,* 18–19.

77. Ludwig Philippson, "Kritik der Verhandlungen der dritten Versammlung deutscher Rabbinen," *Allgemeine Zeitung des Judenthums* 10, no. 34, 35 (1846), 485–89, 501–503. See especially 488–89.

78. Samuel Holdheim, "Offene Briefe über die dritte Rabbiner-Versammlung," *Der Israelit des neunzehnten Jahrhunderts* 7, no. 46–48 (1846), 361–64, 369–72, 377–80. See especially 363.

79. *Protokolle und Aktenstücke der zweiten Rabbiner-Versammlung abgehalten zu Frankfurt am Main,* 19.

80. Geiger himself employed the term "positive historical Judaism" only a few years earlier in 1842 to discuss his rabbinic duties in Breslau. See Abraham Geiger, "Ansprache an meine Gemeinde," in *Nachgelassene Schriften* I, 69.

81. *Protokolle und Aktenstücke der zweiten Rabbiner-Versammlung abgehalten zu Frankfurt am Main,* 21.

82. Ibid., 20. For an excellent summary of Frankel's speech, see Philipson, *The Reform Movement in Judaism,* 164–65.

83. See Brämer's account in *Rabbiner Zacharias Frankel,* 238–42; and Gotzmann, *Eigenheit und Einheit,* 243–77, for a more general account of the relation between Hebrew and modern Jewish identity.

84. *Protokolle und Aktenstücke der zweiten Rabbiner-Versammlung abgehalten zu Frankfurt am Main,* 22.

85. Frankel, "Die Rabbinerversammlung zu Braunschweig," 303.

86. I will discuss Geiger's understanding of liturgical Hebrew in more depth in Chapter 5, on Jewish education.

87. Frankel, "Die Rabbinerversammlung zu Braunschweig," 291.

88. One of the more interesting responses to the rabbinic discussion of Hebrew appeared from Joseph Aub, the Reform rabbi of Baireuth and editor of the liberal weekly journal *Sinai.* He turned the issue of Hebrew language into an attack on rabbinic authority, and in this shares much with Geiger's appeal to local communal differences and customs. Like Frankel, Aub believes that Hebrew grounds Jewish identity, adding that it functions much like the Mass for Catholics and the sermon for Protestants. If one simply removes the "prayer and reading of the holy Bible" in its original language, then Jewish practice loses its distinctive religious source. Yet the rationale for Aub's educational program has less to do with rooting Jewish identity, and more with undermining rabbinic authority. For Aub fears that if the schools and synagogues abandon Hebrew as the common language of prayer and study, then the laity will rely heavily on rabbinic understanding of tradition. A linguistic elite will arise to gain privileged access to the Hebrew sources, and will establish normative readings left unchallenged by a Hebrew illiterate laity. What emerges in Aub's account of Hebrew is a learned and literate community of scholars who no longer passively absorb rabbinic instruction and teaching, but engage fully in communal and scholarly life. See Joseph Aub, "Betrachtungen über die Verhandlungen der diesjährigen Rabbiner-Versammlung," *Sinai* 1, no. 12–20 (1846), 93–95, 101–105, 109–11, 117–19, 125–28, 133–36, 141–42, 149–51, 157–60.

89. Holdheim, "Offene Briefe über die dritte Rabbiner-Versammlung."

90. Ibid., 363.

91. See Philipson, *The Reform Movement in Judaism,* 222.

92. Holdheim, "Offene Briefe über die dritte Rabbiner-Versammlung," 370.

93. Ibid., 363–64.

94. *Protokolle und Aktenstücke der zweiten Rabbiner-Versammlung abgehalten zu Frankfurt am Main,* 86.

95. Ibid., 88–89. Andreas Brämer notes how often the secondary literature highlights Frankel's demonstrative exit from the conference. It has become part of the Frankel lore. See also his discussion of Frankel's "ending his cooperation with the rabbinic conference" in Brämer, *Rabbiner Zacharias Frankel,* 15, 242–43.

96. Brämer, *Rabbiner Zacharias Frankel,* 237.

97. *Protokolle und Aktenstücke der zweiten Rabbiner-Versammlung abgehalten zu Frankfurt am Main,* 91; and Brämer, *Rabbiner Zacharias Frankel,* 243.

98. *Protokolle und Aktenstücke der zweiten Rabbiner-Versammlung abgehalten zu Frankfurt am Main,* 21.

99. Meyer labels his section on the rabbinical conferences as "Rabbinical Reassertion." See Meyer, *Response to Modernity,* 131; see also Schorsch, "Emancipation and the Crisis of Religious Authority: The Emergence of the Modern Rabbinate," 232–33.

100. See Philipson, *The Reform Movement in Germany,* 195–96.

101. Ibid., 207.

102. "'Verwahrung' von Frankfurt," *Der Orient* 7, no. 34 (1846), 261–62. The article was first printed in the *Frankfurter Journal* in August (No. 219) 1846, less than a month after the rabbinic assembly concluded business in Breslau. See Philipson, *The Reform Movement in Germany,* 221; and Meyer, *Response to Modernity,* 140.

103. "Verwahrung," 261.

104. Ibid., 262.

105. Ibid.

106. See *Allgemeine Zeitung des Judenthums* 10, no. 35 (1846), 505–508.

107. Ibid., 506.

108. B. Wechsler, "Briefe von Bremer Zeitung," *Allgemeine Zeitung des Judenthums* 10, no. 36 (1846), 529.

109. Ibid.

110. Ibid.

111. We can see this in other letters that respond to the Breslau conference and reflect views similar to the Frankfurt *Verwahrung.* In a simulated dialogue between "A" and "B" submitted by an anonymous author to the journal *Der Israelit des neunzehnten Jahrhunderts,* speaker "A" mocks the "spiritual leaders of Breslau" as the supposed "men of scientific education." Rather than appealing to "the trust of the community," these "enlightened rabbis" revert to "rabbinism" and the "priestly place." Attracted to office rather than "the learning of humanity," the rabbis in Breslau desire only a "hierarchy" that will ground their religious authority. In this dialogue, too, the critique focuses upon the illegitimate power usurped by rabbis who neglect the knowledge and lived experience of Jewish communities. Unable to trust the communities they represent, the rabbis undermine communal authority. See "Ein Dialog über die dritte Rabbiner Versammlung," *Der Israelit des neunzehnten Jahrhunderts* 7, no. 37, 38 (1846), 289–92, 297–300.

112. "Briefe von Breslau (Sept. 7)," *Der Orient* 7, no. 38 (1846), 295.

113. See Meyer, *Response to Modernity,* 140–41; and Brämer, *Rabbiner Zacharias Frankel,* 246–54.

114. "Briefe von Breslau," 295.

115. See Salomon, *Die Rabbiner-Versammlung und ihre Tendenzen,* 1.

116. Abraham Geiger, "Vorläufiger Bericht über die Thatigkeit der dritten Versammlung deutscher Rabbiner," *Allgemeine Zeitung des Judenthums* 10, no. 35 (1846), 511–12. This article is an excerpt from Geiger's longer essay by the same name.

117. Philippson, "Kritik der Verhandlungen der dritten Versammlung deutscher Rabbinen," 503.

118. This appeal to communal authority is powerfully expressed in another anonymous response to the Breslau conference published in *Der Israelit.* The author wishes to explain "the motive for this dissatisfaction" among "the educated Jewish public." Communal discontent for the Breslau resolutions stems from a sense of abandonment: "The rabbi or preacher is the spiritual official of a *community,* and as such he needs to follow not only his own conviction in his attempts at reform. Rather, he must always keep in mind the religious level of education of his community. The reforms themselves can only be decided by the community." Jewish communities, this author argues, worry little about logical arguments and more about "spiritual writing." But the rabbis in Breslau, with their historical and philosophical training, "take hold of a general and universal historical view" and forget the practical needs of local communities. The site of religious authority remains within the scope of communal standards and decisions, and rabbis cannot flee to abstract thinking to evade

material practices. See "Briefe über die dritte Rabbiner-Versammlung," *Der Israelit des neunzehnten Jahrhunderts* 7, no. 38 (1846), 301–304; and Meyer, *Response to Modernity,* 140.

119. Note Michael Creizenach's position in his *Schulchan Aruch* that, without warrant from Talmudic or biblical sources, moving the Sabbath to Sunday would only split Jewish communities into individual sects. See Creizenach, *Schulchan Aruch* II, 12–15; and Meyer, *Response to Modernity,* 120.

120. Leopold Stein, "Erklärung," *Sinai* 1, no. 34 (1846), 280–83.

121. Ibid., 280.

122. Ibid., 283.

123. See Meyer, *Response to Modernity,* 86.

124. See Schorsch, "Zacharias Frankel and the European Origins of Conservative Judaism," 344–54, especially 349 where Schorsch claims that for Frankel, "the direction that Judaism eventually takes is the outcome of a dialectical relationship between rabbinic leadership and the community."

125. Abraham Geiger, "Die gegenwärtige Lage," 168.

126. Abraham Geiger, "Die zwei verschiedenen Betrachtungsweisen: Der Schriftsteller und der Rabbiner," in *Nachgelassene Schriften* I, 492–504. The essay was first published in Geiger's journal *Wissenschaftliche Zeitschrift für jüdische Theologie* 4 (1839), 321–33. References will be to the text found in *Nachgelassene Schriften.*

127. Ludwig Geiger, *Abraham Geiger: Leben und Lebenswerk,* 49–50.

128. See Geiger, *Nachgelassene Schriften* V, 67, 75–77, 81.

129. Geiger, "Der Schriftsteller und der Rabbiner," 492.

130. Ibid., 493.

131. Pierre Nora, "Between Memory and History: Les Lieux de Memoire," *Representations* 26 (Spring 1989), 16.

132. Geiger, "Der Schriftsteller und der Rabbiner," 494.

133. Ludwig Geiger, *Abraham Geiger: Leben und Lebenswerk,* 108.

134. Eisen, "Constructing the Usable Past: The Idea of 'Tradition' in Twentieth-Century American Judaism," 429–61, especially 429–33: "Geiger's use of history in defining and appropriating a usable past remains at the center of Jewish thought. His marriage of scholarship and faith, like his reliance on and ambivalence toward his chosen ancestors, are still very much with us" (432–33).

135. Geiger, "Der Schriftsteller und der Rabbiner," 494.

136. Ibid., 494–95.

137. Ibid., 495.

138. Ibid., 496.

139. Ibid., 497.

140. Ibid., 497–98.

141. Abraham Geiger, "Die Rabbiner der Gegenwart," *Jüdische Zeitschrift für Wissenschaft und Leben* 1 (1862), 167.

142. Geiger, "Der Schriftsteller und der Rabbiner," 498.

143. Ibid., 499.

144. Ibid., 498–99.

145. Ibid., 500.

146. Ibid., 499–500.

147. Schorsch, "Emancipation and the Crisis of Religious Authority: The Emergence of the Modern Rabbinate."

148. Geiger, "Der Schriftsteller und der Rabbiner," 502–503.
149. Ibid., 504.

5. Jewish Education and the Authority of Personal Meaning

1. See Heschel, *Abraham Geiger and the Jewish Jesus,* 24; and Ludwig Geiger, *Abraham Geiger: Leben und Lebenswerk,* 6.

2. Ludwig Geiger, *Abraham Geiger: Leben und Lebenswerk,* 10.

3. Wiener, *Abraham Geiger and Liberal Judaism,* 4–5.

4. Heschel, *Abraham Geiger and the Jewish Jesus,* 27; Wiener, *Abraham Geiger and Liberal Judaism,* 6–9.

5. Abraham Geiger, "Programmen der jüdischen Religionsunterrichts-Anstalt in Breslau 1844–1863," in *Nachgelassene Schriften* I, 311–51; also see Ludwig Geiger, *Abraham Geiger: Leben und Lebenswerk,* 132.

6. Geiger, "Programmen der jüdischen Religionsunterrichts-Anstalt in Breslau 1844–1863," 319; also see David Ellenson, *Rabbi Esriel Hildesheimer and the Creation of a Modern Jewish Orthodoxy* (Tuscaloosa: University of Alabama Press, 1990), 160–61; and note too Ellenson, *After Emancipation,* 316.

7. See Mordechai Eliav, *Jewish Education in Germany in the Period of Haskalah and Emancipation* (Hebrew) (Jerusalem: Jewish Agency, 1960), 3, 162–73.

8. Geiger, "Programmen der jüdischen Religionsunterrichts-Anstalt in Breslau 1844–1863," 311.

9. Eliav argues that the *maskilim* first raised the issue of female education as a significant problem for Jewish enlightenment. Yet only upper-class German Jewish women took advantage of this new learning, and many of them went to Christian schools. See Eliav, *Jewish Education in Germany in the Period of Haskalah and Emancipation,* 169, 173, 271–79.

10. Geiger, "Programmen der jüdischen Religionsunterrichts-Anstalt in Breslau 1844–1863," 318. See also Eliav, *Jewish Education in Germany in the Period of Haskalah and Emancipation,* 3, 168.

11. Geiger, "Programmen der jüdischen Religionsunterrichts-Anstalt in Breslau 1844–1863," 312.

12. Ibid., 350; also see Ludwig Geiger, *Abraham Geiger: Leben und Lebenswerk,* 136.

13. See Schorsch, "Emancipation and the Crisis of Religious Authority: The Emergence of the Modern Rabbinate," 205–47.

14. Eliav, *Jewish Education in Germany in the Period of Haskalah and Emancipation,* 3, 162.

15. Geiger, "Programmen der jüdischen Religionsunterrichts-Anstalt in Breslau 1844–1863," 318.

16. See Bill Readings, *The University in Ruins* (Cambridge, Mass., and London: Harvard University Press, 1996), 62–69: "As Humboldt puts it, the principle of culture embodied in the University fuses the advancement of objective science (cultural knowledge) with subjective spiritual and moral training (cultivation)" (66).

17. Geiger, "Programmen der jüdischen Religionsunterrichts-Anstalt in Breslau 1844–1863," 342–43.

18. Ibid., 345. Note Michael Meyer's point in regard to the Berlin Jewish community of the 1820s and 1830s: "One either chose *Bildung* or one chose Judaism. The Jewish schools attempted to overcome this dichotomy, relating general culture to Judaism, so that the quest

for *Bildung* would not seem to necessitate the abandonment of Judaism, that, on the contrary, the child would gain general culture within a Jewish framework." See Meyer, *Judaism within Modernity: Essays on Jewish History and Religion,* 175.

19. Readings, *The University in Ruins,* 65–69.

20. Note Schorsch's claim that the "persistent exclusion of young Jewish scholars from university careers in Judaica further enhanced the scholarly character of the German rabbinate. *Wissenschaft des Judentums* soon became the preserve of practising rabbis because the rabbinate provided one of the few professional careers in which it could be pursued." See Schorsch, "Emancipation and the Crisis of Religious Authority: The Emergence of the Modern Rabbinate," 244.

21. See, for example, Martha Nussbaum, *Cultivating Humanity: A Classical Defense of Reform in Liberal Education* (Cambridge, Mass.: Harvard University Press, 1997).

22. Geiger, "Programmen der jüdischen Religionsunterrichts-Anstalt in Breslau 1844–1863," 348–50. Eliav adds that many parents sent their children to private teachers as well. See Eliav, *Jewish Education in Germany in the Period of Haskalah and Emancipation,* 278.

23. See Ludwig Geiger, *Abraham Geiger: Leben und Lebenswerk,* 86. When Geiger arrived in Breslau, private tutors were the norm.

24. See Eliav, *Jewish Education in Germany in the Period of Haskalah and Emancipation,* 3, 278.

25. See Schorsch, "Emancipation and the Crisis of Religious Authority: The Emergence of the Modern Rabbinate," 223.

26. Abraham Geiger, "Die Gründung einer jüdisch-theologischen Facultät, ein dringendes Bedürfniß unserer Zeit," *Wissenschaftliche Zeitschrift für jüdische Theologie* 2 (1836), 18.

27. Ibid., 9.

28. Ibid., 2–4.

29. Ibid., 13 and 14.

30. See too *Protokolle und Aktenstücke der zweiten Rabbiner-Versammlung abgehalten zu Frankfurt am Main,* 15, where Geiger proposes a Jewish theological faculty to his rabbinic colleagues.

31. Abraham Geiger, "Einige Ansichten über die nächste Rabbinerversammlung," *Allgemeine Zeitung des Judenthums* 9, no. 22, 23, 26, 27 (1845), 341.

32. For a review of the rabbinical conferences in Brunswick, Breslau, and especially Frankfurt (where the most intense questions over Hebrew prayer were debated), see Philipson, *The Reform Movement in Judaism,* 140–224.

33. Geiger, "Einige Ansichten über die nächste Rabbinerversammlung," *Allgemeine Zeitung des Judenthums* 9, no. 26 (1845), 386.

34. Ibid.

35. *Protokolle und Aktenstücke der zweiten Rabbiner-Versammlung abgehalten zu Frankfurt am Main,* 32.

36. Ibid., 33.

37. Geiger, "Programmen der jüdischen Religionsunterrichts-Anstalt in Breslau 1844–1863," 318–19, 327.

38. Ludwig Philippson, "Bemerkungen der Radaktion," *Allgemeine Zeitung des Judenthums* 9, no. 26 (1845), 389.

39. *Protokolle und Aktenstücke der zweiten Rabbiner-Versammlung abgehalten zu Frankfurt am Main,* 39.

40. Ludwig Philippson, "Ueber den Gebrauch der hebräischen Sprache beim israelitischen Gottesdienste," *Allgemeine Zeitung des Judenthums* 8, no. 33 (1844), 462.

41. *Protokolle und Aktenstücke der zweiten Rabbiner-Versammlung abgehalten zu Frankfurt am Main,* 40.

42. Philippson, "Ueber den Gebrauch der hebräischen Sprache beim israelitischen Gottesdienste," 462.

43. *Protocolle der ersten Rabbiner-Versammlung abgehalten zu Braunschweig,* 61.

44. For the notion of Jewish identity as "apart" and "a part of," see Arnold Eisen, *The Chosen People in America* (Bloomington: Indiana University Press, 1983), 3–22.

45. Ludwig Philippson, "Die Einheit der Ideen in der Heiligen Schrift," in *Gesammelte Abhandlungen* II (Leipzig: Gustav Fock, 1911), 92. The essay first appeared as "Die Einheit der Ideen in der Heiligen Schrift Israels," *Allgemeine Zeitung des Judenthums* 43, no. 1 (1879). Future citations refer to the Fock edition.

46. Philippson, "Die Einheit der Ideen in der Heiligen Schrift," 95.

47. Ibid., 99.

48. Ibid., 101.

49. Ibid., 117, 120. Philippson at first suggests that only the Pentateuch maintains a consistent view of the covenant (117), but he quickly broadens his view to include the entire biblical text (120).

50. Geiger, "Die Aufgabe der Gegenwart," 34.

51. See Ludwig Philippson, *Der Rat des Heils: eine Mitgabe für das ganze Leben an den israelitischen Konfirmanden (Bar Mizwah) und die israelitische Konfirmandin oder beim Austritt aus der Schule* (Leipzig: Gustav Engel, 1912).

52. Joël, *Zur Orientirung in der Cultusfrage.* I briefly discuss Geiger's opposition to Joël's dogmatic approach in the first chapter.

53. Geiger, "Etwas über Glauben und Beten," 49.

54. Ibid., 2. Geiger cites Joël, *Zur Orientirung in der Cultusfrage,* 11.

55. Geiger, "Etwas über Glauben und Beten," 3.

56. Ibid., 26.

57. Ibid., 8. Note that Geiger does not mention the more problematic cases, such as the excommunication of Spinoza.

58. Ibid., 26.

59. Ibid., 6.

60. Ibid., 13.

61. Ibid., 7–8.

62. Ibid., 9.

63. Ibid., 10. Recall Ismar Schorsch's schema (discussed in the first chapter) in which free inquiry is the second of the five central pillars of *Wissenschaft* scholarship. See Schorsch, "The Emergence of Historical Consciousness in Modern Judaism," 416–19.

64. Samson Raphael Hirsch, *Igerot Tzafon: Neunzehn Briefe über Judenthum* (Altona: J. F. Hammerische, 1836), 96.

65. Abraham Geiger, "Recension: Neunzehn Briefe über Judenthum, von Ben Usiel," *Wissenschaft Zeitschrift für jüdische Theologie* 3 (1837), 74–77.

66. See, for example, Abraham Geiger, "Recension: Neunzehn Briefe über Judenthum, von Ben Usiel," *Wissenschaft Zeitschrift für jüdische Theologie* 2 (1836), 535–37. On Geiger's response to Hirsch's *Letters,* see Liberles, *Religious Conflict in Social Context,* 121–22. According to Liberles, Geiger recognized himself in Hirsch's portrayal of Benjamin and was offended by the picture: "*The Nineteen Letters* represented for Geiger a continuation of the past discussions between the two, but Hirsch had failed in his portrayal of Benjamin to present Geiger's position adequately. Geiger found *The Letters* uncomplimentary both to

himself personally and to the movement with which he identified, and he verbalized this dissatisfaction in a sharp critique of Benjamin's intellectual dullness and of the book as a whole" (122).

67. Geiger, "Recension: Neunzehn Briefe über Judenthum, von Ben Usiel," 3 (1837), 89 and 91.

68. See Eliav, *Jewish Education in Germany in the Period of Haskalah and Emancipation,* 257–70; Jakob Petuchowski, "Manuals and Catechisms of the Jewish Religion in the Early Period of Emancipation," in *Studies in Nineteenth-Century Jewish Intellectual History,* edited by Alexander Altmann (Cambridge, Mass: Harvard University Press, 1964), 47–64; and Andreas Gotzmann, "The Dissociations of Religion and Law in Nineteenth-Century German-Jewish Education," *Leo Baeck Institute Year Book* 43 (1998), 103–26.

69. Petuchowski, "Manuals and Catechisms of the Jewish Religion in the Early Period of Emancipation," 47–48: "It is relatively easy to show that the institution of confirmation, its very name, and the terminology used in connection with it are borrowings from the Christian environment. . . . Some arch-Conservatives, like Salomon Plessner, wrote catechisms, while religious radicals, like Isaac Ascher Francolm, preferred other styles of presentation." Petuchowski cites Eliav, *Jewish Education in Germany in the Period of Haskalah and Emancipation,* 257–59.

70. Samuel Hirsch, *Systematischer Katechismus der Israelitischen Religion* (Luxemburg: V. Bück, 1856).

71. Ibid., i.

72. Ibid., ii.

73. Ibid., 3.

74. Ibid., 95.

75. Ibid., 115.

76. Ibid., 186–88.

77. See Ludwig Geiger, *Abraham Geiger: Leben und Lebenswerk,* 132. The first confirmation class in 1845 graduated three boys and thirteen girls, and this pattern of greater female participation continued throughout Geiger's tenure in Breslau, culminating in 1863 with six boy and fifteen girl graduates.

78. Ibid., 132–33.

79. Ibid., 133–34.

80. Meyer, *Response to Modernity,* 188–91; Geiger, "Die Gründung einer jüdisch-theologischen Facultät, ein dringendes Bedürfniß unserer Zeit," 1–21.

81. Geiger, "Allgemeine Einleitung in die Wissenschaft des Judenthums," 35–245.

82. Ibid., 39.

83. Ibid., 42.

84. Ibid.

85. Ibid., 47–48. See too Abraham Geiger, "Rabbinisches Gutachten über die Abschaffung des Gebetstückes 'Kol-Nidre' am Eingange des Versöhnungstages," in *Zur Judenfrage in Deutschland vom Standpunkte des Rechtes und der Gewissensfreiheit,* edited by Wilhelm Freund (Berlin: Veit, 1843), 313–15. Geiger favorably compares Hebrew to Chaldean, claiming that Hebrew "carries within itself the character of holiness" (315).

86. Geiger, "Allgemeine Einleitung in die Wissenschaft des Judenthums," 53.

87. Ibid., 54–56.

88. Ibid., 57.

89. Ibid., 61.

90. Ibid.

91. Ibid.

92. Ibid., 61–62.

93. Ibid., 63.

94. Ibid., 86. Geiger alludes to D. F. Strauss's notion of "poetic myth" that represents the playful imagination at work. See David Friedrich Strauss, *The Life of Jesus Critically Examined,* edited by Peter Hodgson (Philadelphia: Fortress Press, 1972), 53; Geiger, *Judaism and Its History,* 179; and Hans Frei, *The Eclipse of Biblical Narrative: A Study in Eighteenth and Nineteenth Century Hermeneutics* (New Haven and London: Yale University Press, 1974), 238.

95. Geiger, "Allgemeine Einleitung in die Wissenschaft des Judenthums," 86.

96. Originally entitled *Was hat Mohammed aus dem Judenthume aufgenommen?,* Geiger's book has been translated into English as *Judaism and Islam* (New York: Ktav Publishing House, 1970).

97. Geiger, *Judaism and Islam,* 3. Frei describes the hermeneutical approach to myth by referring to Schleiermacher's claim that the interpreter must understand the author "better than he understands himself." For those in the mythological school, "they believed themselves able to grasp, as it were from within, a mythological writer's necessary and unconscious belonging to, and expression of, the particular primitive consciousness of his era. . . ." See Frei, *The Eclipse of Biblical Narrative,* 243.

98. Geiger, *Judaism and Islam,* 73.

99. Geiger, *Judaism and Its History,* 259.

100. Heschel, *Abraham Geiger and the Jewish Jesus,* 185.

101. Michael Rosenak, *Commandments and Concerns: Jewish Religious Education in Secular Society* (Philadelphia: The Jewish Publication Society, 1987), 129–33.

102. For a reflective and provocative account of classical texts, see David Tracy, *The Analogical Imagination: Christian Theology and the Culture of Pluralism* (New York: Crossroad, 1981), 99–153.

103. See Nussbaum, *Cultivating Humanity,* 50–84.

104. Ibid., 67.

105. Geiger, "Programmen der jüdischen Religionsunterrichts-Anstalt in Breslau 1844–1863," 345.

Conclusion

1. Abraham Geiger, "Jüdische Philosophie," *Jüdische Zeitschrift für Wissenschaft und Leben* 1 (1862), 277.

2. See Cohen and Eisen, *The Jew Within,* 2, 10, 13–42.

3. Ibid., 7; also see Robert Bellah et al., *Habits of the Heart: Individualism and Commitment in American Life* (Berkeley: University of California Press, 1985).

4. Avishai Margalit, *The Ethics of Memory* (Cambridge, Mass.: Harvard University Press, 2002), 133.

5. Ibid., 135–38.

6. Ibid., 65–69, 108–109, 126–31.

7. Cohen and Eisen, *The Jew Within,* 74.

8. Geiger, "Nachschrift: Die Speisegesetze," 65.

9. Cohen and Eisen, *The Jew Within,* 190–92.

10. Geiger, "Programmen der jüdischen Religionsunterrichts-Anstalt in Breslau 1844–1863," in *Nachgelassene Schriften* I, 345.

11. Note the comment cited by Eisen and Cohen on an earlier draft of their book: "[T]he 'self' in the case of moderately affiliated Jews is not nearly so independent as most of them passionately believe. . . . To an astonishing degree, it turns out, moderately affiliated Jews are actually shaped and constrained by their past—their parents, their grandparents, their experiences growing up, and . . . their level of Jewish education (or lack of same)." See Cohen and Eisen, *The Jew Within,* 185.

12. See Margalit, *The Ethics of Memory,* 7–8.

Index

Ken Koltun-Fromm is Associate Professor of Religion at Haverford College and author of *Moses Hess and Modern Jewish Identity* (Indiana University Press, 2001).